DEXTER

INVESTIGATING CULT TV

Series Editor: Stacey Abbott

The **Investigating Cult TV** series is a fresh forum for discussion and debate about the changing nature of cult television. It sets out to reconsider cult television and its intricate networks of fandom by inviting authors to rethink how cult TV is conceived, produced, programmed and consumed. It will also challenge traditional distinctions between cult and quality television.

Offering an accessible path through the intricacies and pleasures of cult TV, the books in this series will interest scholars, students and fans alike. They will include close studies of individual contemporary television shows. They will also reconsider genres at the heart of cult programming, such as science fiction, horror and fantasy, as well as genres like teen TV, animation and reality TV when these have strong claims to cult status. Books will also examine themes or trends that are key to the past, present and future of cult television.

The first books in **Investigating Cult TV** series:

Investigating **Alias** edited by Stacey Abbott and Simon Brown
Investigating **Charmed** edited by Stan Beeler and Karin Beeler
Dexter: *Investigating Cutting Edge Television* edited by Douglas L. Howard
Investigating **Farscape** by Jes Battis
The Cult TV Book edited by Stacey Abbott

Ideas and submissions for **Investigating Cult TV** to
s.abbott@roehampton.ac.uk
p.brewster@blueyonder.co.uk

DEXTER

investigating cutting edge television

edited by

DOUGLAS L. HOWARD

I.B. TAURIS

PUBLISHERS

Published in 2010 by I.B.Tauris & Co. Ltd
6 Salem Road, London W2 4BU
175 Fifth Avenue, New York NY 10010
www.ibtauris.com

Distributed in the United States and Canada Exclusively by Palgrave
Macmillan
175 Fifth Avenue, New York NY 10010

ISBN: 978 1 84885 265 5

A full CIP record for this book is available from the British Library
A full CIP record is available from the Library of Congress

Library of Congress Catalog Card Number: available

Typeset in Minion by Ellipsis Books Limited, Glasgow
Printed and bound in the United States of America
by Edwards Brothers, Inc.

Contents

Acknowledgments   vii

Notes on Contributors   ix

Introduction—Killing Time with Showtime's *Dexter*

Douglas L. Howard   xiii

Part One. First Blood: Interviews

1. An Interview with Author and *Dexter* Creator
   Jeff Lindsay   3
2. An Interview with *Dexter* Writer and Developer
   James Manos, Jr   14

Part Two. Blood Slides: The Structure of the Series

3. Dissecting the Opening Sequence
   Angelina I. Karpovich   27
4. "Serial" Killer: *Dexter*'s Narrative Strategies
   David Lavery   43
5. *Dexter*'s Hollow Designs
   Steven Peacock   49

Part Three. Dexter on the Couch: Family, Friends, and *Frankenstein*

6. Harry Morgan: (Post)Modern Prometheus
   Douglas L. Howard   61
7. Sex, Psychoanalysis, and Sublimation in *Dexter*
   Beth Johnson   78
8. Blood Brothers: Brian + Dexter + Miguel
   Fionna Boyle   96

Part Four. A View to a Kill: Politics, Ethics, and *Dexter*

9. The Ethics of a Serial Killer: Dexter's Moral Character
   and the Justification of Murder
   Simon Riches and Craig French   117

10. The Devil You Know: *Dexter* and the "Goodness"
    of American Serial Killing
    David Schmid   132

11. Neoliberal *Dexter*?
    Michele Byers   143

12. *Dexter*'s German Reception: Why are German
    Networks so Obsessed (and Troubled) with US Shows?
    Vladislav Tinchev   157

Part Five. Dexterity: *Dexter* and Genre

13. The Lighter Side of Death: *Dexter* as Comedy
    James Francis, Jr   175

14. In a Lonely Place? *Dexter* and Film Noir
    Alison Peirse   189

15. The Art of Sp(l)atter: Body Horror in *Dexter*
    Simon Brown and Stacey Abbott   205

16. From Silver Bullets to Duct Tape: Dexter versus the
    Traditional Vigilante Hero
    Stan Beeler   221

Appendices
A: Episode Guide   231
B: Novel Guide   233

Bibliography   235
Teleography   245
Filmography   247
Endnotes   249
Index   259

Acknowledgments

There are a number of people who made this book possible, so, before you (or I) go any further, let me thank them now.

First, I must thank David Lavery. This book actually began as a conversation that David and I had online more than a year ago, and it largely moved forward through his guidance, encouragement, and friendship. Knowing David has been and continues to be one of the highlights of my career in this field.

I must also thank the authors for their professionalism and their inspired essays: Stacey Abbott, Stan Beeler, Fionna Boyle, Simon Brown, Michele Byers, James Francis, Craig French, Beth Johnson, Angelina Karpovich, David Lavery, Steven Peacock, Alison Peirse, Simon Riches, David Schmid, Vladislav Tinchev. Their readings not only brought out the depth and the nuances of the series, but they also demonstrated the vast possibilities of television scholarship and criticism.

Thanks to Jeff Lindsay for kindly agreeing to speak with me about his work, his novels, and his characters and for providing follow-up information thereafter. Thanks as well to Chelsea Lindman and the Nicholas Ellison Agency for making this interview possible.

I would additionally like to thank James Manos, Jr for generously taking time out to speak with me about the pilot, the television series, and television in general. I would also like to thank his assistant, Michelle Trump, for helping me to work out the details of this interview.

Thanks to Philippa Brewster and Stacey Abbott for their help in developing the proposal for this book. I must also thank Philippa for her constant support through every phase of this process, from start to finish, for every e-mail, every answer, and every bit of good advice.

Thanks as well go out to my colleagues at Suffolk County Community College, from the Administration to the Honors Program to the Huntington Library. In particular, I would like to thank Sandra Sprows, Liz Cone, and the rest of my fellow faculty in the English Department for their warmth, enthusiasm, collegiality, and friendship. I continue to admire them for their accomplishments, both in and out of the classroom, and to work toward the example that they have set.

Thanks to my family for all of their love and support. Thanks to my wife Jennifer, for every late-night conversation, every long car ride, every walk, every word of every draft that she ever listened to, and for an accidental phone call 15 years ago that changed my life forever. And, last but not least, thanks to Carolyn Joyce, for every smile that you ever gave from the day that you were born.

Notes on Contributors

Stacey Abbott is a Reader in Film and Television Studies at Roehampton University. She is the author of *Celluloid Vampires* (University of Texas Press, 2007) and *TV Milestones: Angel* (Wayne State University Press, 2009), the editor of *The Cult TV Book* (I.B.Tauris, 2010) and series editor of the *Investigating Cult TV* series for I.B.Tauris.

Stan Beeler teaches film and television studies in the English Department at the University of Northern British Columbia, Canada. His other areas of interest include popular culture, comparative literature and humanities computing. His publications include *Reading Stargate SG-1* co-edited with Lisa Dickson (I.B.Tauris), *Investigating Charmed: The Magic Power of TV*, co-edited with Karin Beeler (I.B.Tauris), and *Dance, Drugs and Escape: The Club Scene in Literature, Film and Television Since the Late 1980s* (McFarland).

Fionna Boyle is the author of *An Unofficial Muggle's Guide to the Wizarding World: Exploring the Harry Potter Universe* (ECW Press, 2004). When not writing about lovable serial killers, she runs The Creative Type, a communications and social media firm in Toronto, Canada.

Simon Brown is Senior Lecturer in Film Studies at Kingston University. A keen biker, he is the author of numerous articles on early and British cinema, as well as American Quality Television. He is co-editor with Stacey Abbott of *Investigating Alias: Secrets and Spies* (I.B.Tauris, 2007).

Michele Byers is Associate Professor at Saint Mary's University in Halifax, Nova Scotia. She has published extensively in the areas of television and identity, most recently in *Atlantis, Canadian Ethnic*

Studies, Shofar, Culture, Theory & Critique, The Essential Cult TV Reader, You Should See Yourself: Jewish Identity in Postmodern American Culture, and *Programming Reality: Perspectives on English-Canadian Television.* Michele is the editor of *Growing Up Degrassi: Television, Identity and Youth Cultures* (Sumach Press, 2005) and co-editor with David Lavery of *"Dear Angela": Remembering My So-Called Life* (Lexington, 2007) and with Val Johnson of *"The CSI Effect": Television, Crime, and Governance* (Lexington, 2009). She and David have also edited a new collection entitled *On the Verge of Tears: Why the Movies, Television, Music, Art, and Literature Make Us Cry.* Her most recent work involves the study of television and ethnicity.

James Francis, Jr is a fourth-year PhD candidate in English with emphases in Children's Literature and Film. His dissertation focuses on the contemporary horror film remake and its influence upon film culture. James grew up on horror films, not children's books, but concentrates on how the two areas complement and influence each other. He is considered a scholar/critic on *Buffy the Vampire Slayer* and serves as a board member to *Watcher Junior—The Undergraduate Journal of Buffy Studies.* James is also a published photographer in London, France, Brazil, Australia, Spain, and the United States.

Craig French is a graduate student in philosophy from the University of London and is currently researching into the nature of Mind and Knowledge.

Douglas L. Howard is Assistant Academic Chair and an Associate Professor in the English Department at Suffolk County Community College. He has written on topics ranging from modern literature to contemporary film and television, and his work has appeared in *Literature and Theology, Poppolitics.com, The Chronicle of Higher Education, This Thing of Ours: Investigating The Sopranos, The Gothic Other: Racial and Social Constructions in the Literary Imagination* (co-editor and contributor), *Reading The Sopranos, Reading Deadwood, Reading 24, Milton in Popular Culture,* and *Modern and Postmodern Cutting Edge Films.*

Beth Johnson is a lecturer in Film Studies and English Literature at Keele University. Her research interests include aesthetics, ocularcentrism, avant-garde cinema, the extreme scene, spectatorship, psychoanalysis and television studies. Beth is the author of various extant and forthcoming publications including "Masochism and the Mother, Pedagogy and Perversion" (forthcoming in a special edition of *Angelaki: Journal of Theoretical Humanities*, Routledge, November 2009), "Realism, Real Sex and the Experimental Film: Mediating New Erotics in Georges Bataille's Story of the Eye" in *Realism and the Audiovisual Media* (Palgrave Press, November 2009), "Viva la Vita" in *Peep Shows: Cult Film and the Cine-Erotic* (Wallflower Press, forthcoming, February 2010) and "Reframing Intimacy: Stranger Sex, Chaos and Contextualization" in *The New Extremism* (Edinburgh University Press, forthcoming, 2010). In addition, Beth is also currently co-authoring a study of sex and post-transgressive cinema with Charlie Blake (Liverpool Hope University), co-editing a collection based on sexual expression, aesthetics and ethics in UK and US television, and writing a monograph on British TV.

Angelina I. Karpovich is a lecturer in multimedia and broadcast technology at Brunel University. Her research concerns the social significance of media texts and non-standard uses of media technologies by professionals and non-professionals. She has published widely on media fandom, cult television, and the relationship between the moving image and tourism.

David Lavery is Professor of English at Middle Tennessee State University and the author/editor/co-editor of numerous essays and books, including *Joss: A Creative Portrait of the Maker of the Whedonverses* (I.B.Tauris/forthcoming, 2010) and volumes on such television series as *Twin Peaks, The X-Files, Buffy the Vampire Slayer, The Sopranos, Lost, Deadwood, Seinfeld, My So Called Life, Heroes,* and *Battlestar Galactica*. He co-edits the e-journal *Slayage: The Online International Journal of Buffy Studies* and is one of the founding editors of *Critical Studies in Television: Scholarly Studies of Small Screen Fictions*. He has lectured around the world on the subject of television.

Steven Peacock is Senior Lecturer in Film at the University of Hertfordshire. He is the author of monographs *Colour: Cinema Aesthetics* (Manchester: MUP, 2010) and "Expressions of Intimacy" in *Close-Up 04* (London: Wallflower, 2010). He is the editor of

Reading 24: TV against the Clock (London: I.B. Tauris, 2007) and has written extensively on television aesthetics, with a particular interest in the American serial drama. He is also co-editor, with Jonathan Bignell, of *The Television Series* (Manchester: MUP).

Alison Peirse is Lecturer in Film Studies at the University of Northumbria. Her research interests are horror film and cult television. Her article "The Impossibility of Vision: Vampirism, Formlessness and Horror in Vampyr" was recently published in *Studies in European Cinema* 5.3 (2009), and her book chapter "Destroying the Male Body in British Horror Cinema," was published in *Mysterious Skin: Male Bodies in Contemporary Cinema* (I.B.Tauris, 2009). She is writing a book on Russell T. Davies for Manchester University Press.

Simon Riches holds a PhD in Philosophy from University College, London and has taught in the Philosophy Department there for the last three years. Before that, he studied philosophy at the University of Southampton. His research interests lie in epistemology, metaphysics, and the philosophy of mind.

David Schmid is an Associate Professor in the Department of English at the University at Buffalo. The winner of the Milton Plesur and the SUNY Chancellor's Awards for Excellence in Teaching, he teaches courses in British and American fiction, cultural studies, and popular culture. He has published on a variety of subjects, including the nonfiction novel, celebrity, film adaptation, Dracula, and crime fiction and he is the author of *Natural Born Celebrities: Serial Killers in American Culture* (University of Chicago Press, 2005). He is currently working on two book-length projects: *From the Locked Room to the Globe: Space in Crime Fiction*, and *Murder Culture: Why Americans are Obsessed by Homicide*.

Vladislav Tinchev has a PhD in Media Studies (Film and Television) from the University of Hamburg, as well as graduate degrees from Germany and Bulgaria. His doctoral thesis on the *CSI* franchise is scheduled to be published this year. He has also published two volumes of poetry in Bulgaria. He is a television critic for *Serienjunkies*, a German internet portal for American TV shows, and his current research involves audio-visual style on television and the economics of television programming.

Introduction—Killing Time with Showtime's *Dexter*

Douglas L. Howard

I remember sitting at my desk in the office at work when the call from my wife came in. "Have you seen the coming attractions for this week's *Dexter*?" she asked. I had not. In fact, I did not even remember seeing them at the end of the previous week's episode. "I'll send you the link," she offered. "You have to see this." After I hung up the phone, I could only wonder what could be so shocking. We normally talked about the show after it aired, but she usually did not call me about it with this kind of urgency. As the promo for "Resistance is Futile" started to run, I stared at the screen, wide-eyed, as Dexter realized that his blood slides were gone, as the FBI knocked at his door, as he apologized to his sister, as Lundy and Matthews glared down at him and demanded an explanation for the rectangular wooden box in the plastic bag. That was it. It was all over for Dexter—no more victims, no more trash bags, no more secrets. Maybe the writers did not have such long-range plans for the show after all. There would more than likely be the drama of a trial and a host of confrontations with horri-fied friends and family, but, in the end, the killer would be brought to justice, whatever that was. Closing out the window, I did not feel that sense of satisfaction, though, that comes with seeing the guilty punished or justice served. Rather, I felt a curious disap-pointment, the kind that goes along with getting caught after breaking curfew as a teen or even watching an underdog sports team getting knocked out of the playoffs, and then a slight bewil-derment at my response, in rooting for an admittedly disturbed serial killer over the propriety of law enforcement. Had television warped my sense of values, or had it just brought out the worst in me?

That the series continues to elicit and tap into such mixed emotions speaks to the compelling nature of *Dexter*, one of the more recent offerings in a provocative line of contemporary quality television dramas (beginning, of course, with HBO's seminal *The Sopranos*). Where so many of its predecessors dealt (or deal) with characters working out significant personality issues, from Tony Soprano's sociopathology to Tommy Gavin's alcoholism to Greg House's cynicism, *Dexter* ups the ante and the burden for us as viewers by providing a hero (or anti-hero) who, for all of his apparent normalcy as a boyfriend, brother, police officer, and Miami native, engages in violent, bloody, ritualistic serial murder. Essentially, *Dexter* dares us to test our moral boundaries and push our sense of ethical tolerance even further by accepting the conditions within which the killer operates. (If we can root for those other characters, for the mobster, the firefighter, and the doctor, can we go along with this one, too?) For some, this test is simply too much to take. Admittedly "nauseated" by the series, the *Wall Street Journal's* Nancy DeWolf-Smith takes the producers to task for their "situational ethics" that work to rationalize Dexter's murders on the audience's behalf ("The Good, the Ugly and the Bad"). Feeling good about serial killing may cross more than just the police line.

Thanks largely to the tutelage of his foster father Harry, Dexter channels his deep-seeded bloodlust toward people who are themselves killers and who have somehow managed to elude the police and avoid punishment from an increasingly Byzantine legal system incapable of catching or holding them. As we learn in Season 1, Dexter's mother was the victim of a vicious murder and Dexter himself, a child crying for his mother in a storage tank bathed in her blood, was, as a result, the product of one (like his brother Brian). As abnormal as his psychological profile might be, Dexter's crimes appear justified and understandable under these circumstances, and, from the little that we learn about his victims, who have no code and are hardly so conscientious, his murders come off as a kind of public service, a bizarre, psychopathic waste management for society, if you will. ("Way to take out the trash," a fan cheers during the fantasy sequence at the end of Season 1 (1.12).)

Nothing should make serial killing okay, but, somehow, *Dexter* does. (See David Schmid's chapter for more on the moral "disavowal" of the series.) I am reminded of Sean Connery's Jim Malone in *The Untouchables* and how he explains to Kevin Costner's Elliot Ness how he will have to go beyond the limits of the law to get Capone. "What are you prepared to do?" he asks him (De Palma). If the killers are out there and the law cannot stop them, then what are we prepared to allow for our own safety?[1] A serial killer with a code and a toolkit lurks in the shadows, his syringe of animal tranquilizer at the ready.

In the same way that we might find ourselves laughing at Nabokov's Humbert Humbert even as we condemn his obsessive desire for Lolita, *Dexter* draws us in and works to make us like the killer in a number of subtle and not-so-subtle ways, even as we recoil from the horror of what he does. From the savagery and brutality of his rather typical morning routine, the playful title sequence could just as easily refer to the violence in our own ritualized behaviors. (For a detailed discussion of the opening sequence, see Angelina Karpovich's thorough analysis here.) Like Humbert, another first-person narrator, Dexter is also immediately open and honest and self-deprecating about who and what he is from the beginning: "a very neat monster" (1.1). Before we can judge him, Dexter has judged himself, beating us to the contempt that we might be inclined to feel toward him, undercutting us psychologically just as our super-egos start to kick into high gear.

Inasmuch as he is the only character on the series with a voice-over narrative, Dexter is also the only one who can explain his thought processes and his actions to us, whether we agree with them or not. He literally speaks to us, a fact that creates a degree of familiarity between Dexter and the viewer. We might well consider the series, in this regard, to be the next evolution of the "serial killer genre." *Psycho* showed us how a mild-mannered man's psychological issues could literally transform him into a deranged killer. As Maggie Kilgour points out, *The Silence of the Lambs* "[left] us siding with Hannibal Lecter, rooting for him as he [set] out for dinner, and [identifying] with the cannibal" (49). *Se7en* gave us a killer whose ritual was so extreme that he was willing to die for it. *American Psycho* brought us into the (pseudo?) killer's mind, allowed us to hear his inner monologue and define exactly what he was. Capitalizing on the audience's interest in such figures, a number of television shows—for example, *NYPD Blue, The X-Files, CSI, Law and Order, Deadwood, Nip/Tuck, The Closer,* and *Bones*—have included "serial killer" arcs or storylines that portrayed the killer as something or someone mysterious, frightening, and destructive. NBC's *Profiler* and Fox's *Millennium* notably revolved around protagonists who, like Dexter, used their unique understanding of serial killers to catch them on a weekly basis. Combining and incorporating these elements, *Dexter* now takes us yet one step closer to the killer, by giving us his perspective on killers and killing, by making his voice the focus of the show, and by making that voice friendly, candid, relatable, understandable (without any special training or paranormal ability on our part), and, at times, even ordinary. But, as James Manos, Jr explains in his interview, *Dexter* was not necessarily developed as a "serial killer" show, with that aspect of his character (or, for that matter, that genre) in mind. Manos, in fact, specifically refers to "his innocence about the world," and his musings on life are often philosophical and insightful. As foreign and as "othered" as he is, through these voice-overs, through these reflections, and in his existential angst, we may well find some of our own general concerns voiced and our own fears expressed.

And we are not the only ones who find something familiar or understandable about Dexter. Clearly, almost all of the other main characters on the show, from Rita to Masuka, have something in common with him and are able to relate to him in one way or another. All of Dexter's primary adversaries or counterparts from season to season, moreover—Brian, Lila, Miguel—see something of themselves in him. Even Doakes, the only one in the Miami Metro Police Department "who gets the creeps from [him]" (1.1) and perhaps the biggest Dexter-hater of them all, sees more in him at the end of Season 2 and believes that he has "a conscience" (2.10). (Dexter, in turn, argues that Doakes only "knew what he was" because he, too, with all of his "officer-related shootings" was a killer at heart (2.10).) These various relationships all work to establish and reinforce our own connection to Dexter and to develop the "disavowal" that Schmid discusses in his chapter.

On top of all that, Dexter, at times, can be darkly comic, again reminding us of Humbert or Hannibal Lecter or Patrick Bateman, or even some of the first-person narrators in Edgar Allan Poe's short fiction, which only adds to the conflict that we feel in watching him do things with stainless steel and Hefty bags that are so very, very wrong. (Working through some relationship issues in "Shrink Wrap," for example, he suddenly decides that he "can't kill [murdering therapist Dr Emmett] Meridian" because he "need[s] another therapy session" (1.8). For more on this aspect of the series, turn to James Francis's "The Lighter Side of Killing.") If we appreciate his humor and laugh at his wry observations, doesn't that laughter amount to endorsement?

But even if we do not like the character of Dexter and instead, like Doakes, "get the creeps from him," the very act of viewing itself puts us in an uncomfortable position, as if any enjoyment that we get from the show at all amounts to complicity on our part. If we watch, doesn't our watching amount to endorsement?

All of these factors clearly contribute to the unusual critical responses to the series. While critics have generally praised the show, they have also felt the need to address, account, and even apologize for their appreciation, as they wrestle with the moral dilemmas that *Dexter* poses. The *Philadelphia Inquirer*'s Jonathan Storm openly admits that the series provokes "a strange feeling": "He's a depraved killer, but you feel like reaching out and tousling his hair, and saying, 'It's OK. You're doing your best'" ("A creepy premise"). Alessandra Stanley, in the *New York Times*, cannot help but condemn it "as the next step in the relentless escalation of eroticized violence on television, a 'CSI' for premium cable" that similarly uses its "forensic science" "as the fig leaf of gross-out pornography"; having said that, though, she must also confess that "she cannot wait to see the next episode" ("He Kills People"). The *Miami Herald*'s Glenn Garvin metaphorically conceives that, if the series is "a weather report on Miami's soul," then "the forecast [is] gloomy—but also a perverse pleasure to watch" ("You gotta love this charming serial killer"). After calling it "easily the best drama in Showtime history," the *Star-Ledger*'s Alan Sepinwall is similarly conflicted about *Dexter*'s appeal: "This is a warped show, don't get me wrong, but it's so engrossing that [, . . .] if I had the other episodes in hand, I wouldn't have gotten anything else done for the rest of that day" ("After hours, he makes a killing"). In her *FlowTV* essay, Bambi Haggins, on the other hand, decides to come clean about her feelings: "I love Dexter, and, if loving him is wrong, I don't want to be right" ("Darkly Dreaming of Dexter"). Love him or hate him (or both), there is something compelling about *Dexter* that demands our attention— perhaps some murmur from our own Dark Passengers in the back- seat—though our other sensibilities might encourage us to turn away.

And, ironically, for all of these critical clarifications and apolo- gies, attention and even devotion are just what this serial killer with a code has received. Now that the series has whetted their appetite for destruction, people just cannot seem to get enough of Miami's favorite murderer. *Dexter* has become the focus of a number of different fansites and message boards online, from the *Dexter Wiki* through Showtime's official website to *Dexter-tv.com* to the Yahoo Group *Dexter Showtime* to a site specifically devoted to *Dexter's Filming Locations*. Fans not only talk about the series, discuss plot twists and character development, speculate about upcoming episodes, post casting news and spoilers, and list their favorite quotes, but they also contribute original artwork and fan fiction, play *Dexter* videogames, create their own *Dexter* videos, share trivia, and even write haikus about Dexter's bloody deeds. (Take this one from "sugarboots" on Showtime's *Wiki*: "Dexter, O, Dexter! / When will you ever be caught? / You're playing with fire" ("Dexter Haiku").) Though he imagines being celebrated by the good people of Miami at the end of Season 1, Dexter actually has an interna- tional following, as Russia, Germany, and Spain have also developed their own websites dedicated to the conscientious killer. Who knew that serial murder could take on such a life of its own?

When the Writers' Strike extended from the fall of 2007 into the winter of 2008 and began to dramatically impact network sched- uling, moreover, CBS, which owns Showtime, decided to turn to this "perverse pleasure" to supplement its existing line-up and provide broadcast viewers with some alternative programming. The network announced that December that it would begin airing edited episodes of *Dexter* on Sunday nights at 10 p.m. starting in Febru- ary. As Showtime noted on their website, this was "the first time [that] a full season of a premium cable drama series [would] make the transition to network television" ("Showtime's Critically Acclaimed Drama"). The controversy surrounding the series resurfaced, when the Parents Television Council denounced CBS for the move. PTC President Tim Winter maintained that the series could cause "irreparable harm" to families who might see the show and that it would only "contribute to [a Columbine-like] culture of violence": "*Dexter* introduces audiences to the depths of depravity and indifference as it chronicles the main character's troubled quest for vigilante justice by celebrating graphic, premeditated murder" ("PTC to CBS"). Not only did CBS not back down from the PTC's charges, but it opted to air the last two episodes together that May, thus moving *Dexter* down an hour and causing the PTC to renew its attack. Winter called it a "slap [in] the faces of parents and families" ("PTC: High Time"), but the network defended the decision and suggested that its latest move would not dramatically affect viewers since they had already determined "whether or not it was an appropriate show for their household" (Eggerton). Like Brian, Lila, Miguel, and the Skinner, the PTC found Dexter a particularly difficult opponent to put down.

For all of DeWolf-Smith's contempt for the producers, *Dexter's* "situational ethics" and its macabre subject matter are also somewhat unique in that they are derived from and inspired by Jeff Lindsay's highly successful Dexter novel series. (*Bones*, based on Kathy Reichs's Temperance Brennan novels, and *True Blood*, based on Charlaine Harris's Sookie Stackhouse series, also share this distinction. And HBO is bringing Alexander McCall Smith's heroine Precious Ramotswe to television in their new offering *The No. 1 Ladies' Detective Agency*.) After publishing a police novel, *Tropical Depression*, in 1994, and collaborating on a number of science fiction novels with his wife Hilary Hemingway (niece of Ernest) as well as an action adventure novel (*Time Blender*) with Michael Dorn of *Star Trek* fame, Lindsay developed the idea for Dexter during a speaking engagement: "I was speaking at a business booster's lunch, I don't know why, and I looked out at the crowd, and thought, 'serial murder isn't always a bad thing'" ("Jeff Lindsay Speaks"). Lindsay brought this same sense of humor and irreverence to the narrative voice of his protagonist in 2004's *Darkly Dreaming Dexter*, the first novel in the series, which was adapted by James Manos, Jr and essentially became the basis for the first season of the Show-time thriller. His second Dexter novel, *Dearly Devoted Dexter*, followed in 2005, with the first season of *Dexter* airing the next year on Showtime in 2006. While the series has made it through three seasons and is approaching a fourth—Showtime renewed it for two more seasons last fall, in fact—Lindsay has completed two more Dexter novels: *Dexter in the Dark* (2007) and *Dexter by Design*, the most recent installment, which was released in the United States this past fall (2009). The novels themselves have definitely inspired the series, and there are a number of key parallels between the two, from the revelation of Dexter's brother as the Ice Truck Killer in Season 1 to Dexter's wedding in Season 3. But the series also departs significantly from the books. Dexter kills Brian rather than letting him go free to kill again. LaGuerta lives, while Doakes does not, and Dexter's engagement is not an accident, as it appears in *Dearly Devoted Dexter*. Fans of one Dexter will find echoes in the other, but, like children raised by different parents (or "Harrys"), these Dexters have gone in slightly different directions and are guided by decidedly different Dark Passengers. Perhaps the only real constant, from Lindsay to Showtime, is blood, which flows red and often both in print and on TV.

Blood, of course, may be a good part of the attraction. We may be sitting down to read and tuning in out of some not-so-subtle bloodlust bubbling beneath the surface and out of some more desperate justice fantasies that hearken back to Hammurabi. Thus, while Dexter may serve as judge, jury, and executioner to those other killers who find their way onto his radar, his own jury will proba-bly stay out, if the controversy that continues to surround him is any indication, and at least as long as the ethical debates regarding the propriety of his actions remain unresolved, and it may hardly be as merciful. But, to the extent that there is an aesthetic at work here (as Stacey Abbott and Simon Brown point out in "The Art of Sp(l)atter") and that art, often very good art, causes controversy and provokes the viewer, *Dexter*, in this age of quality television like *The Sopranos*, *Deadwood*, and *The Shield*, takes us outside of ourselves and places us in a world that, for all of its bright Miami sunshine, is psychologically dark and moody (and noirish, as Alison Peirse makes clear), only to put us in a car with Dexter and his Dark

Passenger and leave us to find some common ground. So, just as *The Sopranos* probably would not make us want to join the mob or *The Shield* would not make us join the force, *Dexter* is not so much an ad for serial killing as it is a show that, in the end, does what television does do in its finest hours: it refers to some unusual commonalities, reflects some general truths about the human condition, and makes us rethink our own sacred codes that we have held so dear. For all of the murders that take place on the series, it is not a bad way to kill time at all.

About this Book

Like Dexter's victims, the body of this collection has been carved into several parts, each of which offers a different perspective on the series. The book begins with two interviews. The first is with author and Dexter creator Jeff Lindsay, who talks about the creation of his main character in detail, the development of the novel series, and some of the issues at work from the novels to the television show. Lindsay also discusses his newest novel, *Dexter by Design*, and gives us a preview of the next Dexter novel, currently in progress. The second interview is with James Manos, Jr, who not only wrote the pilot for *Dexter*, but who also worked on a number of critically acclaimed television shows, including *The Sopranos* and *The Shield*. Manos talks candidly about the ideas that drove the pilot and about his original intentions for the series.

Part Two deals with the general structure and appearance of *Dexter* and how that contributes to the mood, tone, meaning, and success of the show. Angelina Karpovich discusses the evocative title sequence, which won an Emmy in 2007 and has, alternately, been described by *The Onion*'s *A.V. Club* as a "food snuff film" (Gillette). Referring to the work of Saul Bass and the development of title credit sequences as important introductions to the film or television show to follow, Karpovich considers the symbolic and thematic significance of *Dexter*'s title sequence and how it effectively works to introduce us both to the character and the world of Dexter Morgan. From there, in his chapter on "*Dexter*'s Narrative Strategies," David Lavery questions the long-term possibilities of the series and its "flexi-narrative." Will the writers and producers legitimately be able to create any kind of future for Dexter and breathe new life into the series, season after season, Lavery wonders, or will Dexter himself fall prey to the ax and be done in by the seeming limitations of a master narrative about a serial killer? Steven Peacock rounds out the section with a look at "*Dexter*'s Hollow Designs" and how the show's stylized visual surfaces reflect and refer to the drama going on within and around them. Connecting the first episodes from Seasons 1 and 3, Peacock also examines the appearance and influence of Miami itself and draws upon the visual image of the city as it was established by Michael Mann in *Miami Vice*, the film as well as the television series.

The third part considers the psychological issues of Dexter himself, particularly as they are expressed and develop through the trauma of his childhood, his memories of his foster-father Harry, and his relationship with his brother Brian. My chapter specifically looks at Dexter's foster father Harry as a contemporary Victor Frankenstein and explores the often deliberate parallels between Victor and Harry as the creators of monsters. To the extent that both of these figures abandon their creations, my essay goes on to address the ensuing Oedipal rage caused by these rejections and how Dexter reworks the Frankenstein myth in the end through the resolution of this issue. Beth Johnson also takes a psychoanalytic approach to the show, although she interprets Dexter's ritualistic murders as a form of sublimation. Through her application of psychoanalytic theory to Dexter's development, Johnson demonstrates exactly how his horrific childhood loss, his mother-fixation, and his relationship with Harry have all combined to create and inform his complex character. Fionna Boyle adds another dimension to this character analysis through her thorough comparison of Rudy Cooper/Brian Moser and Miguel Prado. Where both Johnson and Boyle point out that Miguel forces Dexter to reconsider the Code of Harry, Johnson sees Miguel as "the real father," while Boyle, instead, argues that he works more as a "surrogate brother" and poses many of the same questions/problems that Rudy/Brian did, albeit at a different point in Dexter's life.

Part Four turns to the political and ethical aspects of *Dexter*, both within and beyond the series. Simon Riches and Craig French open this section with a philosophical reading of the show, as they attempt to interrogate Dexter's moral character. Through their analysis of his background and behavior, Riches and French define the ethical standards that Dexter uses as a justification for serial murder by placing them within the framework of consequentialism. Following up on this discussion, David Schmid suggests that the series enables the viewer to accept its premise and identify with the serial killer by "disavowing" the moral dilemma of this interaction. For Schmid, this disavowal also places Dexter within a distinctly American pop cultural tradition of serial killers; in fact, he specifically calls Dexter "the quintessential American serial killer of the post-9/11 era." Michele Byers, on the other hand, finds a neoliberal political discourse at the heart of *Dexter* and considers his vigilante justice as an expression of "moral self-care" by displaced white masculinity. To reclaim his position of privilege, Byers argues, Dexter must tame and dispose of those Others, i.e. women and Latin and African American men, who have intruded into the social space that he would occupy. From this focus on the series itself, Vladislav Tinchev addresses the question of *Dexter*'s reception in Germany and examines some of the difficulties, in distribution, politics, and dubbing, in bringing an American show like *Dexter* overseas for German audiences. (I should note here that Tinchev's chapter speaks to an issue that I encountered while compiling essays for the book. Although Season 3 of the series concluded in December 2008 on Showtime in the United States, because of differences in distribution and the way that networks are run, British viewers had only recently seen the end of Season 2. As a result, critics contributing from the UK had to find other ways of gaining access to the third season so that they could comment on it for this book.) As Tinchev notes, although American serials are popular in other countries, network politics often prevent those audiences from seeing the shows simultaneously with viewers elsewhere, and, through internet postings and other media outlets, they wind up finding out about the shows and their plots long before they actually air.

The final part of this collection is devoted to genre studies of the series and how *Dexter* flexibly crosses a number of different genre lines in the "execution" of its narrative. As dark as the episodes frequently are, James Francis points out that there is also a great deal of humor in the plotlines, and, through comparisons ranging from *I Love Lucy* to *American Psycho* and even the cartoon *Dexter's Laboratory*, Francis shows us the "lighter side" of Dexter and reveals the comedy beneath the blood spatter and plastic wrap. Alison Peirse conversely sheds light on the darkness of the series by placing it within the context of film noir. Drawing on the cinematic history of noir, Peirse looks at how the series incorporates the genre's conventions before ultimately rejecting them for a domesticity that is more soap operatic. Stacey Abbott and Simon Brown place *Dexter* within the framework of other forensic television shows like *Bones* and *CSI*, shows that specifically function through the proliferation of "graphic body horror." Not only does *Dexter* creatively position itself as a work of horror by subverting or undermining the very conventions that would define it as such, according to Abbott and Brown, but, inasmuch as the series itself is informed by and responds to an aesthetic, Dexter, in the words of The Police, consistently attempts to "turn a murder into art," through his blood spatter and crime scene recreations as well as through the orchestration and construction of his murders themselves. Stan Beeler adds yet another dimension to this genre study by comparing Dexter to other pop culture "vigilante heroes," like the private-eye, The Lone Ranger, and Batman. From Dexter's "public identity" to his code of conduct, the series refers to many of these conventions, too, Beeler argues, just as it reacts and rewrites them as well through his bloody rituals and homicidal temptations.

The book concludes with an episode guide to the first three seasons as well as a novel guide to all four of Jeff Lindsay's Dexter books.

Part One.
First Blood: Interviews

1.
An Interview with Author and *Dexter* Creator Jeff Lindsay

Jeff Lindsay captured readers' imaginations as well as their consciences through the creation of Dexter Morgan in 2004's *Darkly Dreaming Dexter*, a book that largely launched both a novel and a television series. While the Showtime drama has introduced a number of people to the character and the concept of Dexter, Lindsay continues to be the original source for him and provides some interesting perspective on just what makes him tick. In this interview from March 26, 2009, he talked about the development of Dexter, the philosophical and aesthetic ideas behind the novel series, and even some of the challenges that he faces in keeping audiences interested in his work.

Interviewer [Doug Howard]: You've said elsewhere that Dexter came from a Kiwanis Club business luncheon. Is that right?

Jeff Lindsay: Yes. I was getting ready to talk and watching everybody, and, as I like to say when I'm giving my little spiel in public, I was watching them give each other phony smiles and pats on the back and talking with food in their mouth and the thought just popped into my head that serial murder isn't really always a bad thing.

DH: So what were you supposed to speak about?

JF: It was something like, "Why you should read one book in your life or your head will explode," or "The Arts are Important." It was something like that.

DH: And I've read that you were making notes on napkins at the luncheon at that point. Did you always know that this was going to be a first-person narrative? Did you think about writing it in the third person?

JF: I'm not absolutely positive. I know that, when I started writing, the first thing that I wrote was in first person. I don't remember if I had the idea instantly or not.

DH: And *Darkly Dreaming Dexter* wasn't your first choice for the title?

JF: The original title was *The Left Hand of God*. Jason Kaufman, the editor, didn't like it, and I also got a call from my buddy Steve Bogart, who said it was the name of one of his dad's films (yeah, THAT Bogart). So we argued about it for weeks, and one night at dinner my daughter Pookie, who was around seven, suggested *Pinocchio Bleeds*. I opened my mouth to tell her she didn't really understand, since she hadn't read the MS—and it hit me like a ton of bricks that it was a perfect title. Jason didn't like it, though, so we fought a few more weeks before we hit it.

DH: As we were getting ready for this interview, you mentioned that you've been compared to some unusual authors, from P.G. Wodehouse to Poe to Camus. I can understand the Wodehouse connection since you've said that you like Wodehouse.[1] And Poe makes sense because his first-person narrators are also darkly comic, as in "The Tell-Tale Heart." But your real source for Dexter is actually your acting background?

JF: Yes. That's kind of the way that I write it. I get into character, I sit there, and I see it from his point of view while I'm writing. Oddly, though, since you mention Poe, one of the things that I do is I go into the elementary and middle schools and even the high schools, once or twice, and I do a series of shows for the kids. One of them is "The Tell-Tale Heart." I put on make-up, and I talk a little bit about Poe. And then I do the story, which is in the first person.

DH: Would you call Poe a literary influence, then?

JF: No, not really. Wodehouse is more of an influence. I read his stories, but I wouldn't consider it an influence.

DH: Are there any other literary influences that stand out?

JF: None that I can think of. I'm not trying to be disingenuous, but

I just never really thought about that, that, "Oh, I'm going to do something with the characters that he does."

DH: Given the acting influence, then, do you think about the novels cinematically as you write—how they could be staged or how they'd work on screen?

JF: No, not at all. It comes out that way because I did a lot of screen-writing and dramatic writing, in general. That's in there somewhere, and it affects things when I'm writing.

DH: From what you'd said about the more unusual connections that people had made to your work, do you think that they are taking the novels more seriously or in a different way than they should? Are they misinterpreting or misreading you? Have people been reading the novels in ways that you never really intended?

JF: You have to work really hard to misinterpret, I think. There's a story about [the poet Robert] Frost and his poem "Stopping By Woods on A Snowy Evening." While he was still alive, an eighth or ninth grade teacher in New Jersey had her class write about what the poem meant. And, out of thirty-six people in the class, she got thirty-six different answers. She sent them all to Frost and said, "I don't know which one of these is right. Can you tell me?" And he wrote back and said, "They're all right. It's wonderful. Some of them I'd never thought of." So, as far as that goes, it's hard to misinterpret something if you're at least being genuine and pursuing it a little bit. I also made a very conscious choice to write popular stuff, stuff that people would like and not literary, if it's fair to make that distinction. I also think that, if it becomes a guilty pleasure for somebody, then it's possible that they might try to make it more than it is. On the other hand, maybe it is more, and I'm just being too modest. As far as intention goes, my honest-to-God intention is to write something fun to read and maybe thought-provoking at the same time. If people want to make more of it than it is, then, okay, now it is more.

DH: When I spoke to James Manos about his vision of the show, he talked about Dexter as "the most sane and honest" character in a largely dysfunctional world. Do you think about the character that way?

JF: Well, I know that's the way that Dexter thinks of himself.

DH: Would you say that Dexter is the hero of these novels?

JF: He's the protagonist, anyway. Whether that makes him an actual hero in real life, that's one of the things that I'm asking people to think about a little bit. It's not a decision that I'm prepared to come down on one way or the other, except to say that, technically speaking, he's a serial killer.

DH: There is some delicious irony in the fact that Dexter works for the police department. Is that what drew you to the police connection, or were you interested in writing a variation on the police thriller?

JF: Honestly, the whole CSI, lab work, chasing bad guys down dark alleys, all of that kind of bores me. I don't watch those shows. Nothing against them. They just don't interest me. I wanted to make this a little different. And neither the show nor the books really dwell on what I guess you'd call the CSI aspects of it, on the lab work and all of that. If there's a blood sample to look at, it's written as, "I looked at the blood sample." It's not some long thing about using Luminol and all of that.

DH: You did try to track down the blood-spatter expert in Miami as a source for the book though?

JF: I did. Originally, when I started writing the book, I had some good friends who were cops in Miami at the time, and they said, "Oh, you've got to get in touch with this guy Toby, the blood-spatter guy in Miami. He's the guy who has Dexter's job. So get in touch with him, write him, and ask if you can talk to him." So I wrote and I heard nothing, and I wrote again and I heard nothing. And, finally, after like six weeks, I get this very short e-mail saying, "I just don't have time for anything like this. Sorry. Bye." So, when Showtime arrived to shoot the pilot in Miami, he had time for that. And I tell the story, and I was telling the story at the Miami Book Fair. And, to show the difference between books and TV, I talked about how, when Michael Hall first got to town, Toby was there to meet his plane, to carry him around for three weeks, to do whatever he wanted. And, when I finished, everybody laughed and said, "Ha, ha, good story." And then I asked, "Any questions?" And a hand went up in the back of the room, and this guy stood up and said, "Okay, in the first place, I didn't meet his plane . . ." But he was very nice, and he did say, "Now, if you have any questions, you can call me."

DH: Did you speak with him after that?

JF: I didn't because I realize that he is a whole lot busier, and I have a friend on the west coast of Florida who does the same job in this area. Again, though, I try to avoid getting too technical. Just like yesterday, I had to write and ask her, "How hard is it to find out if it's human blood?" And she wrote back and said, "It's easy. You do this." And it took five seconds.

DH: Are the published versions of the novels radically different from the drafts? Have you made significant changes in the plots or in certain scenes from the drafts to the final manuscripts?

JF: I don't really write a lot of drafts because I start every day by rewriting what I wrote the day before. It's kind of in finished condition when the editor gets it. And we work through it, and he'll tell me, "This isn't clear. How about a scene where something like this happens? Can we cut some of this here?" As for doing whole new drafts, that really doesn't happen.

DH: Did you ever write something and decide to take it out because it seemed radically wrong for your vision of the novel or the character?

JF: Not at all. There are one or two things that I'm avoiding, like the whole plot thread where Dexter teaches Cody how to be a serial killer.

DH: That's interesting because that was a significant plot point in the last novel, *Dexter in the Dark*. The TV series hasn't picked up on that specifically, although they did speculate as to the character of Dexter's son in the last season. They never talked about him training his child or Rita's children, though. So you don't want to get into that in the novels?

JF: I kind of have to at some point, because, at this point, I've promised the readers that it's going to happen. And I do readings and appearances where people want to know, "When is this going to happen?" So, they're waiting for it. But, I haven't figured out yet how to do it in such a way that I don't get arrested for literary child abuse or something.

DH: There's an interesting connection there because, for a while, you were writing columns about parenting and fatherhood,[2] and parenting and fatherhood are strong aspects of the novels, from Harry to Dexter. As far as Harry is concerned, on the one hand, this just seems like parenting gone horribly wrong, and I wonder why Harry didn't get this kid into all kinds of therapy when he discovered that he had this dark side. But Harry does love Dexter. Dexter even talks about that in the novels. So what are these novels saying about parenting?

JF: I'm pretty sure what Harry did wasn't the exact right thing to do as a parent. It's not what I would do. Then again, I've never been faced with the problem, either. Harry was a disillusioned cop. Anybody who's been a cop for longer than a week eventually realizes that there's a huge gap between law and justice. I think he saw a chance to save a little bit of his son and his ideals of justice at the same time. It's a solution. Whether it's the right one is a question. I wouldn't have done it, but it worked for him.

DH: You went in a radically different direction in the last novel, both in terms of the serial killer genre and as far as the novel series itself was concerned. You've made it more of a supernatural story now with this whole discussion about the source of the Dark Passenger. Is this where the novels will be going?

JF: Probably not. It was a direction that I wanted to try, and I wasn't really happy with it. I took it in that direction once, and now I'm going to come back. When you're doing a series like this, you've got to keep the mind alive, and I'm not going to apologize to people who think, "Oh, that's false to the character." I have to try new stuff every now and then.

DH: Is that what's difficult about developing a novel series like this, that you constantly have to reinvent it? And you've come out with a number of Dexter books in a short period of time.

JF: I've pretty much had one out every year. The real hard part is making it the same and different each time out. There are a certain number of things that you have to put in because that's what people like about it, but it has to be different enough so that they don't feel like they're reading the same book over and over. I'm not going to mention names, but, in one of the novel serials that I used to follow, by book eight or nine you could tell that the guy just started phoning it in. He was even repeating the same joke two or three books in a row. You could tell he was getting tired. I don't want to do that.

DH: Do you have a vision of where the novels are going to go, or how many novels there will be, or what will happen to Dexter in the end, as Rowling did with Harry Potter?

JF: When I was out in Hollywood, I was in something called the New Talent Development Program at ABC and then at Paramount later. This was for comedy and acting. And one of the things that the guy drummed into our heads was, "You all want to be actors. If you're lucky enough, you'll get a part on a hit sitcom where you're the goofy neighbor. You'll come in every week and say five lines and take the check home and pay the bills. That's success. And it's luck, too, and you owe it to the people who like you to do it as long as they want to see it." I kind of feel like that about Dexter. I want to keep it fresh, and I want to keep it good as long as people want to see it and read them. And if the time comes where they're so tired of it that nobody wants to pay me to write them, I'll go get a job at Wal-Mart or something.

DH: So, where the novel series goes or how it will end up has yet to be determined?

JF: I go book by book. I don't even know what I'm going to do tomorrow. So, five years down, who knows?

DH: You've said that you think Michael C. Hall's doing a great job on the show. In a review of *Hannibal Rising*, one film critic [Ron Henriques] suggested that Thomas Harris had fallen in love with Anthony Hopkins's portrayal of Hannibal Lecter and that this had affected his development of the character.[3] Is it difficult to write the novels now without seeing Hall or any of the other actors in these roles?

JF: Not so far. Every season of the show that goes by, I get more little twinges. To be honest, because I'm doing it from my point of view when I write it, I don't see myself as "Michael C. Hall but bigger." One of the odd things that happens is one or two of the minor characters pop in. He's called "Masuka" on the show, but he's actually "Masuoka" in the novels. And he's played by C.S. Lee on the show. Every now and then, I see his face. And I have to remind myself, "The one in the book is different. Calm down." It's never Michael, though.

DH: While the television series has maintained the flavor of the novels, it's also departed from them in a number of significant ways. One of the key differences and one of the major departures from the novel to the television series is when Dexter decides to kill his brother Brian/the Ice Truck Killer. That moment really spoke to how they would be taking the character in a different direction. What do you think that decision, whether to kill him or let him go, says about the character?

JF: Well, he's coming back again in the novels, the brother. They, of course, don't have that option. I think that it's a key difference, and I think that they did it that way because they fell in love with the character of LaGuerta on the show. They wanted to keep her. She's a valuable member of the ensemble cast, so I think that's why that decision was made. Most of the time in TV, decisions are not made on the basis of aesthetics. They're a lot more practical than that. So, to find a cast member who's that good and who works so well with everybody, you bend a little for that.

DH: I know that you're a fan of the show and that you watch it regularly. Have you ever watched it and thought, "I wish I'd done that," or have you ever watched and thought, "I'd never do that"?

JF: There have been moments of both. TV is a totally different medium. There's things that you have to do on TV that I don't want to do in the books. There've been moments on the show where I've thought, "Well, I wouldn't have done that in the books, but I know why they did that here." I've never gone, "Oh my God! That's horrible! What a bunch of idiots!" I did ten years of hard time in Hollywood, and I know how lucky I got with this group. They know what they're doing, and they're faithful to the material, if they're not literally faithful, and they're always faithful to the spirit of it. They do a great job.

DH: For all of the departures that they have made, they do come back at times to the novels. The wedding comes to mind. So does the question of Dexter as parent.

JF: There are even moments where specific lines from the books come out, where a writer decided that there was something in there that they couldn't ignore. My wife will usually turn to me and say, "That's one of yours." And I'll say, "Are you sure?"

DH: Do you have some kind of agenda, political or otherwise, when you write the novels? Are they making some kind of statement about capital punishment?

JF: No, not really. If there's an agenda, which is iffy, it would be a philosophical one, not a political one. I'd love to have people think about it. One of the examples that I like to give is that, even if you say that you are against capital punishment, there was, in our area, a year or so ago, a little girl and I mean "little," and she was kidnapped, raped, and murdered. What do you want to do with this guy when they catch him? Do you want to just put him in prison? I don't. I want him dead. Sorry. That may make me a bad person. Okay, that's what Dexter's doing. Now, he's doing it without benefit of the courts or anything else, but that's pretty much his agenda. So, whether it's right or wrong is not something I want to come out and say. I would just love it if people would think about it a little.

DH: This makes me wonder about Dexter's popularity, both on television and in the novels. There are websites and fansites from different countries and in different languages. He's internationally popular. Why do you think that is? Do you think that he speaks to some kind of desire for justice?

JF: Here's another literary comparison that we can make. I realized a year or two ago that I was becoming Edgar Rice Burroughs. Nobody in the world knows who Edgar Rice Burroughs is. Everybody knows who Tarzan is; nobody knows who Edgar Rice Burroughs is. The character has obviously hit something with people, some Jungian archetype, ja? I'm in the position where nobody gives a damn about me or the books or the TV show, if it comes down to it, as much as they care about Dexter himself. I think that it's hit some primal nerve somewhere, and I think it's partly because people love to see justice done. If I can go back to this kidnapper again, if I heard that he was caught and shot to death while trying to escape, I'd say, "Yeah, great! Justice is done!" Everybody feels that. A lot of us go, "Oh, that's wrong. Let's move on and not try to get blood for this." But down deep, we all want to see it done.

DH: This reminds me of the recent outcry against Bernie Madoff [4] and how people want justice for what he has done and how negative and violent so many of the reactions toward him have been.

JF: This is a guy who should be tied to a tree and fed Ex-lax. As far as justice fantasies go, though, lots of comic books will give you the same justice fantasy. This is where someone even connected Dexter to Camus. He's so clearly the outsider and looking in and commenting on what he sees. They preserve that brilliantly on the TV show, and I say "brilliantly" because it's an important part of what people like about the character.

DH: Even though he's an outsider, the novels and the TV show work to make him seem familiar. Where he might have been presented from a distance, as the Other, in the past, now we get to hear what he's thinking and what's going on inside of his head.

JF: And one of the points that we come away with is that he's not that different from us.

DH: That's also something that makes the novels and the series so uncomfortable and that creates an ethical dilemma for the reader or the viewer, that we might have something in common with Dexter.

JF: That's one of the things that I spend time thinking about with these books, the ethical and moral dilemmas. It's a lot of what I want to do with the character. I'm glad that it makes people edgy sometimes.

DH: Since you deal with Dexter so much, are there ever any moments that you get tired of the character and want to put your head some place else?

JF: Absolutely. There were moments when I was finishing *Dexter in the Dark* where I seriously thought about killing him. At the moment, I have other projects that I spend some time on, and, if I get totally Dexter-ed out, I'll go tinker with something else for a while.

DH: What can you tell us about the new novel, *Dexter by Design*?

JF: Dexter encounters a killer who kills as a form of performance art. I grew up in a series of art galleries and so on, so this is just a chance for me to play with that a little.

DH: Do you already have the next novel in the works?

JF: I already have two pages of notes for the one after that. I've started on number five. I'm on like page 30. If you want an almost exclusive scoop, I told someone in Australia this. I'm on my way to the Brisbane Literary Festival. The one I'm writing now is called *Dexter is Delicious*, and it deals with cannibalism.

DH: I'm sure that people will be making all kinds of Hannibal Lecter connections there.

JF: It's kind of an obvious perversion to go into this world, but I wanted to wait a couple of books until I felt like Dexter was established, so that people wouldn't say, "Oh, he's ripping off Hannibal Lecter." If you really want to get disturbed deeply, you can look at the Yahoo or Google chat rooms for cannibalism, and they're real cannibals. The worst part of it, and this is the thing I had nightmares about for two weeks, was that about half of the letters are from people saying, "Please consider eating me. I've always fantasized about being eaten." Some of them describe what they want: "As you slowly stick the knife into me and cut out a chunk of my flesh and roast it and eat it while I watch."

DH: Who are they eating? Volunteers?

JF: Yeah, they're eating volunteers.

DH: I guess, just doing research for these books, you wind up seeing sides of the world that you never knew about.

JF: And don't want to know about. And they ask why writers drink. Well, there it is.

2.
An Interview with *Dexter* Writer and Developer James Manos, Jr

In addition to writing and producing the pilot for *Dexter*, James Manos, Jr has worked on a number of critically acclaimed television projects, from *The Positively True Adventures of the Alleged Texas Cheerleader-Murdering Mom* to *The Sopranos* and *The Shield*. In 1999, he won an Emmy Award for Outstanding Writing for a Drama Series, which he received for "College," one of the key episodes in the development of *The Sopranos* narrative. Manos was also Consulting Producer on the first two seasons of *The Shield* (2002–3) before being brought onboard to write the pilot for Showtime's *Dexter* (2006). In this interview from March 19, 2009, James discussed the pilot, the character of Dexter, and his original vision for the show in detail.

Interviewer [Doug Howard]: So tell me about your work with *Dexter*.

James Manos, Jr: I created this show, and I produced the pilot. I cast everybody and put the show together. I figured out a way to turn that novel into a pilot and gave it legs, so that it would have a whole story arc. And I figured out basically the first twelve episodes, some of which ultimately was used and some was not. And that pilot I'm extraordinarily proud of because the pilot that was shot is, basically, word for word what I wrote. And the actors that I cast were all the actors that I wanted. I left the show after producing the whole thing and after the editing process, the music, etc., largely for personal and creative differences. My involvement with the show stopped after the pilot.

DH: As far as television shows go, what kind of shows did you like growing up? David Chase, for example, talked about how he watched *The Untouchables* and *The Fugitive*.[1]

JM: I remember *The Fugitive*. That was great. I watched a lot of *NYPD Blue* when that came out, by David Milch, who is one of the most brilliant men that I've ever met, by the way. He's also one of the most generous and gracious human beings I've ever met in my life. I cannot speak highly enough of David.

DH: When you think about television shows that inspired your work, then, would you list *NYPD Blue*?

JM: Without a doubt. That was the first time where you started to see some really complex characters put into some really complex situations that forced them to make decisions that, ethically, may or may not have been the right decisions for them to make. I was intrigued by that kind of ethical dilemma, that some of these characters faced from situations that they were put in. It was the first time that we saw a real version of life, by way of a cop's view of the world. It was the first time that we were given a sense of reality that was really never done before. There was a cop show with Jack Warden many years ago [*N.Y.P.D.*—1967–9] that comes to mind. That was a really gritty, really cool show—a really interesting piece. When I was growing up, I liked to watch films and tended to go toward the more gritty, realistic movies—the gangster movies, the James Cagney movies.

DH: Are there any television shows that you like to watch now?

JM: It's interesting. Ever since I got into the series world, which started with *The Sopranos*, I really don't watch a lot of TV. More than anything else, I continue to watch a lot of movies. Ultimately, I don't want to be influenced by what's on the air, what people are saying works and doesn't work. I think that, if I had watched a lot of TV, I might not have seen the real opportunity to turn *Dexter* into a series. I might have just said, "Oh, they've never done anything like this, so they won't." I'm not a big fan of being derivative. There are certain fundamental elements of anything that will work well. There are certain fundamental necessities of coming up with a really strong character and putting that character into a unique and compelling world. If you can get those two, which isn't always so easy, then it should work, and the public should be ready for it. I think that the public was ready for a show about a serial killer because of a show like *The Sopranos* and because of *The Shield*, because you started seeing a real anti-hero.

DH: That was one of the things that I wanted to ask you. What drew you to *Dexter* as a television project? What made you think that this would make a good television show?

JM: I actually hadn't thought about that. There were two executive producers who had brought the book *Dexter* to Bobby Greenblatt, who runs Showtime. I had written a black comedy prior to this moment, and I think that Bobby really thought that I would be able to bring some humanity and some humor and some real character and depth to these people, to pull them from the novel and put them into a television world. He thought that I'd be the right one for the job, and I was lucky enough to figure out how to take that book, rework it for television, and ultimately give a sense to Showtime of what the twelve episodes would be. After I left the show, unfortunately, I don't think that they used a lot of them. I think that they took bits and pieces. It would have been a different kind of show in some ways.

DH: What sorts of challenges did you face in turning the novel into a television show?

JM: Novelists tend to have a different kind of ear. It's a different medium, obviously. Let me say that I think that the novel was brilliant. It's a different medium, though, so you have to make certain changes. And I had to figure out a way how to establish, in one hour, a guy that you are going to want to stay with, bring him some humanity, bring him some humor, and allow us into the world that he is in. The way to do that was to have his thoughts, his observations spoken, through voice-over, to try to bring us into his world. One of the most attractive things about that and one of the things that I was most proud of was that all of his observations about the world have a kind of childlike innocence and curiosity about them because he is trying to fit in. That's the irony, though. He has to fit in, but he can't fit in. But within the innocence and the curiosity, there's an unbound kind of thirst of wanting to live, and there's something kind of heroic about that, since he's killing these bad guys. I am a firm believer in that ethical decision. There are people that should be "done with."

DH: *Dexter* makes us confront those kinds of moral decisions, just like some of the other shows that you've worked on, like *The Shield* and *The Sopranos*. And that confrontation makes those shows compelling to watch, in the same way that it makes them controversial. I was reading recently [in Glen Gabbard's *The Psychology of The Sopranos*] about how David Chase argued with HBO over whether or not Tony should kill Fabian Petrulio in that "College" episode (33–4).

JM: I bet you he did. I've got to give an enormous amount of credit to Bobby Greenblatt and his staff because those guys were ballsy. And those guys were very cool with me. They were really good. And they were very respectful and very nurturing. I like those guys a lot. I think that it comes from those people. It comes from the head of HBO. It comes from the head of Fox and FX, who was overseeing *The Shield*, by allowing someone who was as smart and as brilliant as Shawn Ryan to do what he did, to just leave him alone. Shawn is brilliant. He's a great guy. I've been lucky to work with some really good people. I would say the same about Greenblatt and his staff at Showtime. You have to give them credit for doing this.

DH: How would you say that your experiences on *Dexter* compared to your work on *The Shield* and *The Sopranos*?

JM: I probably had more fun in my life working for Shawn Ryan as his Consulting Producer than I've had anywhere. It was a gas. It was so much fun trying to figure out how to fuck up people in ways that nobody had ever seen before—getting to get Vic Mackey to throw someone off a roof. And the rule of thumb on *The Shield* was Vic Mackey could throw anybody off the roof; he could do whatever he wanted as long as the person he was throwing off the roof did something worse than he did.

DH: That's sort of true for Dexter, too.

JM: That's true. This is something that I was going to really stress in the series. His father gave Dexter his life. James Remar in the pilot basically gave Dexter his life by saying, "I'm going to turn this bad thing in you into a positive." That's, without being religious, a truly Christian act, and that relationship between father and son was something that I was going to probably focus on a little bit more than I think they do now. You would've seen more elements of how Dexter became who he was, once the father realized that this kid was a killer, a complete and total sociopath. And you cannot change that. Three per cent of the world's population are sociopathic. They will run over your children without even thinking about it. That's a lot of fucking people. In America alone, that's nine million people that will kill you and not think twice about it, or they will rob you and not think twice about it. So, in the world, that's about one hundred and eighty million people who will do that to you. So, his father, sitting there and thinking about it, instead says, "I'm not going to institutionalize you. I'm not going to kill you. I'm going to teach you how to use your bad for good." And you would have seen more elements of the father training Dexter, where he would take him to a park, let's say, and teach him how to read human behavior—"Who's the bad guy? Who's the good guy?"— teach him how to carve up people, teach him how to cover his tracks. Don't forget his father was a cop. I would've had more of that kind of thing. I think that the audience would have thought that that was kind of cool.

DH: They did break his father down a little bit more in Season 2. They showed how disgusted he was when he finally saw Dexter cutting up a body for the first time. And they revealed that Harry was having an affair with Dexter's birth mother.

JM: Seeing his father's reaction to Dexter killing—that's a very organic thing to do, quite frankly. I think that's probably a very cool element because, at the end of the day, watching your son actually dismember a body, that's going to be disturbing.

DH: But you would have focused more on the training?

JM: I would have focused on the actual upbringing. I probably would have been a little more linear about it. I probably would have been kind of like seeing what it was like and hiding some of these things from his sister. I would have had his sister in more of those flashbacks, young Deb. You would have seen Harry's wife. I would have also done other things with Margo Martindale's character [Camilla], the record keeper in the police department, the one who occasionally hands Dexter files and says, "I don't really want to know what you are doing with these." I was going to have that come full circle and make it clear sooner or later in the episodes that Harry had an affair with her years ago, and she still loved Harry and she kind of knows what Dexter is doing. And, at a certain point, that was also going to turn on Dexter, because the whole trick was to have Dexter be put into situations, first and foremost, human situations, the more human, the more uncomfortable he would be in them. And then, of course, put him into situations where more and more people are suspecting him, not just like Doakes, but other people. And this would just increase the tension. And it would just increase a sense of doom, almost, an inevitability that this may end. And the great irony of the piece, ultimately, is: does Dexter become so human that he loses his serial killing thing? That question, the closer he becomes to being human, by all of his observations, is one of the principle elements of the piece.

DH: How would you compare writing a character like Dexter to writing Tony Soprano or developing Vic Mackey on *The Shield*?

JM: They're totally different elements. I never wrote any episodes for *The Shield*. My job there was to come up with the story ideas, to oversee some of the writers, and basically just to kind of engender, within the writers' room, a kind of sensibility of how this world of criminality exists. And, I also wanted to make sure that Shawn's vision was secured. He had an incredibly strong vision. This guy was a real bright, creative guy. I mean, in the two years that I was there, I don't think there was anything, not a single moment that could be called close to a cliché.

DH: So, thinking about your other work, so many of the shows that you have worked on have dealt with questions of morality and criminals and these different sides of law and order. Are you following a particular theme or area of interest?

JM: Well, Chase was obviously the first one to do it, and he was the visionary of it all. Milch saw it, too. It's kind of a building block of a perception of the world, but I think 9/11 helped create a sensibility in the world, certainly in America, so that there's no longer a black and white. But the reality is, do you really know what's the right thing to do here? I think because of world politics and because of that threat of terrorism and not really being sure if this country is collectively doing the right thing to save us, that all comes into play. Whether we're aware of it or not, I believe that's had an impact. The world now is a much more fucking complicated place. Our enemies are our friends; our friends are our enemies. Is Pakistan a friend of ours or not? Are the Jordanians a friend of ours or not? It's getting really complicated here. I think that there's something to that that has influenced both the creators of shows and certainly the audience that is more willing to accept that complexity as a mirror image of our world. It's not that simple any more.

DH: And you're also drawn to projects with that kind of complexity, where the questions are more ambiguous for the audience?

JM: It also attracts the intelligence of the audience. Nobody's talking down any more, which is a really positive thing.

DH: The other thing that stands out about these shows is that they all deal with domestic life. They're all family dramas, in a way, but with a dark side to them. "College" is a great example of that. On the one hand, here's someone who's a family man, and, on the other hand, here's someone who's a killer.

JM: But who isn't? You can't think that these characters have a separation, where someone's in the mafia or they're a cop or they're a serial killer and they go home and they separate it out, and it doesn't have an impact. The truth of the world is that what you do for a living will impact your home life. For these characters, it all boils down to the personal character relationships that they have with these other people and how it hurts or benefits these other people. You can't make that separation any more.

DH: So these shows are reflecting that complexity of life?

JM: Without a doubt.

DH: Do you think that the audience's tastes are changing?

JM: I think that audiences are getting brighter. I think that audiences are demanding more, both in terms of production value and in terms of more well-drafted characters.

DH: Audiences, then, are looking for something more provocative?

JM: They're definitely looking for something, and, if it's not reality TV, then you better be doing something good to keep your audience. It's getting tougher for people like me and anybody else out there that does what I do. This reminds me of something else that would have been different at the end of the first year. The cliffhanger, the ending episode would have been different than what they ended up doing. But, most importantly, you would have realized, the audience would have realized after ten, eleven, twelve episodes, that all of the satellite characters, that being Batista, that being Doakes, that being Lieutenant LaGuerta, that being Deb, everybody else, all the satellite characters—if you put them in a circle with Dexter in the center—you would have realized that all of those people are infinitely more fucked up and more dysfunctional, that, in fact, Dexter is the most sane of them all.

DH: Even being a serial killer, then, you would have said that he's the healthiest one on the show?

JM: I would have said that he's the most honest, even though he's living a secret life. But, ultimately, I would have presented these other characters so that you would have seen them becoming more idiosyncratic, more dysfunctional, more kind of fucking crazy, more kind of making more mistakes than even Dexter does.

DH: Like *The Sopranos* and *The Shield, Dexter* has generated its share of controversy. [The Parents Television Council's campaign against the public broadcasting of the series comes to mind here.] How would you respond to critics who are upset with the way that the show "empathizes" with a serial killer or who believe that it glorifies serial killers?

JM: I would tell them, "If you don't like it, don't watch." You hear rumors that the Fairness Doctrine is going to be imposed once again on radio, and I find that absurd. Turn off the fucking radio, and turn off the television station. Change it. No one has a gun to your head. Dexter's not going to come over and kill you if you don't watch it. Watching the evening news is, in some ways, more horrifying and more violent and more threatening than anything that's created out of fiction. Pick up the *New York Times* and read between pages 7 and 13 or between pages 3 and 7 about how the world is falling apart. That's pretty harrowing stuff. And in the total scheme of things, it's a lot more harrowing than some fictional guy who is killing other killers. If other people don't like it, they always have the freedom to create what they want to create and try to get it on the air.

DH: There are a number of successful serial killer films out there, like *The Silence of the Lambs* or *American Psycho* or *Se7en*. Were you thinking about those films or influenced by them when you wrote the pilot for *Dexter*?

JM: I didn't think about those, primarily because my focus was not thinking about the killing, but about thinking of him as a human being. I did not think of him as, necessarily, a killer. That was almost a by-product. It was more important for me to focus on his innocence about the world. I didn't really think about him as a killer because that would have been somewhat one-dimensional and also somewhat truncating.

DH: Were you thinking about any specific political agenda when you wrote the pilot? Were you thinking about making some kind of statement about capital punishment?

JM: No. I personally don't believe in capital punishment, which sounds contradictory because I earlier said that I think certain people should be dead, but I don't believe in it whatsoever. And I did not set out to write a political statement at all. I think that most people don't. When that happens, the politics supersedes the storytelling, so you have to be careful.

DH: Did you watch the show when it was put on broadcast television?

JM: No.

DH: What did you think about the idea of editing the show for broadcast television?

JM: I thought that it was a lousy deal for everybody involved. None of the actors got any residuals, and I didn't make any money off it. It was a lousy deal, quite frankly. I think that it was a smart move on [CBS President] Les Moonves's part to do it during the [Writers']

Strike. But it's showbiz. It's money. CBS has to make money. I may not like it. I have no control over it. It's a business, so what are you going to do?

DH: In writing the pilot, did Jeff Lindsay have any input at all?

JM: None. He's a very nice man, and I invited him to the set once, and he seemed to be very pleased. The novel was bought from him, though, so creatively, we could do whatever we wanted to do to his characters. We didn't have any obligation whatsoever to what was in his novel, and I wrote the pilot by myself.

DH: In your version of the first season, did you also have Dexter killing the Ice Truck Killer?

JM: In my version, his brother was going to escape so, in year two, the audience would sit there and think, "My God, his brother knows that Dexter is a serial killer, and Dexter knows that his brother is a serial killer." It's going to become a cat and mouse game. The brother was going to be exposed, and Dexter was going to be exposed. But ultimately, Dexter was going to be absolved of all of the suspicions that everybody in his police station thought of him until the very end. So it gives him a kind of pass, a freedom.

DH: From all that you've said here about Dexter, do you think that he is the hero, then, of the show?

JM: Without a doubt, he's the hero of the show.

DH: I guess that's the thing about many of these newer dramas. They make the audience rather conflicted about these characters and their heroism. Thinking about Vic on *The Shield*, for example, in some ways he's the best cop on the force. In other ways he's the dirtiest cop on the force. At one point, [creator Shawn] Ryan said that one of the main questions the show posed for the viewer was, "What would people be willing to accept for their own safety?"[2] In terms of the killer's heroism, *Dexter* seems to ask that same question. On the one hand, he's obviously got severe psychological issues, and he's committing ritualistic murders. On the other hand, he's killing other killers, ones that the police haven't caught, and he's taking them off the street, so isn't this a good thing?

JM: Who wouldn't kill a pedophile who's killing little kids? Who in their right mind would say, "Oh, let him go"? This guy's obviously not being incarcerated. That's the opening scene of the pilot, and it really endears the audience to this character. Nobody can accept a kid getting hurt. We have to stop that.

DH: Where do you see the show going? What do you think its future will be?

JM: I hope the show lasts forever, for the actors' sake because they're all nice people and they're all great at what they do. I hope it continues forever. I wish them all well.

Part Two.
Blood Slides: The Structure of the Series

3.
Dissecting the Opening Sequence
Angelina I. Karpovich

What does an opening title sequence do? It sets the mood of the piece, conveys essential information about the genre, setting, and characters, and it "hooks" the viewers in by building up anticipation for what is to follow. Additionally, as Hall (2000) suggests, title sequences can be viewed retrospectively, to gauge "something of the prevailing state of the film industry" in a given time period ("Opening Ceremonies"). Title sequences also act as unique "calling cards," which (if they are successful) instantly create a distinctive visual and thematic identity for the film or television programme. The work of Saul Bass, the graphic artist who crafted the title sequences to some of Alfred Hitchcock's most successful films, is commonly invoked as a paragon of creativity in the field of title sequence design. Bass' work, instantly recognizable for its clear lines and use of block colors, became intrinsic to Hitchcock's Hollywood-era style.

Bass' deceptively simple credits aimed to revolutionize the audience's experience of the beginning of the cinematic narrative. Previously, most title sequences had been considered a necessary but "dull" interlude, dictated by industrial and legal requirements, rather than any narrative or aesthetic considerations:

In the beginning, the function of a film's opening credits was simple: To list, literally, the makers of and contributors to a movie. Thematic links to the movie were achieved by a simple combination of score and typography itself—delicate script for a romance, bold sans serif for a crime picture, etc. "Artsy" credits might be ripped away one by one by a hand, appear on an antique map or be blown away, but they were still distinct from the movie proper and remained relatively static. Early titles, really a holdover from theatrical playbills, functioned like a book's title page: When they ended, the movie started. (Weed, "Using Movie Title Sequences")

The audience was rarely expected, even by the filmmakers themselves, to pay attention to the screen during the title sequence. Saul Bass' breakthrough was to convert opening credits into "a positive introduction to the film":

[W]hen the film itself begins, there is usually an initial "cold" period. However, titles can be sufficiently provocative and entertaining to induce the audience to sit down and *look*, because something is really happening on the screen. . . . [A]t this moment it is possible to project a symbolic foretaste of what is to come, and to create a receptive atmosphere that will enable the film to begin on a higher level of audience rapport. (Bass 200, emphasis in original)

Using graphics, music, and editing, Saul Bass crafted credit sequences which forced the viewers to pay attention, and thus engaged them in the narrative, from the very first frame. Bass' experiments with the medium rapidly produced both practical and theoretical results: "While the title of a film is a rather small appendage to the larger organism that is the film, I soon discovered it contains, in miniature, many of the procedures and problems that are characteristic of the body of the film" (200). Reflecting on his work in the documentary *Bass on Titles* (1977), Bass elaborated on the myriad creative possibilities offered by treating the opening title sequence as an integral part of the film: "[T]he title could make a more significant contribution to the storytelling process. It could act as a prologue; it could deal with the time before. . . . [It could] actually create a climate for the story." The success of Bass' pioneering approach to credit sequences is apparent from the way his contribution to, and influence on, the moving image, is recognized and persists to this day.

Geffner (1997), writing primarily for a readership of professional independent filmmakers, discusses title sequences in terms which are clearly inspired by Bass:

[T]he ultimate questions when designing a main title sequence are, much like any other aspect of a film, centred on theme, content, and the viewer's desired emotional response. . . . [T]itles are the very first images the audience absorb after the lights go out. They form a kind of contract, outlining the filmmaker's intentions and, for better or worse, setting up expectations that the audience, almost subliminally, will demand be met ("First Things First").

Geffner is echoed by Allison (2003) in a discussion of contemporary film title sequences which deliberately invoke the historical (and cinematic) past. Allison suggests that the title sequences can signal both the content and the "filmmaking sensibility" of the film that is about to follow. In so doing, they forge "a contract with the audience at the outset, instructing them of the parameters within which the film operates, alerting them to the tonalities of the film to come, and encouraging them to approach that experience in a frame of mind where they will be receptive to the pleasures it has to offer" ("Catch Me If You Can"). Finally Hall (2000) asserts that "[The] early days of film title sequence design laid the conceptual groundwork for all subsequent innovation in the field. There is hardly a title designer practicing today who doesn't refer back to the work of Bass and his sixties successors" ("Opening Ceremonies").

Conceptually, opening sequences are the most complex moments in most films and television programs. In an opening sequence, the reality of the production process (the names of the actors and production personnel) is literally superimposed over the fictional setting of the narrative. A modern opening sequence is, in effect, a reverse Brechtian device: a liminal moment, and a visible boundary between the real and the fictional, which ushers in the fictional world, leaving real life behind until the closing credits roll. In television in particular, where the flow of content is now almost entirely constant, the opening sequence serves a purpose which is doubly liminal: not only does it set up the distinct fictional universe of a particular series, but it also serves to distinguish the program from the program (or more likely, advert) which immediately preceded it in the television schedule. Arguably, television opening sequences have to encapsulate the essence and identity of the program to an even greater degree than film opening sequences: a film will be watched once, or in rarer cases, a number of times; a television program, if it is successful, will span multiple seasons over several years, running to dozens or even hundreds of episodes, each of which will be prefaced with opening credits which will become intensely familiar to the viewers.

Television opening sequences, then, share the main aims of opening sequences in film, but have an added dimension in their design: as well as providing instant impact, television opening sequences have to continuously engage the audience over multiple, weekly, repeat viewings. In practical terms, this means that an opening sequence for a television series will usually address the wider overarching thematic and narrative concerns of the series, rather than addressing the plot of individual episodes. Thus, opening title sequences for contemporary television series provide a particularly rich topic for in-depth analysis.

In the case of *Dexter*, the creative agency behind the opening credits, Digital Kitchen (which had previously produced the credit sequence for HBO's *Six Feet Under*, a similarly dark, complex, and often controversial series which coincidentally also starred Michael C. Hall), followed Saul Bass' maxim in producing a credit sequence which manages to reveal essential information about the character and plot, set up the themes and visual style of what is to follow, and yet produces enough tension and mystery to "hook" the viewers into following the narrative that is to come.

Dexter opens with a close-up on a mosquito. Retrospectively, the mosquito can be interpreted as a curiously apt metaphor for the protagonist: simultaneously dangerous and fragile, and utterly compelled to seek out and feed on human blood, despite the fact that humans usually fight back, and, more often than not, kill mosquitoes. So it is here: Dexter swats the mosquito with a precise, well-aimed, deadly blow, without even opening his eyes. We are only five seconds into the series at this point, but the central theme is already established: Dexter Morgan disposes of parasites, with a deadly efficiency. Moreover, we, the audience, are also already complicit in identifying with Dexter's actions: which of us has never killed a mosquito? The protagonist is unseen at this point, remaining either out-of-focus or in extreme close-up, but his actions so far are entirely understandable and familiar.

The title appears next, and several key inferences can be made about it: the color is strikingly red, easily assumed to be, or interpreted as, "blood-red." Indeed, the smudges and a droplet of the same color next to the title suggest spilled blood, as does the association with the mosquito which appeared immediately before the title. It is important to remember that while the color of the title is not coincidental, it may still, at this stage, represent something that *looks like* blood, rather than actual blood. *American Psycho* (dir. Mary Harron, 2000) does this in its opening moments, focusing on drops of a blood-red liquid, fully aware of its audience's expectations, before revealing that the blood-red liquid is in fact a sweet sauce being poured onto a dessert, and thus delaying the horror of an encounter with actual blood until after the opening sequence. In any case, even if the color of the title isn't representing actual blood, the red is still evocative. Without a doubt, red is the most evocative, connotation-rich color in the spectrum. In addition to blood, it is associated with passion, love, danger, beauty, celebration, excitement, political extremism, and illicit or illegal sexuality. The simple choice of blood-red for the show's title gives a clear indication of the type, and perhaps genre, of story that is about to unfold.

The graphic design of the show's title is just as deliberate and telling as the color; the design and the color of the title, taken together, both encapsulate and become symbolic of the show. The word "DEXTER," in thin, blood-red, block capitals, becomes the show's singular and defining graphic identity across all visual media, linking the series with its extensive promotional materials. The simple, clear, balanced, squared design of the letters, block capitals centred on a white background, is entirely undermined by the uneven and smudged distribution of the color in the letters. This contrast is another metaphor for one of the central themes of the series: Dexter's constant meticulous planning and the rigid boundaries he has set up in his life are like the solid contours of the letters; the way the world interferes with Dexter's plans, the constant external challenges to his routine, the tension of trying to contain his compulsion within a rigid exterior of "normalcy," are all represented by the uneven color, which smudges and escapes beyond the orderly straight outlines of the letters. We zoom in on the letters, slowly and slightly, almost imperceptibly, as the color drips and smudges further and further beyond the outlines of the letters, particularly the "X" in "DEXTER." "X" is significant both visually and conceptually: visually, it is almost in the center of the screen, so it naturally becomes the focal point of the frame; conceptually, the letter has its own connotations—it is associated with mystery, it signifies the unknown, it "marks the spot." Through color, typography, and composition, the title, although glimpsed only for a few seconds, contributes to establishing the mood of the narrative, and provides early signals of some of the series' central themes.

We move on to Dexter's morning routine. Still out-of-focus, he stands in front of the bathroom mirror, looking at his reflection. Then, in a disorientatingly uncomfortable close-up (combined with an audio close-up, a significantly amplified sound, which makes the touch of human skin sound harsh and intrusive), he drags a fingertip over his stubble, and begins shaving. Even this briefest of sequences is open to interpretation. Dexter is performing the same action as millions of other men, but something about the way he does it is clearly marked as extraordinary. Firstly, there are the close-ups, which signify a focus, a level of precision, in carrying out every task, however mundane, which clearly set Dexter apart from most men. Secondly, there is the fact that at this point, the audience still hasn't seen Dexter, apart from the extreme close-ups and the brief out-of-focus shots, which could suggest that his morning routine, which begins with shaving, is a ritual of making himself presentable to the outside world. For Dexter Morgan, "fitting in" with other people is a constant performative act, and his morning rituals are therefore a complex preamble to a performance. The practiced nature of Dexter's actions suggests that the routine is always the same, always this elaborate, and that he is somewhat incomplete and somewhat unready until it is finished.

The composition of the shaving scene once again invokes the themes of danger and vulnerability. Dexter's neck is exposed, and he tightens his skin with one hand, while holding a razor with another. The close-up, however, disembodies both the neck and the hands, so that we're not entirely sure—in the context of this particular frame—whether the body part being shaved is actually a neck, or whether the hands are Dexter's own. The trail of the razor upwards across the skin is once again accompanied by an audio close-up, an over-emphasized sound which invokes scraping, rather than gliding, as the movement of the blade. Even the most mundane activities take on a disembodied and violent quality where Dexter is concerned; and even the most mundane activities take an unusual amount of physical effort.

A drop of blood (an unusual instance of carelessness in Dexter's shaving routine, perhaps?) appears on the skin, before a quick cut to an extreme close-up of a drain. The shiny metal of the drain, together with the spotlessly clean white of the sink around it, invoke sterility, but that sterility is short-lived, as the drop of blood lands on the white surface of the sink, its perfect roundness in momentary symmetry with the roundness of the drain. The symmetry is almost immediately disrupted by two more drops of blood, each messier than the one before. The last drop, more of a smudge of blood, encroaches on the glistening metallic surface of the drain, completely undermining the initial spotlessly sterile composition of the shot, and serving as a reminder of the unruly splodges of blood-red color which disrupted the uniformity of the title.

As (presumably yet another) drop of blood glides down Dexter's neck, he catches it with a piece of tissue. An extreme close-up shows the white of the tissue (yet another symbol of fragility) rapidly changing to red as it absorbs the blood. The red overwhelms the white. Red, the color of danger and passion, rapidly replaces white, the color traditionally associated with innocence and purity.

In another rapid close-up, a large sharp knife cuts a piece of meat wrapped in plastic, cutting through the plastic and the meat at the same time. Once again, the sounds of the cutting, the unwrapping, the snapping of the meat are over-emphasized, as is the sound of the sizzling butter in the frying pan and the sound of the cooking once the meat hits the frying pan.

Another extreme close-up fleetingly focuses on Dexter's eyes and then cuts to an extreme close-up of his mouth as he devours the meat he's just cooked. He chews with precision, efficiency, but without any apparent enjoyment.

In yet another extreme close-up, an egg is broken, and ends up in the frying pan, being prodded with a knife. More red drops appear on a white surface. This time it's ketchup on an omelet, but

33

the color and composition clearly recall the blood in the sink and the blood on the tissue of a few moments earlier. There is a series of fast cuts of blood-red ketchup splashing on the omelet, and the omelet being efficiently dissected with a knife and fork. Once again, the sequence takes a familiar action, one probably done by most of the viewers, and suggests a sinister undercurrent through the use of extreme close-ups, unusual framing, and rapid editing.

This defamiliarization continues in the next shot, of a coffee mill from above. The coffee beans swirl, rapidly and uncontrollably, becoming less and less recognizable, losing their shape and texture, accompanied by the insistent mechanical sound of the coffee mill and the slow, deliberate beat of the theme tune. There is a cut to an extreme close-up of Dexter's fist as it tightens around the top of the cafetiere, and pushes the filter down, into the murkiness of the coffee.

Another (or perhaps the same) large sharp knife cuts an orange, in close-up and in slow motion, so that we see the orange's juice spray at the moment when its skin is broken; the moment is accompanied by yet another audio close-up. We follow the knife all the way through, as the fruit splits and falls apart. It is, of course, a blood orange. Another series of quick cuts shows Dexter using a manual juicer, forcing the juice out of the orange, and leaving behind the orange skin, with its pulp looking like mangled, twisted flesh.

In another extreme close-up, dental floss is wrapped precisely and tightly around fingers. Back at the bathroom sink, there is another set of extreme close-ups of Dexter's neck and teeth. The character is still disembodied, though by now we have plenty of information about him from the brief glimpses of his morning routine. From the rope imagery of the dental floss, we move on to more ropes, and close-ups of Dexter's muscles flexing as he tightens the ropes, which turn out to be shoelaces, once again in extreme close-up.

A piece of white fabric goes over the character's head, invoking suffocation through the simple everyday act of putting on a t-shirt, before it is pulled down, letting us see Dexter's face for the first time. He looks straight into the camera, underscoring the identification between himself and the audience, which will form one of the central devices of the show.

A key is taken out of a lock, and Dexter is outside, smiling at someone off-screen, and strolling to work. The exterior forms an immediate contrast to the interior shots: firstly, it is sunny, unlike the constantly murky and somewhat desaturated interior sequences, and secondly, Dexter is finally framed in a mid-shot, rather than the partial close-up glimpses of his body which punctuated the interior sequences.

There are four themes which appear to be central to this sequence, their importance signified by prominent repeated references. Firstly and most obviously, there is the theme of blood, which either physically appears or is invoked as an association on seven occasions: firstly, by association with the mosquito, secondly in the color of the title, then during the shaving sequence, as a separate close-up spreading on the tissue, and then as a color associated with the meat, the ketchup, and finally the orange.

If blood alone was the central repeated theme, it could be interpreted (relatively) innocuously. Dexter is, after all, an expert on blood-splatter patterns, working in the police department. The prominent presence of blood, or blood references, in his morning routine may be disconcerting, but could be explained as a professional preoccupation. Yet, another prominent theme is suffocation and/or strangulation: references include the wrapped-up meat, the rope symbolism of the dental floss and the shoelaces, and even Dexter's t-shirt, which momentarily appears to suffocate him. It is the combination of the imagery of blood and strangulation which pushes the opening sequence beyond the innocuous and into the territory of the unequivocally sinister. Both blood and strangulation are generally associated with extreme violence, and both feature prominently in the series, as part of Dexter's preferred method of murder: he binds his victims, and then cuts them up. The opening sequence thus prefigures the central elements of a ritual which will be featured, in one way or another, in almost every episode of the show.

At the same time, there is a conflicting set of imagery, which invariably appears in close proximity to imagery associated with violence, providing a contrast and raising questions about motivations and subjectivities. This is the theme of fragility, which again re-appears in multiple contexts throughout the sequence, suggesting its overall importance to the show. Dexter himself provides the first fleeting moment of fragility, asleep and vulnerable to the mosquito's bite; the mosquito, in turn, is transformed from assailant to victim when it is squashed by Dexter. Next, Dexter cuts himself while shaving, underscoring the fragility of his own skin, before a series of rapid cuts (in both senses of the word) destroy the egg, the coffee beans, and finally the orange. What is powerful about this study in fragility is that on every occasion the audience gets to see the object just before the moment when it is cut, broken, or otherwise destroyed. It is that repeated glimpse of completeness before the moment of destruction that illustrates just how fragile Dexter himself, and the world around him, is. The moment of destruction is also a moment of liminality, and the opening seconds in particular illustrate a fluidity of movement between categories, as Dexter and the mosquito switch between the roles of hunter and prey, victim and perpetrator of violence.

As discussed previously, Dexter's killing of the mosquito serves multiple narrative and structural purposes: it places the protagonist in danger and shows that he's capable of protecting himself; it demonstrates his efficiency in disposing of parasites; and it provides a moment of identification between Dexter and the audience. In addition, the role reversal seen in these opening moments introduces the notion of character complexity, of a wide range of motivations. Throughout the credit sequence, Dexter becomes the focal point for the representations of both violence and fragility, often in the space of the same moment. Apart from the interlude with the mosquito, this theme reappears in the shaving sequence (Dexter is seemingly in control of the blade, and then cuts himself), and while he gets dressed (seemingly struggling to breathe while putting on a t-shirt). The first time the audience sees his face properly, he looks directly at the camera, once again appearing fragile, despite the quite bloodthirsty way in which he has just dealt with his breakfast.

Thus, the three central thematic and visual refrains of the credit sequence combine to produce a complex and conflicting set of inferences about the central character. It is precisely the juxtaposition of the three themes (blood, suffocation, and fragility), which, like a cinematic montage, allows the viewers to begin to make links which would explain how these diverse elements fit together. In Dexter's case, the juxtaposition clearly points to some level of internal conflict. It may also point to another juxtaposition, which is a central formal device in the series, between Dexter's verbal interactions with other characters and his own internal voice, which serves as the narrator of the series. These two voices, which at times contradict each other, but also complement each other in giving the viewers a complete picture of Dexter's personality, invoke both juxtaposition and the idea of fluid movement between different social roles, thus developing the thematic concerns first identified in the title sequence.

Dexter is, of course, not the only conflicted character in the series. One of the series' main attractions is the complexity of almost every major character (though none is as complex as Dexter himself). Conflicting motivations drive Harry Morgan, LaGuerta, Doakes, and of course Dexter's nemeses, the Ice Truck Killer in Season 1, Lila Tournay in Season 2, and Miguel Prado in Season 3. Yet, in the opening sequence, Dexter is conspicuously alone (save for the mosquito, which he immediately kills). Indeed, the partial and out-of-focus shots of Dexter throughout the credit sequence serve both as a teaser to the audience and as an indication that he will ultimately "face the world" on his own terms, and only when he is ready.

Another visual refrain, already mentioned above, is the contrast between (blood-)red and white. In each case (blood drops in the sink, on the tissue, and ketchup on the egg white, as well as the graphics of the show's title), the red serves as a disruption, providing both a conceptual and a sharp visual contrast to the white. White may signify anything from sterility, to calmness, to innocence; the point is that even a single drop of red destroys it. Indeed, the image of a single drop of blood may also be a significant reference to the wider narrative of the program: a single drop of blood is all that Dexter keeps as a morbid memento from each of his victims.

There is one more persistent theme in the title sequence, which becomes more apparent retrospectively, in the context of having watched the show. Everything Dexter does seems to take effort, much more effort than it should. The shaving and tying of shoelaces—typical mundane activities that barely take any time or notice for most men—are accentuated with the unusual device of the audio close-up. The tying of shoelaces and filtering of the coffee require Dexter to flex his muscles, once again in extreme close-up, suggesting far more force than those activities would ordinarily require. Perhaps unexpectedly for a character already established as efficient (through his disposal of the mosquito), Dexter uses a manual razor and a manual orange juicer, rather than time- and effort-saving electronic devices, so that once again, we are shown aspects of his morning routine which require effort. Two interpretations are possible. The first is that Dexter enjoys, perhaps even fetishizes, the minutiae of each process, relishing the very physicality of an action like manually squeezing the juice out of an orange. This interpretation is not supported by the rest of the title sequence: Dexter's actions consistently appear as methodical, and not emotionally motivated; for instance, in the close-up footage of him eating breakfast, he chews the meat thoroughly, but without any trace of enjoyment (and it is not until the final episode of Season 2 that Dexter himself appears to realize how much he actually enjoys his morning routine). A second, more likely, interpretation for the repeated signs of excessive physical effort in the title sequence is that they serve as a metaphor for the constant strain which Dexter is under, in his efforts to appear to be living a "normal" life. Returning to the concept of juxtaposition, Dexter's struggle to consistently maintain a performance as "normal" and "ordinary," revealed mostly through his narration, is juxtaposed in the first season with the apparent ease with which Rudy maintains a public façade of easygoing normality while carrying out his elaborate campaign as the Ice Truck Killer. Dexter is not like "normal" people; this is established very early on in the series, in the title sequence, through his wildly over-elaborate performance of mundane everyday tasks; but neither is he like other killers, as the series reveals more gradually, through the juxtaposition with the Ice Truck Killer and other murderers.

The juxtaposition with other serial killers is both deliberate and ultimately intertextual. The structure and themes of the opening sequence powerfully and, I would argue, very consciously recall two earlier cinematic openings, from films both of which also centered on serial killers: *Se7en* (dir. David Fincher, 1995) and *American Psycho*. As a series, *Dexter* is aware of its pop cultural heritage, and of the need to both confront and confound its audience's genre expectations. Indeed, the partial, incomplete glimpses of Dexter which characterize the early moments of the title sequence may be a deliberate nod towards *Se7en*, whose own serial killer protagonist is unseen until the final moments of the film. However, whereas the opening credits of *Se7en*, created by Kyle Cooper (seen by some as the modern-day successor to Saul Bass (Geffner)), convey the precision and menace inherent in a killer's meticulous preparation for a deadly crime, the opening sequence of *Dexter* suggests that the very same careful, violent, and, above all, clearly deadly precision is present throughout all aspects of the protagonist's life, however mundane these may be.

Indeed, precision is a key defining characteristic of Dexter's behavior which runs from the mundane (his morning routine, his work) to the abject (the rituals surrounding his killings). The opening sequence hints at Dexter's darker rituals, but is also a ritual in itself.[1] Cinematic techniques such as extreme close-ups, distorted sounds, and rapid editing serve to deliberately decontextualize Dexter's morning ritual, yet it remains recognizable and relatable for the viewers—we may not share Dexter's precision, but most of us perform a vaguely similar morning routine ourselves, or have other small and innocuous rituals of our own which render Dexter's behavior in the opening sequence as somehow familiar. The opening sequence thus foreshadows Dexter's murderous rituals, and yet provides a point of identification for the viewers through a focus on seemingly everyday behavior.

The focus on the mundane thus erodes the boundary between the extraordinary, abject protagonist and the viewers. Not only does the audience of the series get to experience the world through Dexter's perspective and narration, but from the opening moments, his morning routine serves not so much to "normalize" him, but to suggest that the difference between him and everybody else is only a matter of degree. He may be a serial killer, the opening sequence says, but he still puts his shoes on one at a time.

Seeming blood drops, apparent violence, overly precise food preparation, and an incongruously upbeat soundtrack are all features which *Dexter*'s opening shares with the opening credits of *American Psycho*. Indeed, the series is so playfully aware of the parallels with Mary Harron's film and Bret Easton Ellis' novel, that Dexter uses the name "Patrick Bateman" as an alias in the show.

American Psycho, like *Se7en*, is both a point of reference and a point of departure for *Dexter*. The initial narrative hook, the idea that Dexter Morgan is not like other serial killers, can only be contextualized through actual comparison with other serial killers. The show itself gives us Dexter's victim-of-the-week (most of whom have little screen time or character development) and, in the first season, Rudy/the Ice Truck Killer, whose motivations are shrouded in mystery for most of the season. The audience's points of reference thus become extra-textual: Dexter Morgan is not like other serial killers we have previously seen on screen, in either fictional or factual representations. Like *Copycat* (dir. Jon Amiel, 1995), a film about a serial killer who is "inspired" by extra-textual events, *Dexter* assumes its audience's familiarity with the serial killer genre. Unlike any of the previous entries in the serial killer canon, *Dexter* then inverts the generic conventions to make the protagonist not only sympathetic, but the central figure of audience identification. Through this identification, the audience is ultimately made complicit in Dexter's crimes; significantly, the process of audience identification begins in the title sequence, from the very first frames.

In order to appreciate the success of *Dexter*'s opening sequence in fulfilling its aims, it can be broken down further, into distinct elements, both technical and thematic, so that we may appreciate the effects produced by the combination of these elements. In technical terms, the sequence is characterized by extreme close-ups and out-of-focus shots, rapid and somewhat disorientating camera shifts and cuts, a pace which looks like slow-motion but is, in fact, for the most part, real-time slow and meticulously performed action, and over-emphasized sounds, which correspond to visual close-ups. It is difficult to get any real sense of the mise en scène, due to the proliferation of extreme close-ups and rapid cuts; Dexter's apartment, perhaps even more than Dexter himself, is largely unseen during the title sequence. The lighting used in the sequence gives an overall impression of darkness, despite the key lights focused on the objects in the close-up shots. The color schemes appears slightly desaturated, so that, for example, the color of the sink and the tissue is an overly, spotlessly white, highlighting the contrast between it and the spots of blood-red which appear on it. The lighting and color schemes of the interior sequences provide a sharp contrast to the excessively bright, summery exterior, revealed when Dexter leaves his apartment. The interior, which is predominantly dark and only partially seen, can be seen as a synecdoche for Dexter's internal world, which he also keeps unseen, and which is a sharp contrast to his public persona.

These technical elements combine to produce a range of general themes, which the viewers can use to orientate themselves in the narrative that is about to unfold. The most obvious effect of the cinematography and editing is an unsettling uncertainty about the setting and the actions taking place within it. When actions which initially seemed sinister are repeatedly revealed as "normal" everyday activities, the audience may begin to doubt the innocuousness of mundane activities. The cinematography, editing, sound and mise en scène combine to produce a study in the shadowy and sinister side of everyday actions: shaving is disruptive and dangerous, preparing breakfast is bloodthirsty, a healthy appetite is highly suspicious. Moreover, the constant dwelling on extreme close-ups of slowed-down mundane activities produces a conceptual contradiction: on the one hand, it drives home the idea that every single aspect of the protagonist's life, however minute, requires absolutely meticulous preparation; on the other hand, the disjointed sequences, rapid cuts, and shaky camera movements produce an overall picture of the morning routine as devastating destruction. The title sequence simultaneously conveys Dexter's attempts to control his life, and the futility and destructiveness of these attempts.

The title sequence thus packs an enormously dense amount of information about the central character, style, and themes of the program into a remarkably short period of time. Indeed, the sequence can be said to encapsulate the essence of the central character and main themes of the show. Following in the best traditions of title design, it reveals just enough to allow the viewers to form expectations about the narrative, and thus to "hook" them into following how the rest of the narrative will unravel. It makes deliberate intertextual references which, if they are recognized, will enhance the viewers' appreciation of the sequence and the rest of the series. Above all, as a television title sequence, it stands up to multiple repeat viewings, allowing the audience to appreciate some new aspect of the sequence's design on every occasion. Indeed, in another playful (self-)reference, the title sequence eventually becomes fully incorporated into the narrative of the series: in the Season 2 finale, "The British Invasion," a variation on the title sequence appears a third of the way through the episode, as Dexter wakes up on the morning after Doakes' body is found and Doakes is assumed by the FBI to have been the Bay Harbor Butcher. At this moment, crucial both to the episode and to the story arc of the entire season, Dexter reflects on the simple everyday pleasures that he would be missing out on had he turned himself in, and finally voices—indeed, revels in—his enjoyment of the mundane activities which constitute his morning routine.

4.
"Serial" Killer: *Dexter*'s Narrative Strategies

David Lavery

I. "You think it ends here?"

> **Miguel Prado:** You think I'm done with you? You think it ends here?
> **Dexter** (as he garrottes the ADA): It does for you.
>
> ("I Had a Dream," 3.11)

Perhaps this exchange between our beloved anti-hero Dexter Morgan and his first-ever "friend" and apprentice vigilante Miami Assistant District Attorney seemed redolent with not only the series' signature pungent wit but also televisual significance because of the assignment I chose for myself for this collection. I wanted to hear in its ironic humor the sort of self-reflexivity so many television shows now exhibit as they think aloud—within the diegesis—about themselves and their missions—and their ends—while still in medias res telling their tales. Those ingenious episodes of *Buffy*, for example, taking as their subject the show's very narratology,[1] or that *Lost* hour in which the medium's most labyrinthine narrative buries (literally) on screen its misguided plan to add two new characters for the indeterminate seriality of a multi-season marathon.[2]

The inextricable questions of *Dexter*'s end and Dexter's fate have nevertheless been with us from the beginning. What would the series' longevity be? Would it become a "long haul" show (the term is Sarah Vowell's) or just have a short run? Could Dexter himself endure his impossibly dangerous existence without being done-in by the likes of his fellow serial killer brother, or a psychotic British woman, or the sadistic Skinner, or being caught by his law-enforcement colleagues?

When this not-yet-viewer first learned about *Dexter*'s existence, before I had seen anything but its bloody opening credit sequence, I recall being struck at once by both the ingeniousness of the idea and its limits. As I became a serious, loyal viewer of its first season, I still remained skeptical of its potential for a long run. But my track record as a prognosticator was not that strong. I had predicted *24* (FOX, 2001 –) would be a one-day wonder and doubted *Prison Break* would make it beyond the Fox River Penitentiary (FOX, 2005 –), but both series have had long runs, with *24* remaining riveting for at least its first five seasons (out of seven to date) and *Prison Break* continuing to enthrall even on the lam.

Still, the challenges, the "peaks and valleys" as Marc Dolan calls them in a magisterial essay, facing a long-term serial narrative of any kind are massive and often fatal. For every success there are ten failures. One more inclined to cheap puns than myself might even suggest that television narrative is ever threatened by a "serial" killer, part industry force, part imaginative limitation, running loose in the medium, ready to cut down many a promising series in its prime. "Brilliant but cancelled" has almost become its own genre.

A serial narrative about a serial killer—that would seem to be courting undue risk, and yet *Dexter* has survived now for three 12–episode premium channel seasons.[3] Season 1, drawing substantially on the origin story laid down by Jeff Lindsay in *Darkly Dreaming Dexter*, was strong from start to finish as our hero did battle with his brother-in-crime the Ice Truck Killer. It seemed difficult to imagine *Dexter* ever achieving a more brilliant moment than the blood-spatter specialist's triumphant, imaginary walk through the throng of adoring, "Way to take out the trash"-ing fans—a plane overhead trailing a "We ♥ Dexter" banner. If *Dexter* had been a miniseries, this would have been a sensational, unforgettable ending to a limited narrative. But *Dexter* would go on, preparing for the long haul. For example, the decision was made to leave dead-at-the-end-of-the-first-novel Lieutenant Maria LaGuerta, a central character in all three seasons, still alive.

Season 2, in which Dexter, aka The Bay Harbor Butcher, becomes the hunted, began somewhat slowly (or was that perception really projection, the side-effect of my initial skepticism?) but gained momentum with the introduction of Lila and the spiraling antagonism between Dexter and in-house nemesis Sergeant Doakes. Some of the B and C stories of the season would earn the snark of bloggers at sites like *Television Without Pity* and *The Onion TV Club* (it seems not everyone cares for Dexter's sister Debra), but for the most part *Dexter*'s sophomore outing was critically well received and ended well. The future of the series seemed promising indeed. When Dexter insisted with a pride touching on hubris that he had now outgrown his father—"I'm no longer his disciple. I'm a master now. An idea transcended into life" (2.12)—my meta-commentary Geiger counter sounded again. James Manos' adaptation of Jeff Lindsay's fiction had, in the hands of Clyde Phillips and company, found its stride, achieved mastery. Would it last? Would it transcend?

Season 3, on the other hand, characterized by Heather Havrilesky as "dark but capricious," really did seem different—and not nearly as adroit. Season 3's dual story—Dexter's growing friendship and then war with the manipulative and more evil Prado/his expectant father domestication and eventual season-ending marriage to Rita—nevertheless prompted *Salon*'s television critic, fonder of the season than I, to wonder:

> does Dexter really have anything but ice water flowing through his veins? Is he capable of being a remotely decent husband and father, given his utter lack of feeling for everyone and everything in his life, not to mention his tendency to disappear on nefarious errands with clock-like regularity?

Asked by *TV Guide* to speculate on the future for her character and Dexter, Julie Benz (Rita) suggested that "The success of their relationship will depend on how good Dexter is at multitasking and juggling. Most men aren't very good at that." Neither, my meta-commentary Geiger counter prompts me to add, are television shows.

II. *Dexter* as a Narrative

What kind of narrative is *Dexter*? Television scholars like Marc Dolan, John Tulloch and Manuel Alvarado, Horace Newcomb, and Robin Nelson have helped us sort out the multiple narrative modes television series come in, starting with the Traditional/Episodic, in which each episode stands alone, adding little or nothing to the cumulative memory of the show over seasons/years. In sharp contrast, serial narratives, relegated for most of television's first three decades to the mediacosmos of daytime—"another world"—told open-ended, linear stories "designed to be infinitely continued and extended" (Dolan 33).[4]

The advent of night-time soaps like *Dallas* (CBS, 1978–91) broke the mold and introduced new hybrids. The sequential series, for example, shows "that, had they been made a decade earlier, would almost certainly have been constructed in almost purely episodic terms," made broadcast order of prime importance, "since events in one episode clearly led to events in another" (Dolan 34).[5]

The last two decades of television, however, have seen the initially experimental but now common adoption of what Robin Nelson terms the "flexi-narrative," a "hybrid mix of serial and series forms . . . involving the closure of one story arc within an episode (like a series) but with other, ongoing story arcs involving the regular characters (like a serial)" (82). Appealing both to those wanting long-term relationships with television and the less faithful, no-appointment-necessary occasional viewer, the growing popularity of flexi-narratives for audience and producer is not hard to understand.

Dexter is a flexi-narrative. Like *The X-Files*, it has blended discrete "monster of the week" (MOW) episodes with an ongoing story arc. In MOW mode, "the dark avenger" investigates, tracks, and murders this or that enemy of society, be they gigantic Cuban thug, murderous used-car salesman, or psycho-stalker psychiatrist. Like *Buffy the Vampire Slayer*, however, the series has opted for constructing each season primarily around Dexter's clash with a particular "Big Bad" (as *Buffy* deemed the Slayer's foes): the Ice Truck Killer in Season 1, Lila/Doakes in Season 2, Miguel Prado in Season 3, with none of these conflicts spilling over into subsequent seasons. At the end of *Darkly Dreaming Dexter*, the Ice Truck Killer goes free; the series, true to its medium, kills him off.

On the other hand, *Dexter*'s master narrative—*The X-Files* deemed it "mythology"—has essentially been the incremental, over an individual season and the course of the entire series, humanization of Dexter Morgan. Its twin multi-season line tracks his continuing dialogue with his dead father and his education as the right kind of serial killer and his developing relationship with Rita.

The legacy of his dead-by-his-own-hand-before-the-series-begins father has been of great importance to the ongoing narrative. Harry Morgan has appeared in every episode to date, either in flashbacks or as a spectral presence serving as his monster stepson's very special conscience, which gives Dexter someone to talk to in addition to us. Clyde Phillips admitted in a Season 1 interview that the voice-over evolved in order to solve the problem of Dexter's extreme loner status.[6] Not until his friendship with Miguel Prado in Season 3 can Dexter find another human being to confide in, but from the first he unburdens to us, and his often black-humored commentary, brilliantly done by Michael C. Hall, is the best, the wittiest on television, never becoming as cloying or pedantic as that of, say, Meredith Grey on *Grey's Anatomy* or *Desperate Housewives'* Mary Alice Young.

But to what end? The recent mega-controversial example of the culmination of *The Sopranos* reminded us that the narrative eschatology (as I have deemed it elsewhere) of a television series is a matter of great complexity.

III. Happily Ever After?

But have a real relationship with a person that goes on for years—well, that's completely unpredictable. Then, you've cut off all your ties to the land, and you're sailing into the unknown, into uncharted seas, and I mean, people hang onto these images of father, mother, husband, wife, again, for the same reason, because they seem to provide some firm ground. But there's no wife there. What does that mean? A wife. A husband. A son. A baby holds your hands, and then suddenly there's this huge man lifting you off the ground, and then he's gone? Where's that son?

André Gregory in *My Dinner with André* (Louis Malle, 1981)

Julie Benz has strong feelings about how she sees *Dexter* turn out. The Dark Defender and Rita, she hopes, "will find happiness." "In Season 1," Benz recalls, "they talk about being normal. That's all they want, and I think that's what really holds them together. I'd love to see them get married, and then have babies, and live happily ever after. I'm a bit of a romantic." Could this be the end of *Dexter*/Dexter?

The typical American narrative Leslie Fiedler famously argued in *Love and Death in the American Novel* (1960) involves the male hero's flight from civilization and from the force of women. From the henpecked Rip Van Winkle of Washington Irving, to James Fenimore Cooper's averse-to-the-feminine Natty Bumppo, to Mark Twain's Aunt Polly-defying Huckleberry Finn, the American hero prefers the company of a primitive, homoerotic "other" (Rip's little people, Hawkeye's Native Americans, Huck's escaped slave Jim) and usually finds himself "lighting out for the territory" (like Huck, who wants no part of Aunt Polly's "sivilizing").

Set in America's southernmost major city, *Dexter* remains distinctly American in Fiedler's sense. His other, of course, is found within, not without, in the form of his "Dark Passenger." His marriage to Rita, his settling down, complete with stepchildren and a baby on the way, is precisely the opposite direction for an American hero as charted by Fiedler.

Now supremely good at his life's work, Dexter dispatches his enemies, from Prado to the Skinner, with relative ease. Whether he can master the ordinary, the pursuit of happiness, remains to be seen. The futures of both the character and the ongoing narrative are riding on the unprecedented nature of that project. Clyde Phillips and company may have painted themselves into a corner, and nobody, nobody puts Dexter (*Dexter*?) in a corner.

But perhaps it won't be a corner. A "real relationship with a person that goes on for years," after all, as *My Dinner with André's* brilliant conversation reminds us, "well, that's completely unpredictable. Then, you've cut off all your ties to the land, and you're sailing into the unknown." On Dexter's boat, *The Slice of Life*, no doubt. "An idea transcended into life" indeed.

5.
Dexter's Hollow Designs

Steven Peacock

> My name is Dexter. Dexter Morgan. I don't know what it was that made
> me the way I am, but whatever it was left a hollow place inside. People
> often fake a lot of human interactions, but I feel like I fake them all. (1.1)

Dexter paints a slick sick picture. Set in Miami, the city's glitzy flare
has never seemed so seductively glossy and shallow: true-blue pools
glisten in the sun's refracting glare, while the neon nightscape fizzes
in day-glo jets. Identical whitewashed blocks jut against an oceanic
sheen; window panes stare glassily at impossible pastel skies. As the
serial celebrates its setting's shiny urban veneer, it also embraces
the radiant possibilities of high-end television. The use of cinematic lighting, filming, and editing techniques creates a smooth set
of visuals and a highly polished aesthetic. Whereas other, lesser
works of television garner such a look for meretricious gain—
dipping each shot in a thick glaze of color and gleam to coax critical
coos of "quality"—*Dexter* skillfully uses its filmy luster to present
its main protagonist's illicit lust.[1] Some of the most compelling
designs of the series stem from the way the surface materials of the
external world—settings, décor, landscapes, look—reflect Dexter
Morgan's synthetic sensibility.

A play on surfaces binds the character of protagonist and
program. This is a place of fakery, shallows, and hollows. Dexter's
hardened psychological masking fuses with *Dexter*'s lacquered outer-
world reflections of plastic, glass, water, and metal. Both present a
façade of cool charm with nothing underneath. Holding his steely
gaze and tempered grin, led by bloody compulsion, Dexter has no
access to his own or others' emotional depths. He has been left with
"a hollow place inside." Within a shell of his making, he (initially)
shows no signs of breaking. In presenting us with a self-contained

serial killer, Dexter and *Dexter* refrain from hysterical scenes or obtrusive displays of delirium. Instead, each scene, each victim, remains tightly cut, framed, and wrapped. Across the series, patterns of clinically stylized business—these slick slices of life—start to chill. In a rare televisual instance, signs of superficiality create a composite study of complexity.

To show how *Dexter* not only adopts an expressive interest in stylistic surfaces from the outset, but also across its duration, this chapter focuses on examples from the first episodes of Season 1 (1.1) and Season 3 (3.1). These instances rhyme across time; they also declare the series' development of concerns, and the main protagonist's shifting designs.

In the pilot episode's inaugural glimpse of *Dexter*/Dexter's worldview, in place of the subsequently applied credit sequence we are presented with fragmentary sights of Miami from a car window. A Gothic moon beams through red-stained rain; palm-tree fronds jag in splintering shots saturated in deep pinks, greens, and blues. A figure, Dexter, is cast in shadow in his car: the city portrait comprises passing glances from the window and reflections in the mirror. The effect is kaleidoscopic, with hints of the hallucinatory. Immediately, the series crafts an impressionistic sketch of Miami "on the go" in which many of its key concerns swirl. This is a fantasy of surface pleasure, from which Dexter is held at one remove by the car's glass and metal shell. Increasingly, as the camera moves further in on the milling crowds outside bars and clubs, aspects of vice (and, perhaps, traces of *Miami Vice*) start to stain the sketch: a wretched figure grimaces from, it seems, drug withdrawal. Contempt for decadence mired by corruption inflames Dexter's desire to kill.

The painterly combination of street gloss and grime coming from the detached perspective of a driver recalls the opening moments (and wider stylistic tendencies) of Martin Scorsese's *Taxi Driver* (1976). Scorsese's film presents not only warped atmospheric impressions of the New York cityscape—all hot smoke, colorful spills, and seedy street-corners—but also the disconnected yet disturbed viewpoint of cab-driver Travis Bickle (Robert De Niro). Moreover, the moment and the film as a whole suggest that the setting's portrayal reflects the character's mindset. And, on the surface, Bickle is blankly cool until a final hellish crack-up.

The comparison assists a deeper understanding of *Dexter*'s hollow designs, particularly when considered in relation to Robert Kolker's views of Scorsese's artistic sensibility. In *A Cinema of Loneliness*, Kolker makes compelling claims for the director's elemental fusion of setting, mise en scène, and characterization. The critic raises the idea that, "The spaces [Scorsese's characters] inhabit are places of transition, of momentary situation" (180). This is certainly true of Bickle's cab and Dexter's car. Moreover, the views from these metal shells present similarly warped orchestrations of particular cityscapes. As Kolker continues:

> These places are not . . . abstract ideas of places. The Manhattan of *Taxi Driver* and *After Hours*, the Little Italy of *Mean Streets*, the Las Vegas of *Casino* are perfectly recognizable, almost too much so. . . . They represent, to borrow a notion of Roland Barthes', a New York-*ness*, a shared image and collective signifier of New York that has little to do with the city itself, but rather expresses what everyone, including many who live there, has decided New York should look like. (180)

In turn, *Dexter* gives us a Miami-*ness*, two parts glitz to one part gore. Finally, Kolker (and Scorsese) intertwine the two aspects, suggesting that the handling of city locales is "reflective of the energy of the characters . . . colored by the characters' perspective," as indicative of "a method of integrating the character with the space he occupies so that the two become reflections of each other in a mutually defining mise-en-scène" (181–3). The remainder of this chapter looks at exemplary instances in *Dexter*, suggesting ways in which the series displays such a precise cinematic inheritance to equally expressive effect.

Shows, Shells, Skin, Slides, Skimming

The first victim of Dexter's to whom we are privy is child-molester and murderer Mike Donovan. Again, the pilot episode presents a swift and intricate overture of concerns under the sign of "the surface." A cut moves from Dexter's car-view to a neatly uniform tableau of singing schoolboys (in neat uniforms). They grin towards the camera: a proscenium-style chorus line on display. A slight tilt of the camera reveals the boys are performing for Donovan as conductor. The implication that the children are exhibiting themselves openly (on show, in a show) to Donovan, while he conceals his true dreadful intent in a mask-like smile is held in the angle. Later, when Dexter forces Donovan to look at the dead boys' decaying bodies, they are lined up and arranged on the same line in the frame. The rhyme inverts the dynamic of power. Dexter's ritualistic method of murder creates another kind of theatrical display, placing Donovan as dramatic tableau, ready for (de)composition.

Lights and color create further inflections of surface covers and glimmering desires. The children conclude their recital. The camera cranes to disclose strings of twinkling white bulbs: a customary affectation of social performance. While adding another thread of decorum to Donovan's own performance of propriety, the surface decoration also suggests a bright (too bright) flicker of excitement, reflective of the character's murderous energies. The series develops this suggestion and couples the killing instincts of Donovan and Dexter, as the two finally meet. As Donovan walks to his car, a shard of electric blue light cuts across the body of the vehicle while a block of red casts over the metal shell, blinking on and off. Here is a little abstract hint of things to come, playing off surfaces: glinting cuts in clean lines and a menacing presence.

The colors carry with Donovan into the car. As Dexter whips a cord across Donovan's neck, slabs of blue light fill the windows. Again taking a cue from Scorsese, an exaggerated saturation of deep colors—reds and blues—forms an expressionistic manifestation of the protagonist's stark psychological intensity. The excited twinkle of bulbs at the beginning of the scene meets in a final refraction of lights in the frame, as Dexter pulls the cord tight. The multicolored splinter of streetlamp light stems from the use of a certain type of "gel" on the camera lens: a showy effect from a glass surface. Yet, again, the series turns a standard of television drama's visual repertoire—a trick of the light—to expressive effect. Overlapping hints of meaning are put in play. Like the cord, they bind the two murderers: the light carries a jolt of Donovan's alarm and, perhaps, the hallucinogenic effect of oxygen deprivation. It also, rhyming with the earlier display, gives out a flash of Dexter's bloodlust, animating anticipation.

As Dexter and *Dexter* move to the kill, they perform a formal show about surfaces: first stripping them back, then building them up again, in tiers and gradations. Inside his hideaway cabin, Dexter demands that Donovan looks at, acknowledges, his own murderous designs. The boys' bodies are laid out on the floor, victims in front of the victim, presented as dreadful evidence in this courtroom-cum-execution chamber. The series develops the theme of "looking" in dialogue and peripheral designs. Dexter spits out his command: "Open your eyes and look at what you did. Look or I'll cut your eyelids right off your face" (1.1). The physicality of this gruesome threat is reinforced in the mise en scène. Donovan is pinned by his neck to the wall; his head is aligned with one of the cabin's windows. Slats of moonlight cut through the window's metal shutters. The image associates eyelids and shutters as blinds to looking outwards. Harsh slits of light point up Dexter's dire warning, make it tangible.

In contrast, the handling of Donovan's murder is a matter of clinically layering (rather than violently removing) surfaces between the camera, Dexter and the victim. From Donovan's POV, Dexter's face looms large overhead, strapped into a clear plastic mask. The first, ritualistic slit of the knife down the side of Donovan's cheek creates a much-treasured blood sample. Here is the second set of surfaces, held square in the center of the frame: two glass slides squeezing the prized droplet for keeps. Then there are Donovan's binds, tying him to the table in opaque plastic wrapping. In later kills, the walls of the scene will also be masked by thick plastic sheets, covering the massacre in a wipe-clean coating.

Dexter is skillful in using props as both sensibly present in the world of the drama and as dramatically meaningful. It makes sense to find such objects as masks and sheets in this scene, in this serial, as the killer chooses certain materials to cover his tracks. The trappings also become tools in a carefully timed visual detachment and protection of the viewer from Donovan, to encourage empathetic alignment with Dexter even in death-dealing. Again, in the preparation and execution of the kill, the aesthetic coating of varying clear plates and covers is expressive of Dexter's complex emptiness. From the cinematic tradition of serial killers, one might expect the moment of murder to be representative of a euphoric release in the protagonist; such acts of wicked liberation are often channelled in spurts of textual stylization (consider, for instance, such moments in *Natural Born Killers* [Oliver Stone, 1994] or, gloriously, *Serial Mom* [John Waters, 1994]). Here, though, act and aesthetic are ascetic. The careful arrangement of surfaces indicates Dexter's chillingly dispassionate methodology, but also, more complexly, a buttressing of his psychological armor. The act holds him from everyone else; the layering of surfaces inspires a reflection of isolated detachment, made all the more acute in combinations of synthetic materials. Even in the darkest act, Dexter's unnatural entrapment behind a mask is transparent.

When a cheekily wry variation on "release" finally arrives, the serial holds on Dexter's relationship with surfaces. *Dexter* releases the viewer from the sight of Donovan's slaughter in abruptly changing scenes: we see Dexter next enjoying an early morning boat-trip, having dumped Donovan's body in the water's depths. Yet we are not fully allowed to breathe easy. The move between scenarios creates a viscerally playful association: of Dexter's electric knife-blade gliding into Donovan's throat, and the boat's smooth skim across the water—cuts in a cut. There *is* also the suggestion that Dexter finds pleasurable release in the murder's aftermath: the sunshine, upbeat musical accompaniment, his beaming smile, and voracious bites of snack-bar all point to a bright mood. Yet we should beware the crocodile grin. It appears as Dexter's voice-over declares, "People often fake a lot of human interactions, but I feel like I fake them all" (1.1). Further, the serial is exacting in its perspective: Dexter's facial expression of happiness is only viewed through the boat's windshield. Even an apparent display of exhilaration is all front. To cap the suggestion, Dexter's boat—*Slice of Life*—skims across the water's frothy surface.

As the pilot episode moves from the boat-ride to the first view of Dexter's sea-front apartment, ripples of another filmmaker's style and signification are felt. In a meticulously composed (and often repeated) moment, Dexter walks across the balcony to his front door. As a marker of his necessary (and incarcerating) duplicity, the shot shows the anti-hero's reflection caught in the wide apartment windows; equally, suggestive of his isolation and emotional obscurity, he is positioned, on the overhang, by the ocean's opaque expanse. Invoking again the spirit of *Miami Vice*, this is also the preferred worldview of director Michael Mann. In "Gravity of the Flux: Michael Mann's *Miami Vice*," Jean-Baptiste Thoret notes Mann's involvement in both *Miami Vice* the Eighties television series (as executive producer) and 2006 film (as director). Crucially, Thoret observes a deepening of Mann's interest in Miami's surface designs from television to film productions:

> Created by Anthony Yerkovitch and supervised (very) closely by Michael Mann, *Miami Vice* was, let's remember, one of the leading television series of the 1980s and for the director of *Heat* (1995), chastened by the failure of *The Keep* (1983), the laboratory where he was going to forge a new aesthetic, founded on an extreme sophistication of *mise en scène*, an excessive taste for design and advertising kitsch . . . From the credits, the tone is set . . . the wings of pink flamingos in slow motion, tracking shots on gleaming limousines [as a world of] arrogant successes and cheap flashiness . . . Finally, Michael Mann brings *Miami Vice* to the big screen and, in doing so, the greatest contemporary filmmaker proves once again his ability to bend the logic of the blockbuster (*Miami Vice* was thus oversold) to his personal universe . . . A flash of lightning that stripes the sky, a palm tree that bends under the weight of the wind and an incandescent night that Mann's camera relentlessly pursues convey the feeling of a hallucinatory film where man and nature dissolve in each other, quivering with the same tragic breath. ("Gravity of the Flux")

In its handling of Miami in precise visual arrangements, *Dexter* shows it has the various *Vices* in mind, its absorption in veneers equally complex.

Thoret hones in on his subject to closely survey a close study of surfaces. He interprets Mann's patterned interest in modes of transient transportation and bodies placed against backgrounds similar to those patterned across *Dexter*:

> As a counterpoint to the chaos and confusion of human relations, Mann multiplies surface effects (bay windows, villas on the border of the sea) and sliding (offshore, in the plane, in race cars). They are impeccable images from a world where survival depends on the capacity to remain on the surface (and superficial). ("Gravity of the Flux")

The sea, according to Thoret, is the "eternal utopia of Mann's characters" ("Gravity of the Flux"). They stand by, or with their back to, the vastness of the ocean, but must always return to the "flux" of surface life. Here, too, is Dexter, held close to the water's edge, or skimming across its surface, but never reaching utopian depths. Even the choice of the ocean as receptacle for his victims' bodies is illustrative of his bind when the black bags bob back to the surface in Season 2.

In another article, Thoret points to Mann's presentation of a "world of . . . neon signs that flicker day and night, a world that seems resigned to the omnipresence of glass and concrete" ("The Aquarium Syndrome"). This emphasis on impersonal places as illustrative of a disembodied world, of the disappearance of human feeling, takes us to the heart of *Dexter*'s complex heartlessness. The protagonist's patterned position by the sea and mirrored representation in windows reflects his personification of the "Mannian imaginary . . . a mental and geographical extension" ("Gravity of the Flux"). There are echoes here of Kolker's spaces "colored by the character's perspective." Both readings enrich interpretations of *Dexter*'s architectural designs. With its wide bay windows and seafront situation, Dexter's apartment block (like many of those in Mann's films) has an aquarium quality. The external aesthetics carry inside, creating a telling merger of exterior and interior states. In 1.1, as Dexter moves to slot away his prized blood-blot slide with the others in a boxed collection, the camera reframes to nestle him next to an array of glass vases and containers, in front of blue-hazed windows. Just as the series presents us with false externalizations as expressive of the impenetrability of Dexter's "hollow place," the omnipresence of glass surfaces (slides, vases, windows) bleeds inside and outside spaces together in a mutual blankness. Ultimately, in its neon glimmer, watery glare, and glass coating, Dexter's world in Season 1 comprises a shallow, hollow simulacrum of lived human experience.

Settling In

In "Our Father"—the opening episode of Season 3 (3.1)—*Dexter* holds true to its significant superficiality, while suggesting depths also emerging from new expressions of deepness. Dexter now considers himself master of his killer craft and in charge of the cultivation of his personal relationships. No longer caught in a perpetual disconnection from the world (willed or otherwise), Dexter sees himself as "an idea transcended into life" (2.12). The episode's opening sequences playfully twin moments with those described above from 1.1—the clear plastic mask used when murdering Donovan is recast as a dentist's visor. The same Latino music accompanies Dexter on his boat, riding the waves; the shot of Dexter walking across the balcony to his apartment also reappears outside of the credit sequence. There is a sense of return but also revival and transformation. The dentistry scenario gives a self-reflexive "nod" to a past episode. There may also be the suggestion that the character is able to view his past life from a knowing distance. Equally, the return view of the boat skimming the water comes with a subtle change: this time a smiling Dexter is framed in the open air, from the side, no longer caught behind the windshield's protective surface.

As Dexter declares early on in the episode, "For someone who has to go through life *pretending* to be normal, I've finally been able to *settle in* to a nice normal world" (3.1). Here, a developing tension crystallizes: the character remains close to (and so still at one remove from) surface orchestrations of human emotion. At the same time, there is a sense of "settling in"—a voluntary easing into forms of deeper experience, albeit in shallow ways. The character (and actor's) pressing intonation on the words "settle in" forms a saucy pun; the scene moves to a view of Dexter and Rita making love in bed. For Dexter, it is a physical act of intimacy (and a semblance of emotional proximity) only rarely rehearsed in prior times with Rita. In many ways, he appears to be getting deeper into an embodiment of life.

Surface aspects of mise en scène begin to take on the problematic deepness of settling in. A later instance of "mental and geographical extension" finds the post-coital couple in the kitchen huddled by the open refrigerator, spooning chocolate pudding into their mouths. The scene *appears* as one of domestic happiness, yet quietly gives way to complications. The metallic slab of the fridge is now cracked wide open; the door swings with the concerns of the series and Dexter's personal circumstances, from a hard case of surfaces to a clutter of contents. While suggesting an emotional development (letting others, letting himself in), the scenario hints at a muddling in the act of exposure. Opposed to the ascetic order of ritualized routines molded in glass and steel, the mixed jumble of chilled goodies inside the metal box hints at a growing organic unruliness. The open fridge door provides a half-rhyme to the later sight of Dexter's "innocent" victim (Oscar Prado) lying in an open-cask coffin after our anti-hero's botched hunt. Finally in the episode, a messy pot of chocolate pudding becomes a revelatory signifier of Rita's surprise pregnancy: the ultimate sign of life penetrating Dexter.

After this extraordinary news, a handling of spaces expresses the father-to-be seeking to slide some of the surfaces of his brittle world back into place. To provide a final impressionistic sketch: harking back to earlier bits of business in the previous seasons, patterns develop around computer screens, the frames of office windows, the donning of dark sunglasses. There is the suggestion that as well as Dexter wanting to withdraw under the cover of simulacra, the series, too, seeks solace in prior examples of significant superficiality. Yet, like the square of flesh taken from Teegan's shoulder, there is a growing relationship at work in *Dexter* between surface coverings and deeper attractions, epidermal and emotional.[2]

In its sophisticated attention to surface designs, *Dexter* presents us with proof that critical concentration on the style of a particular program (an approach still rarely undertaken in Television Studies) might allow for vital aspects to emerge from seemingly frivolous visual arrangements.

Part Three.
Dexter on the Couch: Family, Friends, and *Frankenstein*

6.
Harry Morgan: (Post)Modern Prometheus

Douglas L. Howard

At first glance, this seems like an extreme story of a father's love, a love that goes beyond blood and blood spatter, as police officer Harry Morgan takes young Dexter in after rescuing the child from a horrifically blood-drenched storage container. And knowing that the boy is deeply, darkly, decidedly disturbed, Harry nevertheless does all that he can to keep him from that electric chair that would otherwise be his destiny. In Lindsay's *Dexter in the Dark*, the eponymous serial killer makes it clear that "Harry had run on love" (299) and that his ghoulish guidance, in the end, came from this place of compassion and tenderness. Would Mike Brady or Cliff Huxtable have ever gone so far if one of their own had developed a taste for blood slides and duct tape? But, as the television series continues to plumb the darker depths of Dexter's Dad and uncover the truth about just who and what he was, Harry becomes less and less of a candidate for Father of the Year. He had an affair with Dexter's mother, who was working for him as an informant, and he purposefully manipulated Dexter to become this Dark Defender, only to find himself disgusted when he finally saw his son in action and only to leave a bloody string of Oedipal issues for the fledgling killer to cut through subsequently. Inasmuch as he "forms" Dexter through his blind devotion to some abstract ideal informed by personal pain and frustration, Harry is really more Victor Frankenstein than Ward Cleaver (although this might have been a good name for him), another man who would be God through the act of creating, and *Dexter* becomes yet another cultural variation on the Frankenstein myth,[1] where the sins of the creator are revisited upon the creation and give birth to a different kind of monster.

It's Alive

While she may have called it her "hideous progeny," Mary Shelley's *Frankenstein* has become, after all, the "father" of all great monster creation stories, echoed in every cautionary tale of science and artificial life gone wrong from James Whale to James Cameron and from *Alien* and *Blade Runner* to *X-Men*. But for all of the emphases on castle laboratories, electrical equipment, and hunchbacked manservants, Shelley's original is, "at heart," actually a very "human" text, a tale of misguided passions, self-destructive ambitions, Oedipal motivations, forbidden knowledge, and the deep-seeded need to conquer death. Where Walton puts to sea at the beginning of the novel in search of a Paradise up north, in spite of his "father's dying injunction [. . . against] embark[ing] in a sea-faring life" (8), Victor Frankenstein studies alchemy against his father's better advice,[2] and, in his own search for the elixir of life, he dreams of that discovery that will "render man invulnerable to any but a violent death" (22). This preoccupation wanes, however, until the all-too-real pain of death is brought home to him for the first time by the loss of his mother, a loss that he describes as "that most irreparable evil" (25) and that may well be the true inspiration behind Victor's obsession to create life from death.[3] As he reflects on his grief over his mother, Victor's pain is palpable: "It is so long before the mind can persuade itself that she, whom we saw every day, and whose very existence appeared a part of our own, can have departed for ever—that the brightness of a beloved eye can have been extinguished, and the sound of a voice so familiar, and dear to the ear, can be hushed, never more to be heard" (25). Lest we doubt the importance of his mother's death here, both Shelley and Victor remind us of it after he gives life to his creation. From "nearly two years" of tireless work and research, the exhausted creator sleeps, only to dream of his Elizabeth, "in the bloom of health," transforming into "the corpse of [his] dead mother in [his] arms" (34). In many ways, then, the creature becomes Victor's symbolic attempt to resurrect or recoup the loss of his mother by "conquering her killer." Aside from the Oedipal significance of Elizabeth's transformation—the connection between the two in his dream is clearly no accident[4]—Victor nevertheless subconsciously realizes that he has not created life from death, but, instead, has turned life, in all its beauty, into death and brought the reality of his mother's loss literally back home with more horrifying clarity.

Caught up in his obsession, Victor is unable to see the awful truth of what he has done, however, until his creation comes to life, until he has transformed the abstract idea of life into the actual thing itself. As he explains to Walton, he "had selected [the creature's] features as beautiful" (34), and, in the planning stages of his experiment, they may well have appeared that way. But, in stark contrast to "Henry" Frankenstein's iconic, hysterical sense of accomplishment in Whale's 1931 film—in a nod to it, the Season 2 opener of *Dexter* is even titled "It's Alive"—Shelley's Victor, upon seeing the creature's "yellow skin," black hair, and "watery eyes" at work for the first time, is, conversely, overcome with "breathless horror and disgust" (34). The creature can be nothing but horrific because it is, as Mary Poovey points out, "the product of the unnatural coupling of nature and the imagination" (258). As it moves toward him, as what he has made, as what his desires and ambitions, conscious or otherwise, have wrought confronts him "in the flesh," Victor flees his apartment in abject terror and psychologically breaks from what Dexter calls "an idea transcended into life" (2.12).

Whereas so many critics anticipate the "transcendence" or the reinvention of Shelley's Gothic vision in the form of the biological, the mechanical, or the virtual, the more likely and frightening possibility is that the artificial creature will be methodically constructed in a suburb somewhere, by a policeman foster father with the best of intentions for the worst in his adopted son. Like Victor, Harry certainly does not think that he is creating something so monstrous or "evil" (2.11), as Dexter later describes himself. Rather, his plans for Dexter often sound less sinister and gruesome and more like some kind of stereotypical father-son bonding (albeit with more emphasis on weapons training and stalking). Realizing that the young boy has been killing animals in the neighborhood and burying them in a private grave, Harry is quick to confront Dexter and ask him about his "urges" (1.1), a conversation that he compares, in Lindsay's *Darkly Dreaming Dexter*, to the parental "talk about sex dreams" (40). Soon thereafter, Harry and Dexter are out on private hunting trips, practicing ambushes, and visiting death penalty electrocutions (a unique take on the fishing trips or the baseball games that are a part of most father-son excursions), all in an effort to keep the troubled teen from a similar fate himself. Harry talks to Dexter about girls and dances, although this conversation turns into a lecture about appearing "normal" (1.5). In "Shrink Wrap," he even teaches him the important lesson about not killing the playground bully.[5] And though he maintains that he does not "want to teach [him] these things" (1.8), Harry still does because, through it all, he deeply cares for his son. Promising Dexter that they will work through his problem, again a problem that sounds like something more mundane, like breaking a neighbor's window or getting a bad grade in math, Harry poignantly reminds him, "You are not alone, and you are loved" (1.1).

But, as the series suggests, Harry's motivation for training Dexter is based on more than love alone. He is not just interested in keeping Dexter alive. The other part of his plan involves raising someone who can address those injustices in the world, to solve those crimes and punish those evil-doers, to accomplish beyond the law what Harry himself could not accomplish within it.[6] Early on in Season 1 of *Dexter*, we see Harry's pain as he tries to come to grips with the murder of his partner, Davey Sanchez—he "was my partner," he says as he practices his eulogy in front of a young Dexter, "[and he] was my hero" (1.2)—and we hear it in his vow to "catch the bastard who did this to [Davey]" (1.2). For Harry, Dexter's inherent homicidal impulses become, in part, an opportunity, a chance to bring some moral order into the world and perhaps even satisfy his own "something deep inside" (1.2) unquenched by the deaths of people like his partner. Along these lines, his "creation" and education of Dexter becomes more like the secret origin narrative of a new superhero. "We can't stop [your urge to kill]," Harry tells the teenage Dexter, "but maybe we can do something to channel it, use it for good [. . .]. Son, there are people out there who do really bad things. Terrible people. And the police can't catch them all" (1.1). As a police officer himself, Harry must admit the limitations of his role and the frequent failure of the system and acknowledge that, sometimes, the guilty get away and go unpunished. Like Victor's experiment, Dexter, or the idea of Dexter, becomes an attempt to give life to an abstraction. As a dying Harry predicts to him in *Dearly Devoted Dexter*, "Your sister will be a good cop[, but] you will be something else. Real justice" (94). Dexter will become the living embodiment of a concept, justice incarnate. And after all of his lessons, when his health begins to fail him, Harry, seeing that the time is right and that his son/student/disciple has come of age, finally sets Dexter loose on the nurse who has been overdosing her patients so that he can stop her "before she hurts anyone else" (1.3). Though Dexter subdues the nurse, though Harry lives another year as a result, and though "justice" is apparently served, Harry never sees Dexter's initial missteps or the kill itself, a fact that the series explores in more detail in Season 2.

Just as Victor aspires to God-like glory and adoration—he initially looks forward to that day when "[a] new species would bless [him] as its creator and source" (32)—Harry becomes God the father to Dexter—in *Darkly Dreaming Dexter*, he calls him "the all-seeing, all-knowing man" (43)—and the "Code of Harry" virtually serves as a Ten Commandments for him, a sacred set of principles that restrains and directs his desire to kill. (At the start of Season 3, in the religiously titled "Our Father," Dexter makes these connections clear when he defines the code as "twisted commandments from the only God [he] ever worshipped" (3.1).) But, while Dexter remains devoted to Harry in the novels, even after the revelation of Harry's betrayal and the existence of his brother Brian, the series dares to knock Harry down from this pedestal in Season 2 by offering yet another motive for Harry's creation of the self-righteous serial killer. As Dexter learns in "The Dark Defender," much to his shock and dismay, Harry was having an affair with his mother, Laura Moser, while she was working for Harry as a criminal informant and passing on information about the drug dealer Estrada. (Her killer, Santos Jimenez, admits to Dexter that this was the real reason behind her murder (2.5).) As much as Dexter would like to believe that Harry's interest in him, then, was largely pure, genuine, and benevolent, this connection casts a pall over his character and leads Dexter to doubt the true nature of his intentions. As he wonders at the beginning of "Dex, Lies, and Videotape," "Did [Harry] blame himself for [Laura Moser's] death? Is that why he took me in? Did he love her, or was he just using her? Was he using me? [. . . M]aybe he planned for me to settle the score all along" (2.6). For all of Dexter's memories of Harry as the loving father and dedicated family man, in the end he may have felt a responsibility toward Dexter out of guilt, for putting his mother in harm's way, just as he may have deliberately turned Dexter into a killer of killers out of a personal desire, if not to bring her back like Victor's experiment, then to avenge the murder that, essentially, gave "birth" to his dark side.[7] In this regard, Dexter's "education" really becomes the ultimate act of selfishness, as Dexter later realizes when he describes himself as Harry's "own personal vendetta machine" (3.1). So, rather than finding the divine in his father's case file and through his dealings with his mother's killer, Dexter, like Shelley's creature, instead discovers a significantly flawed creator, a man prone to temptation and weakness, a liar, a cheater, and a manipulator. After breaking the code and impulsively killing Oscar Prado at the start of Season 3, he expresses his subsequent disappointment with Nietzschean succinctness: "[M]y God is dead now" (3.1).

To the same extent that Harry's character and morality are called into question through his connection to Laura Moser, the self-control and self-assuredness that he demonstrates in his plans for Dexter in Season 1 give way to the portrait of a man more on the edge in Season 2. In "There's Something About Harry," one of the most pivotal episodes, if not *the* most pivotal episode, in the series to date, the history, the narrative, the creation story of Dexter, that initially appears so justified and righteous, is revisited and revised to reveal yet another side to the policeman-father-patriarch. As he learns that Juan Ryness, a sadistic pimp who beat and murdered some of his prostitutes, was released on a technicality, Harry, in a moment of frustration that we never see in the first season or the novels, smashes a beer bottle against a kitchen cabinet during Deb's birthday party, and bemoans the fact that the police can do nothing more than "just wait for him to kill another girl!" (2.10). Disheartened and disappointed, he notes that this incident only proves that he "did the right thing in training [Dexter]" (2.10), an assertion that he makes as much for Dexter's benefit as to convince and reassure himself. So, while Dexter specifically remembers him as "always firmly in control" (2.10), this flashback suggests otherwise and refers to the instability brewing beneath the surface,[8] an instability that perhaps helps to explain how a father could knowingly cultivate his son's homicidal inclinations. As Dexter later begins to look into the mysterious circumstances behind his foster father's death, even Harry's friend and colleague (now Dexter's boss), Tom Matthews, remembers him, at the end, as a man plagued by the failure of the system to punish the guilty, and, unaware of Harry's accidental encounter with Dexter and the body of Ryness, readily believes that this is why he took his own life. ("[It] just got harder and harder for Harry to deal with" (2.10), Matthews explains.) The creation of this monster, then, like the creation of Victor's, is not so much a measured response as it is an act of panic or distress, the last gasp of a drowning man, an absurd attempt to create order when the chaos has already done its damage.

When Harry finally sees Dexter in action, however, his reaction is not one of elation or pride or satisfaction; rather, it is Victor's "breathless horror and disgust" in *Frankenstein*. To please his father and right an apparent wrong, Dexter kills Ryness, "an evil bastard," as Harry calls him, but, walking in on the sight of his son cutting up the lifeless, bloody body of the killer and walking in on the monster that he has made, Harry instead throws up and, like the caged Doakes, begs Dexter to "stay away" (2.10). As Dexter himself perceptively realizes through the return of this memory, "The idea of a code [is] one thing—a grand idea, a noble cause. But the reality of it [is something else]" (2.10), something that Harry literally cannot stomach or live with. In the abstract, turning Dexter into a serial killer with a conscience, for Harry, kills several birds with one stone (or knife), from his guilt and frustration to his concerns over Dexter's future. And if justice cannot be served in the court of law, then, at least, it can find a home in the court of Dexter. But, as he sees the end result of his training, as he sees the living, breathing, murdering truth of it all, as he sees the monster, not with black hair and yellow skin barely covering its muscles, but with a detective's code and the ruse of normalcy, there is only blood and body parts. For all of the lessons that he teaches Dexter, the final lessons are Harry's, and these are the lessons of *Frankenstein*, lessons that "spin his world out of control" for one last tragic time. Violating moral and social laws in the name of an ideal does not lead to retribution or vindication. Ryness's murder does not make up for all of the other killers who got away or for Davey Sanchez or the dead prostitute or even Dexter's mother. Justice is not served by injustice, and death does not lead to rebirth. Harry is horrified by what he has done and rightly so. "[Gazing] into the eyes of his creation"— another "product of the unnatural coupling of nature and the imagination"—he sees "evil, pure and simple" (2.11), Dexter's as well as his own, perhaps. Three days later, he kills himself, ironically making Harry yet another one of Dexter's victims (as Victor is the creature's)[9] and crystallizing the Oedipal issues lurking within his psyche, issues that become the focus of the rest of Season 2 and all of Season 3.

That Harry has created a monster is something that really is never in doubt and perhaps should not come as such a surprise to him. In *Skin Shows*, Judith Halberstam argues that *Frankenstein* "presents itself not as the making of a monster but as the making of a human" (32). The horror of the creature comes from those moments and those descriptions that point to Victor's failure and the creature's inhumanity, behaviorally as well as in Halberstam's visual sense, from his creation to the murders that he commits, just as the creature's nobility is demonstrated in those speeches and scenes from the text when he appears (or sounds) the most human, as when he begs for De Lacey's friendship or explains himself to Walton at the end of the novel. In the same way that Victor believes that he can "make a human" by sewing together dead body parts, Harry also believes, in addition to his love for the boy and his dreams of justice, that he can take the monster-child born from the bloody storage container and make something human or something that appears to be human out of it. So many of Harry's lessons, like smiling for pictures and going out on dates, are all about getting Dexter to fit in and appear normal specifically, as Harry explains, "because [he is] not" (1.5). But, like the creature, Dexter is, when all is said and done, only a more advanced form of artificial life, a bizarre cross between Robbie the Robot and Michael Myers or Mr Data with a butcher's knife, and, for all of Harry's instructions, he still lacks the feelings that would make him whole. He admits, right from the beginning, that he "fakes" all of his human interactions "very well" and that he does not "have feelings about anything" (1.1). During a candid conversation with teen killer Jeremy Downs, who also suffers from this lack of feeling, the best advice that Dexter can give is to "pretend the feelings are there for the world, for the people around [him]," an act that may one day lead to the feelings themselves (1.7).[10] He is drawn to Lila in part because she, too, is "emotionally color-blind" and has "no idea of what [emotions] actually feel like" (2.12), just as he admires serial killer Roger Hicks because he can lie so effectively and jump "from one lie to the next" like "someone ski[ing] moguls" (2.3). And for all of its apparent sincerity, Dexter's proposal to Rita in Season 3 is similarly an act, inspired by the emotional appeal of deluded murderer Fiona Kemp (3.4). Even Harry cannot help but call Dexter what he is by name. After Dexter fakes his way through a psychological exam, an exam that his foster mother requested as she, too, became suspicious of him, Harry proudly notes that "the doctor didn't even see the monster inside [him]" (2.4). In both Lindsay's first novel, *Darkly Dreaming Dexter*, and the first episode of the series, Dexter introduces himself as "a very neat monster" (12 and 1.1) and is consistently honest with himself about just who and what he is, just as brutally honest, in fact, as he is with his victims. From his conversation with a vision of Rudy, a product of Dexter's psyche, in Season 2, he comes to a conclusion about himself in the most direct terms: he is "not human"; he is "just fucked up" (2.2).

The Sins of the Father

For all of the psychological motivation behind the creation in *Frankenstein*, Victor's creature ironically becomes the son that he never had or, for that matter, wanted. (In spite of the unusual circumstances behind his "birth," the creature, through his own first-person narrative, often sounds like Victor in his allusions to Adam and Satan, in his love of nature, and in his self-centered view of his own pain and misery.) And, like the other fathers trying to restrict or control their children and the other children defying their parents in the novel, Victor soon finds himself drawn into an Oedipal conflict of a different sort, as the creature, having been rejected by his creator and spurned by mankind, returns to request a mate. From his vicarious experience of domesticity with the De Lacey family and his reading of Milton's *Paradise Lost*, the creature, as Collings explains, "just wants to be another person" (291). But normalcy is not something that the creature, a grotesque composite of limbs and organs, can, realistically, ever have, not in Geneva nor in South America, where he promises to go, and neither is it something that Victor is, upon reflection, willing (or able) to grant, as he now better understands the responsibilities of creation and how individual lives come with individual wills. ("I was now about to form another being," he realizes during his creation of the creature's mate, "of whose dispositions I was alike ignorant" (114).) Victor's destruction of the second experiment sets off an Oedipal fury that essentially turns the creature, still very much an emotional child, into a monster (and a serial killer of sorts). Having already murdered Victor's younger brother William, he kills Clerval and Elizabeth, Victor's best friend and his wife respectively, and forces him to share in the pain of his isolation. Victor's dream becomes prophetic, as his attempt to create gives birth to death. In the end, Victor and the monster, creator and creation, father and son are left with only their hatred, both for themselves and one another, a hatred that ultimately consumes them both, as Victor dies in the obsessive pursuit of his creation and the monster, with no other reason to live, destroys himself by Promethean fire, "ascend[ing] his funeral pile triumphantly" (156).

After he is cast out, though, the creature is at least able to (re)turn to Victor and to focus on him, both as the source of creation and loss. As he torments Victor through the destruction of those he holds dear, he finds a strange satisfaction in his creator's prolonged misery. From the death of his father to the memory of Harry's disgust, Dexter, however, is afforded no such focal point and no such sadistic pleasures. Instead, he is left to work out his Oedipal anger on a purely psychological level and to resolve his conflict by himself, without some dog-sled chase through the Arctic. Shaken by the thought that Harry's teachings amounted to nothing and that he is something twisted and evil rather than heroic, Dexter nearly surrenders to the authorities, only to rededicate himself to his purpose and to embrace the Code of Harry as a law all his own. "My father might not approve," Dexter muses at the end of Season 2, "but I'm no longer his disciple. I'm a master now, an idea transcended into life" (2.12). Where the thought of disobeying Harry might previously have seemed like blasphemy and where Harry's disappointment was so devastating, Dexter no longer appears to work for his father's approval. He now takes strength from his disobedience and from his existence as a living abstraction, and, in his dismissal of Harry, he finds self-affirmation.

But, as *Frankenstein* suggests, the influence, the effects, and the legacy of the creator are not so easily abandoned or discarded. Victor's creation certainly cannot ignore or dismiss his existence and is determined to get his undivided attention if he cannot command him to make a female counterpart. And, though Dexter asserts his "mastery" and buys himself a new box of blood slides, the memory of his father continues to haunt him. Drinking with Miguel Prado (who has rather significant father issues of his own)[11] outside of his apartment early on in Season 3, he still reflects, forlornly, on Harry's horror, even though he became "exactly the man [his] father molded [him] to be" (3.3). In fact, since Harry is dead, Dexter must resurrect him in his mind, so that he, like Frankenstein's monster, can continue the conflict and wrestle with the Oedipal demons released by his final memories of Harry and his subsequent suicide. Harry reappears in a variety of brightly lit visions and dream sequences in Season 3, often disrupting their appeal, spiking his son's anxiety, and serving to remind him of his monstrosity in the face of more domestic fantasies. As Dexter contemplates fatherhood, Harry cuddles "Dexter, Jr" in one vision and waves a toy blood-filled syringe at the infant (3.2). When he imagines his future son playing with Rita, Cody, and Astor, Harry turns up to point out the inconsistency in the dream, that Rita's children "would be older" (3.2). Though Dexter, still bristling at Harry's rejection, notes that the possibility of Dexter as a family man was something that Harry could never "picture" (3.2) or consider for him, the vision again ends badly, with Astor gone missing and the young boy, with dark gloves and a length of wire, suddenly manifesting his father's killer impulses and looking very much like the culprit. During a CAT scan, Harry shows him how his brain compares to another serial killer who "snapped" and "killed his wife, two kids, and the neighbor's dog" (3.3), and, as Dexter considers moving to a bigger house with Rita and the kids, Harry points out that "central air" could affect his ability to hide his box of blood slides (3.5). When he dismisses Rita's request to go house-hunting so that he can put down wife killer Ethan Turner out on a cruise ship near Bimini, Harry again appears to suggest that Dexter is "cheating on her, even if [he] doesn't realize it" (3.5), just as Dexter's birth mother turns to ask Harry for more suntan lotion. And when Dexter starts to include Miguel in his work, Harry, dressed like Dexter, quips that he should also "swing by and pick up Rita and the kids" (3.6), and later waves Ellen Wolf's dead hand at him after Dexter suspects that Miguel has violated the code for personal reasons. Clearly, in death, Harry has an odd sense of humor that he never had in life.

As sarcastic and upsetting as Harry is in these daydreams, however, he, as the originator of the code, also serves as the voice of Dexter's conscience or super-ego, reminding him of the consequences of his actions as he attempts to move beyond the code and expand on his world. When Dexter thinks about taking Miguel on as a "full" partner, Harry's tone becomes more serious and, for lack of a better word, parental. "Don't think about it" (3.8), he warns, a warning that could just as easily have (and, psychologically speaking, ultimately does) come from Dexter himself. Later, as Dexter and Miguel search through murderous gambler Billy Fleeter's house for evidence, he returns to chastise Dexter for his poor judgment. "I didn't teach you the code to share with your buddies," Harry admonishes. "I taught you the code to keep you alive" (3.8). Staring into his father's eyes (or a vision of them), Dexter rebelliously turns to show Miguel Fleeter's ledger, the final "nail in the coffin" that satisfies the code and justifies his death. As reasonable as Harry's advice may be and as insightful as his assessments are, Dexter deliberately rejects them, largely because they come from this source and because he still smarts from the memory of Harry's betrayal in Season 2. And for any doubts that he may have, consciously or subconsciously, about "sharing the reins" and taking their partnership to this level, Dexter summarily dismisses them when Miguel talks about his own dark side and "knock[ing] [his father] down a flight of stairs" (3.8),[12] an act that Dexter symbolically recreates by letting him make the kill on Fleeter.

Deb suggests that Dexter's sudden rejection of Harry amounts to "You gotta-kill-your-father-so-you-can-become-your-own-man kind of bullshit" (3.1), and she may well be right. After embracing the code as his own at the end of Season 2, Dexter goes on to break its terms repeatedly in Season 3, as much to adapt it to the changing demands of his life as to take a stab at Harry and the legacy that he left for his son. Not only does Dexter share the code with Miguel and teach him how to kill, essentially creating a killer like his father,[13] but he also kills several people who do not meet the code and are not killers themselves—Oscar Prado, "sexual predator" Nathan Marten, family friend and Miami Metro record keeper Camilla. And getting married and having a child also amount to attempts to surpass Harry's expectations. ("I could have surprised you," Dexter tells him during the vision of his son with Rita and the kids (3.2).) But, while these may be the more pronounced examples of Dexter's denial of Harry, they are clearly not the first. Inasmuch as Harry's disgust and physical repulsion were the most direct commentaries on Dexter's murders, his continued indulgence in ritualistic murder after this fact as well as his dutiful service to the Miami Metro Police Department amount as much to honoring Harry as to outdoing him. Dexter brings those criminals to justice that Harry never could, in the same way that he dreams of saving his mother in "The Dark Defender," a murder that Harry was unable to prevent. In many ways, Harry may well be the one that he has been trying to kill all along.

With the revelation that Miguel has killed Ellen Wolf and gone outside of the code (even as Dexter now more broadly defines it), he, begrudgingly, begins to see the value and the intent of Harry's lessons, just as he better understands the responsibilities of creation, like Victor when he tries to make the creature's mate. "I created this" (3.9), Dexter confesses from an open grave, as he stares down at Wolf's dead, dirt-covered body. Horrified, he encourages Harry to say that he "told him so" and warned him about the consequences of these actions, but Harry instead opts to show him a more disturbing sight, the many graves of Miguel's future victims and the many deaths for which he now will be additionally responsible. After finally realizing that Harry has "always been right" from his heated rooftop meeting with Miguel (3.10), a struggling Dexter, kidnapped and apparently heading toward his end at the hands of the Skinner at the start of "I Had a Dream"—Masuka actually grabs him for his bachelor party—goes on to tell him as much from the confines of the car trunk, yet Harry does not appear there to bury

Dexter but to praise him for aspiring to normalcy. (Collings's quote about the creature in *Frankenstein* again comes to mind here: he "just wants to be another person.") As Dexter comes around in his relationship with his father, imaginary or otherwise, his vision of Harry becomes more supportive, if only to give him the more gruesome, absurd advice that he "still can [kill Miguel]" and that he should not "give up" (3.11).

Perhaps the most conspicuously absent emotion in *Frankenstein* is forgiveness. Neither Victor nor the creature is capable of forgiving the crimes of their adversary (or themselves, for that matter), again another character trait that they share, and, as their conflict destroys all of those around them, they are left with nothing more than hatred to inform and inspire them. Victor is willing to abandon his own safety and well-being in pursuit of the creature— stranded on an ice floe, he is ready to reject passage on Walton's ship to continue the chase—and, on his deathbed, he openly admits that he "may still be misled by passion" (152) in calling for the creature's death. Conversely, the creature has no purpose beyond his torment of Victor—he asks Victor "to pardon him" (153) only after he is dead—and, with Frankenstein's death, he has nothing more to look forward to than his own death by fire and "the agony of the torturing flames" (156). Dexter, by contrast, is ultimately able to forgive Harry and resolve his Oedipal anger, even as he lies helpless at the hands of the Skinner, largely because he has achieved at least the guise of normalcy and the companionship and family life that the creature aspired to, but was denied. (From Victor's death, the creature is again only reminded of this lack. "[E]ven the enemy of God and man [Satan, as he learns through his reading of Milton] had friends and associates in his desolation," he considers; "I am quite alone" (154).) Unlike the creature, Dexter's monstrosity is more internal than external, and so he is able to blend in and mingle with his Miami neighbors, even as he contemplates chopping some of them up and sending them down the Gulf Stream in a series of Hefty bags. (Deb and Rita, the people who are closest to him, never really suspect the dark side that he hides. In Season 1, Rita goes so far as to describe him, ironically, as "the one good, truly decent man left on the planet" (1.2).) And not only has he "found a mate" and not only is he about to marry Rita, a suitable substitute for the mother that he has lost,[14] but Dexter is also about to become a father, and, through this change, he makes his admiration of and identification toward Harry crystal clear: "I hope to be half as good a father to my son" (3.12), Dexter tells him, as the Skinner looms menacingly in the background. Where Harry's rejection of Dexter led to Dexter's rejection of Harry, his experimentation with the terms of the code, Miguel's betrayal, and his impending fatherhood now make him view the creator in a different light. Though his God may be dead, he can accept the man himself. Inasmuch as Executive Producer Clyde Phillips, in thinking about this season, recalls "the old Jungian phrase that you have to kill your father to forgive him" (*Dexter 25: SHORunner*)[15]—a rather ironic phrase in light of Dexter's role in his suicide—Dexter may also be able to reconcile with Harry or Harry's memory here because, psychologically and through these experiments, he has successfully made this kill, too. And so, with the final episode, Harry is "dying" to be forgiven.

While Season 3 ends on a high note, with Dexter and Rita's wedding, with a vision of Harry and his mother toasting their son, and with Dexter's reflection that "life is good" (3.12), this sense of optimism and resolution is betrayed by the dark realities beneath, like the dark red blood stream that runs down the back of Rita's white wedding dress at the end of the episode. For all of his appearances during the season, Harry is never actually there. Though he admits, in Masuka's trunk, that he is "proud" of Dexter's attempt to create "a normal life" for himself (3.11), and though he is apologetic and remorseful in the Skinner's lair over the mistakes that he made and uncharacteristically cries as he thinks about his role as Dexter's father (3.12), Harry himself might not have had these reactions. His responses to Dexter's behavior, like his tears, are Dexter's creation, a manifestation of his psyche, a monster's monster. In the end, they become a coping mechanism for him, an imaginative way of resolving what would otherwise remain unresolved and of dealing with those painful, horrific last memories of his parents, that his mother was chainsawed in a storage container, that his foster father was having an affair with her, that he "gazed into the eyes of his creation and saw evil" (2.11). Unable to confront Harry or his mother in person, Dexter can exercise this freedom and comfort himself with the belief, however illusory, that they would toast him and that Harry would seek and need his forgiveness, an option that the creature in *Frankenstein*, fully aware of Victor's hatred and constantly reminded of his disgust and rejection, can never enjoy. If "the sins of the father" do go on and are perpetuated, as Dexter tells Ramon Prado, "from kid to kid to kid, unless . . . someone chooses to end them" (3.12), then, in choosing to reconcile with his father's memory and absolve him, Dexter is paving the way for the future, his son's as well as his own. A creation now becoming creator, he thus wills his own resolution, lets go of his resentment, and, within the span of this final episode, ties up all of the loose ends in his life, physically as well as psychologically—a very neat monster, indeed.

(Post)Modern Prometheus

In a recent call for papers on the *Independent Scholars* website, Tuna Erdem referred to what she called "the father problem in contemporary television fiction" ("It Has Happened Before"), that unusual preoccupation with fathers and children that has become an integral part of so many television narratives. If you look closely at the television landscape as it now stands, you will find it littered with a host of TV dads gone wild, of deadbeats, users, abusers, drug addicts, crooks, liars, fakers, cheaters, beaters, imposters, and a few who are just downright mean. In addition to *Dexter*, in fact, fathers play or have played rather disruptive or negative roles in the lives of the main characters on so many shows lately—*Heroes, House, Fringe, Prison Break, Monk, Bones, Deadwood, The Shield, Mad Men, Rescue Me, The Sopranos,* and *24*, to name a few. If television fathers were all the rage from the '50s through the '90s, from insurance agent Jim Anderson on *Father Knows Best* (ironically, also the title of a Season 1 *Dexter* episode) to level-headed minister Eric Camden on *Seventh Heaven*, they inspire nothing but rage now, and, behind House's irreverence, Jack Bauer's cold determination, or Tony Soprano's sociopathic toxicity, there are hints of the childhood pain and emotional scars that make their characters so intriguing.

But, even if there is, arguably, a good Frankenstein myth at the heart of contemporary quality television, a creation story gone wrong that has given birth to a dysfunctional hero/villain, the father problem is more than just a fashionable plot hook. Rather, it speaks to that constant and particularly relevant cultural need to plumb the depths of the myth of origins and to understand exactly what the patriarchs of the past have done to get us to this point, both good and bad. If these figures are, in some small way, representations of ourselves, of our desires, fantasies, fears, and beliefs, then their Oedipal struggles are, more generally, our own, and, in their attempt to reconcile (or perpetuate) them, we find our own conflict as a culture replicated and expressed. As we navigate this world laden with moral ambiguity, political uncertainty, and financial chaos, we have a need to know, now more than ever, who made us this way and how we came to be, just as we want to know the creator/father behind it all.

In *Dexter* as in *Frankenstein*, those answers bring little comfort, as they reveal "accursed origin[s]" (Shelley 87) and disappointed creators, and add to the general sense of alienation that these creations already feel toward mankind. But, where Victor's experiment clearly is a failure, at least in the immediate sense, the consequences of Harry's still are not so readily apparent. While he certainly has made a monster, a killer who poses as a friend and family man to hide the bloody work of his Dark Passenger, Dexter satisfies the need for justice beyond the judicial system, both within the confines of the series and the novels and, like Vic Mackey or Tony Soprano, as part of the contemporary audience's ongoing fantasy of moral accountability. So, while we continue to cringe at what Dexter does in the name of the code and at what Harry has wrought through his crime of stealing fire from the gods, we still continue to watch as the fire burns and the monster runs loose, perhaps because, through the flames and from our vantage point on this side of the television screen, we see something recognizable, if only in our darkest dreams.

7.
Sex, Psychoanalysis, and Sublimation in *Dexter*

Beth Johnson

> **Dexter:** There are no secrets in life, just hidden truths that lie beneath the surface.
>
> ("Crocodile," 1.2)

Sex, the Sublime Object, and Psychoanalysis: Season 1

As the reflective voice-over above denotes, Dexter Morgan, handsome blood-splatter analyst and serial killer, is represented as a complex character, both man and monster, public and private, villain and victim. He is, perhaps, initially represented in the pilot episode of the series as sublime—in the Burkean sense (54)—remote, alien, and terrifyingly outside, even beyond human. Dexter however proves to be dynamic, ever-changing, emerging and regressing at various points through various relationships, experiences, and punctums. Undoubtedly, Dexter embodies duality. Most obviously, he looks quite beautiful on the outside, and it is this beauty which aids him to conceal his inner deviance, his "Dark Passenger." While this duality can, of course, be interpreted in various ways and via various theoretical frameworks, the following essay argues that a psychoanalytic reading of Dexter is appropriate and resonant due to the self-referential nature of Dexter's own psychological reflections. That is to say that Dexter continuously self-analyses, reflects, and nominates psychological shifts in his thinking. In voice-overs and through flashback scenes, Dexter soothes the viewer with his revelatory admissions of emptiness, anxiety, and urges, drives, demands, and dreams. The psychoanalytic approach

78

explored in this chapter is thus grounded in the fact that *Dexter* itself engages with psychoanalysis and theoretical assertions concerning desire, death, and drives. Most significantly, Dexter recognizes the framework of psychoanalysis while visiting an analyst in the episode ironically entitled "Shrink Wrap" (1.8).

Several questions come to mind when considering Dexter's identity and his desires; however, as the title of this essay indicates, Dexter's sexual desires are particularly pertinent as this aspect of his character is never fully explained. Indeed, as Michel Foucault asserts: "Whenever it is a question of knowing who we are, it is this logic that henceforth serves as our master key . . . Sex, the explanation for everything" (78). Viewers of Season 1, particularly episodes one–seven, may well ask why or if, in fact, sex is really that integral to understanding Dexter. Dexter shows, at least initially, very little interest in sex, nominating in the pilot episode that sex "never enters into it": "I don't understand sex. Not that I have anything against women [. . .] But when it comes to the actual act of sex, it's always just seemed so undignified" (1.1). It is, I suggest, precisely for this reason, however, that gaining an understanding of sex in *Dexter* and to Dexter is so important. Psychoanalysis is concerned with that which is out of place in the image—that which blindingly "sticks out"—and that which is missing or off-screen. It is the latter which, precisely, organizes ways of seeing and, as such, the lack of sexual desire that Dexter exhibits is principally important to understanding his character.

The pilot episode brings several questions to bear: Is Dexter asexual? Does Dexter avoid sex as it threatens his own mortality? Does Dexter sublimate his sexual desires into a violent murderous drive? These are the questions which this article both asks and attempts to answer. Alongside these questions, it is also important to discuss and define (if possible) the nature of Dexter's sublimation and analyse the sexual desires of other characters, specifically those whom Dexter has sexual relationships with, namely in the first and second series, Rita and Lila. I will argue that psychoanalysis, sex, and sublimation are primary themes of significance in Dexter which help to explicate an understanding of this slick, sublime serial killer.

In line with the aforementioned schema of analysis, it is useful to define the primary terms I invoke in this article and explain the capacity in which they will be used. Firstly, the term "sublimation" is to be utilized here in a psychoanalytic sense. As Dylan Evans argues, sublimation in Freud's work is "a process in which the libido is channeled into apparently non-sexual activities such as artistic creation" (198). If we invoke this definition of sublimation, then Dexter's murderous "hunger" can be seen as a re-formed or perhaps de-formed manifestation of sexual desire. For Freud, sublimation is the process of transforming libido into "socially useful" achievements. While it may seem strange in the first instance to consider Dexter's murderous activity as an achievement, it is repetitively noted by Dexter to be "justified" and, further, is nominated as a craft—as "art." In the pilot episode, Dexter tells the viewer that: "Miami is a great place for me to hone my craft" and, on gazing at a fragmented, beautifully packaged, bloodless female murder victim, he declares the killer to be "an artist," noting that his "technique is incredible."

It is also in this episode (1.1) that we see Dexter initiating sexual intimacy with his girlfriend, Rita. She is, we are told, "damaged" due to the emotional scars of her former marriage in which she was repeatedly raped and beaten by her estranged husband, Paul. Dexter explicates that he, like Rita, is damaged: "Rita is as damaged as me," he laments. Perhaps because of this recognition of damage, there appears to be an intimacy between Dexter and Rita. One could surmise that intimacy here exists at both a conscious and an unconscious level. As Aunt Sally, an "agony aunt" for the British publication *The Sunday Times Magazine*, writes: "Intimacy is the admission of human frailties on both sides [. . .] two people who recognise the damage in each other [. . .] We are attracted to fragilities in other people that we know, often at an unconscious level, we share ourselves" (39). While this is illuminating, Rita's restricted knowledge regarding Dexter's dark deeds facilitates and induces a reliance by her upon Dexter. He is, in her eyes, a stand-up guy with a "good heart," kind, trustworthy, and patient regarding her deferral of a sexual relationship. As aforementioned, later in this episode we observe Dexter (subconsciously) attempting to engage in a sexual act with Rita. While reflecting upon the sublime beauty of the aforementioned crime scene in a car with Rita, he places his hand beneath her skirt. When Rita runs from the car, disturbed, Dexter sits, appearing shocked at his actions. "Why did I do that?" he asks himself, genuinely mystified.

The answer, I suggest, is that Dexter is turned on by the beauteous bodily object he remembers at this crime scene. Though outwardly attempting to touch Rita's leg, Dexter is, in fact, trying to appropriate, to re-create intimacy with the sublime "art" he has seen. Dexter's desires are not however directed towards the object—the bits and pieces of the body he analyses—but, rather, are invested in the work itself and the artistic beauty of it. It is in this artistic beauty that Dexter finds pleasure. In essence then, as the artistic beauty is not concrete, cannot be physically touched, Dexter displaces his desire onto an actual visible object—Rita's thigh. Indeed, the inner thigh connotes intimacy—it is an object, a pathway that leads toward a familiar yet estranged pleasure. The same of course could be said of Dexter's intimate relationship with his "victims" in the kill rooms he creates. Both in a physical and psychological sense, Dexter engages in intimate relationships with each of his victims, stripping them, physically containing them, demanding that they look at him and at images of those they have murdered. Dexter often forces his victims to acknowledge the fear and pain they have caused others and immediately afterwards (while they are conscious), penetrates his various victims with knives or other sharp objects—a penetration that could arguably be read as phallic.

Returning to Rita, Dexter appears to work hard in order to sublimate his sexual desires, to quell or repress this aspect of his identity lest he actually makes real a connection with another. The purpose of such repression is two-fold. Arguably, Dexter needs to protect himself, to prevent himself from being "caught." Via this self-control, Dexter is able to protect others from the irrational danger of the world. Dexter, of course, kills only those who have killed others and escaped justice. This is the code by which he lives. While warped, it is rational of sorts—an alternative version of morality. The act of sex, alternatively, can transcend rationality. As Georges Bataille argues in *Eroticism*: "[sexual] pleasure is so close to ruinous waste . . . Anything that suggests erotic excess always implies disorder" (170). Of kissing Rita Dexter admits: "making-out with Rita was interesting, but if I don't keep a lid on this, it could be the end

81

of us." Dexter desires order and control. As such, sex is dangerous, "messy," and has the ability to make him anxious. Dexter has, we infer, been engaged in romantic sexual relationships before. In episode two ("Crocodile"), he laments: "When I feel comfortable with a woman, it all goes wrong" (1.2). Sex has previously, then, it is relayed, resulted in loss.

The concept of loss is again a crucial one in terms of psycho-analysis. Loss can be best understood here in relation to the Oedipus complex as theorized by Freud. As Dylan Evans explicates, the Oedipus complex is defined as "an unconscious set of loving and hostile desires which the subject experiences in relation to its parents; the subject desires one parent and thus enters into rivalry with the other parent" (127). In relation to Dexter, this complex can be understood thus: the child, Dexter, chooses his mother as the object of his libidinal investment. This relationship is threatened by the anger of the father who, Dexter imagines, may castrate him in order to prevent this relationship from developing. The fear of castration leads the child to internalize the rules of the father and identify with him. If a positive outcome is achieved, the child (Dexter) must select an alternative object of desire. If this complex "malfunctions" in any way, psychopathological structures can form inducing neuroses. Significantly, this complex is experienced by all children and first emerges, Freud nominates, in the third to fifth year of life. This is significant in relation to Dexter as we find out in episode eight ("Shrink Wrap") that Harry, Dexter's foster-father, took him in at the age of three after a traumatic event.

During a regression session with a psychoanalyst, Dr Meridian (whom Dexter visits in order to prove his participation in the supposed suicide of three powerful professional women), Dexter accesses for the first time a horrific memory which he has repressed. In a flashback scene, we see Dexter as a small child, sitting in a vast pool of blood, drops spattered on his angelic young face. He cries and screams, looking off-screen and then back, a large, bloody tear rolling down his cheek. Forcing a return from this traumatic state he opens his eyes, breathes hurriedly and deeply before running from the office. The sequential events that follow this horrific remembrance—Dexter's appearance at Rita's home and their subse-quent sexual engagement—will be discussed shortly. Before this, however, it is important to clarify how this memory, a memory that prompts for Dexter the traumatic return of his mother's murder, is connected to the Oedipus complex.

Clearly, if Dexter's mother was murdered when he was aged three, it is arguable that while Dexter may have considered his mother, Laura, as the object of his libidinal desire, this relationship may have failed to progress beyond this stage. If, as is indicated, Dexter repressed any knowledge of his mother's horrific murder and his own witnessing of this event until regression "brought it back," Freud suggests that identity would indeed be affected in terms of suffering from a "mother-fixation." And, as Dexter so aptly points out in episode nine ("Father Knows Best"): "Trauma can distort the memory" (1.9).

The "mother-fixation" is again connected to the concept of loss and associated with a need or desire to control. Through control of his environment (for example, his apartment is meticulously clean and ordered) and, further, through his blood-splatter control (both his expertise at his "day" job and his control over his own crime scenes), Dexter simultaneously evokes and fulfills Harry's demand that he "must not get caught." However, in psychoanalytic terms, fulfillment also brings a sense of loss, which itself is a desire for what has passed—the opportunity to love his mother, be loved by her, or maybe the chance to confess his crimes, to break away from Harry's demands—an appropriation of an unbearable pleasure.

The mother-fixation is also manifested in Dexter's choice of the beautiful, young, white Rita as his girlfriend. Notably, the face of Dexter's mother is not revealed until episode ten ("Seeing Red"), in which the blood-filled room Dexter is called out to analyse throws up for him (again) the sickening memory of his mother's desperate, weeping, and terrified face prior to her imminent murder. The reveal here is interesting on many levels. Firstly, Laura, Dexter's mother, is startlingly similar in appearance to Rita. Both women are fair, with virtually identical hairstyles and colors, similar face shapes and bodily statures. According to Freudian theory, the mother-fixation is often identified in this way, through choosing sexual partners who are discernible surrogates for their parent. Like Dexter's mother, Rita requires saving from male violence and terror;

like Rita, Laura was mother to two young children and was desperate to protect them, giving her life in order that they should be saved. In a conversation between Rita and her estranged husband, Paul, she says to him: "You cheated on me, you broke my heart, you broke my bones, and I took it so those kids wouldn't have to" (1.11). Likewise, we infer, Laura did the same. Like Rita's husband Paul, Laura's husband, Joseph Driscoll (Dexter's biological father) was an addict. Commenting on the unknown past of Joe, Dexter suggests that: "Joe spent some time in prison and mixed with some bad people. Maybe he had to hide from it." Rita pitches in, clarifying the similarity between the two men: "Whatever it was, drugs were involved," she says, looking at some medals belonging to Joe. "Narcotics Anonymous," she announces. "Paul used to get these" (1.9).

It seems almost ironic that Dexter knows nothing of his real father until he is laid out, cold and lifeless before him, until the relationship, or any potential for one, is already lost. The past Dexter knows consists of Harry, his foster-father, instructing him and training him to avoid capture. It was Harry who knew most poignantly the duality of Dexter. It was Harry who, Dexter considers, was the only one "who ever really knew me" (1.8). Reflecting on his psychoanalysis sessions with Dr Meridian, Dexter admits to "sexual hangups and control issues." Meridian, unaware of Dexter's traumatic past or his current murderous activity, identifies that Dexter is afraid. Referring to Dexter's sexual deferral of an intimate relationship with the now willing Rita, Meridian remarks that Dexter is afraid that she won't like what she sees. His specific psychological assertions on Dexter's sexual, or lack of sexual, behavior are articulated thus: "The reason that you avoid sexual intimacy is because you don't want to surrender control [. . .] The minute you accept who you are you might feel free to share that intimacy again" (1.8). Later, of course, after Dexter's regression—his recognition of the origin of his loss and pain—he makes the journey to Rita's house. Startled by the pain in Dexter's eyes, Rita asks if Dexter is okay. He does not reply, instead kissing her hungrily before fucking her, stood up, face-to-face.

Significantly, the next day, Dexter does not reflect on what, or if, in fact, the act made him feel. Instead, his lack of description and reflection regarding this indicates that it is "unknowable." What does Dexter recognize, feel, and find through this new sexual relationship? Does he find himself? Does Rita suddenly become the object of his desire? These are important questions—ones that Dexter himself refuses to answer through speech. Psychoanalytic theory can be utilized here, employed to reveal what words—or the absence of words—cannot. If Dexter's mother is to be understood as his "lost object," perhaps, through Rita, Dexter attempts to re-find her. This would of course explain the initial deferral in sexual relations with Rita beyond evasion of capture. If the mother exists as Dexter's origin of being and origin of loss, then Rita—through her similarity to Laura—may be elevated into the place of the mother. Indeed, Rita may take on the status of "the Thing"—what psychoanalyst and theorist Jacques Lacan defined as: "das Ding—in other words, the forbidden object of incestuous desire: the mother" (*Book VII*, 67). Dexter perhaps then makes real the connection that he longs for through the messy connections he makes—both sexual and non-sexual. His blood-splatter analysis functions as a way of finding meaning in the trauma of his past. In episode eleven ("Truth Be Told"), he reflects a self-awareness—a need and desire to understand his past: "My mother was murdered before my eyes. It makes sense I choose a life where I find meaning in blood—when the sole memory I have of her is being covered in it" (1.11).

The acts of murder Dexter undertakes are not merely about the breaking up of the body, but can be seen as a deeper, more intimate attempt to gain access to something beyond the human body—a connection perhaps, linked to the origin of his loss. "I find people around me are all making some kind of connection, like friendship or romance but human bonds always lead to messy complications . . . I can't let that happen" (1.4), he avers.

In Freudian terms, Dexter can also be understood to sublimate his sexual desires into work or, the "honing his craft"; tracking down, evidencing, and murdering murderers. Further, Dexter's desires, I suggest, are also sublimated onto other killers. Dexter elevates the status of his victims to fascinating objects which must be destroyed so that he can follow Harry's code and, via these acts, make sense of and honor the relationship between himself and others: "[T]here was something Harry didn't teach me. Something he didn't know, couldn't possibly know. The willful taking of life represents the ultimate disconnect from humanity. It leaves you an outsider, forever looking in, searching for company to keep" (1.3). Dexter is, we infer, isolated and, as he himself explicates, "empty" and "disconnected." In episode twelve ("Born Free"), the Ice Truck Killer reveals himself to Dexter as his biological brother—Brian. Having begun a relationship with Dexter's (foster)-sister, Deb, in order to get to know Dexter, he kidnaps her, intending that they should murder her in the same manner as Dexter's other victims.[1] Brian, attempting to connect with Dexter, requires Dexter to recognize the similarities between them via their shared knowledge of their mother's murder and their own murderous urges: "I know what you've been through all these years. The isolation, the otherness, the hunger that's never satisfied. You are not alone anymore Dexter. You can be yourself" (1.12). This relationship, potentially at least, facilitates the fulfillment of Dexter's earlier nominated desire, explicated in episode seven ("Circle of Friends"): "I used to pride myself on being an outsider but now I feel the need to connect with someone" (1.7). Dexter, however, rejects the blood connection with Brian, choosing, albeit uncertainly, to murder him and bleed him out. Unlike Dexter's other victims, he does not take a sample of blood from Brian, clearly demarking that Brian is not a trophy kill. Instead, Dexter looks mournfully at his work, recognizing the deadly scene as a re-enactment of a former experience that both he and Brian shared. As the blood flows from inside Brian's body to outside, Dexter holds his head in his hands, covering his eyes. His mother's last words, her command to him recalled in episode ten, "Don't look Dexter. Close your eyes" (1.10) are, perhaps, finally adhered to here.

This messy leakage between the inner and outer, the unknown and the known is pertinent in bodily and psychological terms. As Bruno Snell notes: "Knowledge is the state of having seen [...] as it suggests a degree of reasoned perspective" (Jay 24). This recognition begins to address two distinct visual orders: pro (connected to the outer eye) and anti (connected to the mind's "I") visual regimes. The distance between these two regimes in Dexter constitutes a violent unhinging of the singular perspective.

The leakage of repressed knowledge is, even when consciously "known," distinct in Lacanian psychoanalytic theory from Freudian understanding in that Lacan views language as an index of loss. For Lacan, the conscious and unconscious overlap and repetition occurs to unify the ego. Desire for Lacan then is an effect of language: yet, the subject does not seek knowledge, but rather, seeks satisfaction via language (*Book II*, 288). Through demand having to be uttered, for example the cry of a child to its mother, it is alienated. The child, in essence, does not want satisfaction from food but the presence of the mother in and for itself. Desire, then, is what is left over after demand has been satisfied. Desire is also, for Lacan, always unconscious and, as Evans clarifies, always concerned with sex: "the motives of the unconscious are limited . . . to sexual desire" (36). Desire can thus only be recognized when it is articulated—appropriated via speech. It is speech, Lacan insists, that gives birth to the existence of desire: "In naming [his desire], the subject creates, brings forth, a new presence in the world" (Evans 36). For Lacan, the realization of desire does not concern fulfillment, but the repetition and reproduction of desire. That is to say, desire exists in relation to lack.

This theory can be understood in Dexter thus: Brian's identity, like Dexter's own, is built on lack—the loss of the maternal body. As Toril Moi explains in *Sexual/Textual Politics*, the concept of lack is fundamentally important to a Lacanian understanding of order, both imaginary and symbolic:

> The Imaginary corresponds to the pre-Oedipal period when the child believes itself to be a part of the mother, and perceives no separation between itself and the world. In the Imaginary there is no difference and no absence, only identity and presence. The Oedipal crisis represents the entry into the Symbolic order. This entry is also linked to the acquisition of language. In the Oedipal crisis the father splits-up the dyadic unity between the mother and child and forbids the child further access to the mother and the mother's body. The phallus, representing the Law of the father (or the threat of castration), thus comes to signify separation and loss to the child. The loss or lack suffered is the loss of the maternal body, and from now on the desire for the mother or the imaginary unity with her must be repressed. (99)

Dexter's loss can be understood through this theory as a lack which he continually attempts to rectify or fulfill through symbolic substitutions. Since, of course, the original loss manifested itself both through Dexter's acquisition of language and the actual physical loss of Laura, the mother, Dexter's remembrance of her demonstrates an acknowledgment of her desires above and beyond him. Her unknown desires are of course a source of anxiety for Dexter, which he does not attempt to explain, simply nominating in episode twelve (aptly named "Born Free"): "Laura Moser— addict, dealer, my mother" (1.12). If desire is to be found in the unspeakable gaps, the silences of life, then Dexter's repetitive murderous actions can be understood as a form of self-destruction. The compulsion to repeat can thus be understood as an attempt to produce jouissance (an unbearable pleasure) through absence. The opening lines of the pilot episode highlight the significance of repetition in and to Dexter: "Tonight's the night and it's gonna happen, again and again . . ." (1.1). In episode twelve, Dexter questions his compulsion to repeat the life he knows rather than accepting the freedom his brother Brian offers:

> What did I just do? I drove away a brother who accepts me, sees me, for an adopted sister who'd reject me if she knew . . . and a foster-father who betrayed me. That's what it was—a betrayal. The most important single fact about me—I'm not alone—and Harry kept it from me. What do I really owe him after that? [. . .]Sometimes I wonder what it would be like for everything inside me that's denied and unknown to be revealed. But I'll never know. I live my life in hiding. (1.12)

Sex, Biology, and Spectatorship: Season 2

In Season 2, episode three ("An Inconvenient Lie"), Dexter meets the next woman with whom he will form a sexual relationship— Lila West. Lila takes on a maternal role in the sense that she acts, initially, as Dexter's sponsor in a Narcotics Anonymous Program, due to an "inconvenient lie." Lila, unlike Rita, is dominant, assertive, and an illegal alien in the visible and audible sense—she is tall, slender, ghostly white with dark hair, has a distinctly British accent, and lives in Miami under an assumed identity. Like Dexter, she desires control, often using her body to try to capture Dexter's attention. Dexter's sister, Deb, remarks that she is "obviously a vampire. A gross, English titty vampire" (2.8). This description, while humorous, evokes notions of the Gothic, the uncanny, and the grotesque. As Philip Thompson argues: "The grotesque ha[s] always tended to [be] associate[d] with either the comic or the terrifying […] Those who emphasize the terrifying quality of the grotesque often shift it towards the realm of the uncanny, the mysterious" (20). Lila is indeed mysterious, powerful, and boundary breaching. Failing to respect borders and rules, Dexter terminates his relationship with Lila, causing her to demand he take responsibility for himself:

> Jesus, Dexter, what are you so fucking scared of!? You make yourself into a monster so you no longer bear responsibility for what you do! "Ah, I can't help it, I'm a monster," or, "Of course I was gonna do that—I'm a monster." It's sad! And it's pathetic! And it breaks my heart (2.4).

This notion of the monster inside is linked here to the act of looking. As the title of this episode, "See-Through," consciously denotes, the look is a projection of power. When Dexter asserts that he will show Lila evil (2.4) in order to prove to her that monsters exist, he takes her to a mass-morgue where the reconstructed bodies of the Bay Harbor Butcher (Dexter) are laid out as part of an ongoing police investigation. Looking at the fragmented bodies Lila relays her perception of them—as objects—and her perception of the perpetrator of the crime: "It's … incredible," she notes, echoing Dexter's initial response when confronted with the first Ice Truck Killer victim. Dexter, attempting to force a condemnation of the monster, is clear. "But the person who did this," he begins. Lila asserts her opinion, interrupting, dominating the conversation: "Is a person just like me. Like you. We're all good, Dexter. And we're all evil" (2.4). Dexter is forced by Lila's judgment, her way of seeing, to recognize her power and her subversive potency.

In "Morning Comes," just four episodes later, Dexter rejects Lila's power—her potential to appropriate an alternative vision of the monster. Exorcizing her from his life, his vision, he notes that: "Lila almost had me believing it was possible. To change, to become something else—as if that ever really happens" (2.8). Declaring Lila to be an experiment which he has terminated, he nominates in "Resistance is Futile" his desire to reaffirm his relationship with Rita, promising that "It is over [with Lila]. If I ever see her again it will be too soon" (2.9). Lila's monstrous and powerful acts of looking at and fucking (with) Dexter function as a potentially traumatic threat to his identity and sense of self. Her insistence that he would benefit from self-reflection is finally dismissed and undermined when he notes that such acts are "unhealthy" (2.9). The unhealthiness Dexter nominates can, perhaps, be considered in line with Lila's sexual aggression, her destruction of property and her own monstrous urges which threaten Dexter's own. As Linda Williams argues in "When the Woman Looks": "precisely because this [woman's] look is so threatening to male power, it is violently punished" (65). Lila's true monster is unveiled in "The British Invasion," when Dexter nominates her difference, her otherness, stating that she is vacuous, devoid of feelings: "To know what it's like. To feel something, that deeply. Anything. That's why you hang out in recovery groups. You're emotionally color-blind. You use the right words, you pantomime the right behavior. But the feelings never come to pass. You know the dictionary definition of emotions. Longing, joy, sorrow. But you have no idea what any of those things actually feel like" (2.12).

Later, after breaking into Dexter's car, Lila steels his GPS in order to replicate his journey. This homage to him—to travel the same path as his Dark Passenger—is configured in order to access his inner secrets and locate the places and spaces that he has denied her entry to. On arriving at Dexter's pre-programmed destination, Lila finds Sgt James Doakes, one of Dexter's colleagues, caged. Instructing her to free him from a "psycho," Lila inquires as to the identity of his captor. Dexter is, she is told, the Butcher—the monster. Rather than enacting revenge on Dexter for his rejection of her, she avers that he is her "soul-mate" and turns on a gas-tap, aware that the imminent explosion will kill Doakes and protect Dexter. She is then finally revealed as deluded, passionate, an intersection of good and evil. Thus, Lila's sex, her difference, her refusal to look away, changes and informs Dexter's own transformation; from disciple to master. Dexter recognizes his (Lacanian) semblance—the philosophical opposition between appearance and essence. Reiterating Lila's reconfiguration of difference, her acceptance of it, he asserts, finally: "Am I evil? Am I good? I'm done asking those questions. I don't have the answers. Does anyone?" (2.12).

The answer is of course indeterminate . . . There are, as this essay initially cites and conceives, "no secrets in life, just hidden truths that lie beneath the surface" (1.2) . . . waiting, perhaps, to be reborn, rediscovered, revised, rewritten.

Sex and Paternities: Perverting the Parable: Season 3

Season 3 heralds a continuation of Dexter's rebirth in the role of the father, inviting, again, a psychoanalytic reading. Dominantly focusing on paternity and perverting the father's "code," this series makes visible from episode one, "Our Father" (3.1), the significance of control, ritual, and routine. From the outset, we see that the relationship between Dexter and Rita is back on-track yet, simultaneously, is changed. Rita appears to be (sexually at least) in control, taking position "on-top" of Dexter, fulfilling her own sexual desires and bodily needs. In the bedroom, Dexter tells Rita that she is "on fire," to which she replies: "Are you complaining?" Humorously, Dexter notes that he is merely "complying" and as such, firmly re-establishes Rita as the mother figure, himself doing (in the bedroom at least) as "he is told."

Dexter's presence in Rita's bed, home, and family life (particularly, his position in her children's lives, Cody and Astor), sets up and informs the significance of the role of the father even further. In episode one, Rita's son, Cody, asks Dexter if he will attend and give a talk at "Dad's Day" at his school. Again, Dexter complies and goes on to reflect upon the significance of the father-son relationship. Dexter's voice-over nominates the complexities of his own relationship with Harry, and the problematic nature of Harry's "code," a code Dexter refers to as the "twisted commandments handed down from the only God I ever worshipped." Significantly, Dexter laments: "My God is dead now."

Asked by his sister, Deb, to meet in a bar to remember the anniversary of Harry's death, Dexter fails to turn up, provoking a heated discussion between Dexter and Deb in which he informs her that he is "moving on." Deb's response is profound, invoking and (again) inviting a Freudian/Lacanian psychoanalytic reading of the text: "What is it—you gotta kill your father so you can become your own man, kind of bull-shit?" she asks. According to Evans (2003:62) who explicates a Freudian understanding of the symbolic father: "the symbolic father is also the dead father, the father of the primal horde who has been murdered by his own sons." Indeed, as Dexter painfully nominates in Season 2: "I killed my father" (2:10).

Dexter's acknowledgment of the difficulties of the father-son relationship in the first episode of Season 3 is swiftly followed by Rita's own "eureka" moment. Contemplating her increased sexual and food-related desires (in particular, a craving for chocolate pudding after sex) she tells Dexter that: "I've had this before . . . I'm pregnant" (3.1). Dexter is thus interpolated into the role of the father himself. From this point at the end of episode one, the intimacy seen between Rita and Dexter is rapidly transferred onto and into Dexter's next intimate relationship—that between himself and the character Miguel Prado, an Assistant District Attorney and the brother of an innocent man whom Dexter has murdered in error. This murder goes against "Harry's code," again breaking the paternal bond and laws established by Harry. This relationship between Dexter and Miguel is to be discussed in detail later. However, what is particularly significant about the relationship on a general level is that throughout the third series, Dexter goes against Harry's code in several ways, teaching Miguel his skills, his routine, and his murderous rituals in order to make "a friend" (3.6).

In line with other psychoanalytic explorations relayed in this chapter, it is appropriate here to consider the "father" in full as a psychoanalytic concept. In terms of psychoanalyst Jacques Lacan's theories, the concept of the "father" is to be understood via three distinct strata. These are, according to Lacan, the symbolic father, the imaginary father, and the real father.

The symbolic father is notably not real, but rather, can be understood as a paternal function. In essence, the symbolic father's function is to regulate the desire of the son by imposing law upon the child. Relating this back to the Oedipus complex aforementioned in relation to Season 1, the function of the symbolic father is to impose a healthy distance between mother and son. As noted above, the symbolic father is also "the dead father" (Evans, 2003:62). In the third series of *Dexter*, the symbolic father is Harry. It is Harry who continuously appears to Dexter in flashback sequences stressing the importance of the code and warning of the potential consequences, the responsibilities, the implications if the code is broken.

The disapproval of the father or the inability to "live up to" the code inscribed by the father is discussed in "The Lion Sleeps Tonight" (3.3). In a heart-to-heart with Miguel Prado, Miguel confesses that: "in his [father's] eyes, I was a failure." Dexter's response is equally emotive: "My father was disgusted by me," he says. Later, in episode five, Dexter experiences another painful visit by Harry in which Dexter asserts: "I'm nothing like you!" (3.5). Harry's response to this outcry from Dexter forces Dexter to acknowledge the similarities between them. While Dexter is angry with Harry for lying to him about his brother Brian and the (sexual) nature of his relationship with Laura (Dexter's murdered mother), Harry makes the cutting remark that Dexter is also a "cheat." Referring to Rita and Dexter's murderous passion, Harry notes that: "You're cheating on her and you don't even know it [...] You're going to have to choose which one is your mistress and which one is your wife—and more importantly, which is your priority' (3.5). The issue of priorities or, more specifically, to whom Dexter ultimately listens or prioritizes, can be explicated further through a consideration of the imaginary father in this third series.

The function of the imaginary father is equally complex according to Lacan. As Lacan notes, the imaginary father can be construed in two polarized ways: "as an ideal father" in the first instance, and "as the father who has fucked the kid up" in the second (Evans, 2006:62). Ultimately, while Harry can of course be seen to fulfill the aforementioned positions in several ways, it is, I suggest, also Dexter himself who can be positioned as the imaginary father in the third series. Dexter's impending fatherhood and his paternal role in the lives of Rita's children in this series indicate repetitively his paradoxical nature. Reflecting on the news of Rita's pregnancy (3.2), Dexter considers the risk of his actions in terms of "fucking the kid up": "Why do parents take the risk?" he asks. Increasingly fearful of his impending paternal responsibilities and the potential for him to both hurt his child through omitting the truth (repeating the pain that he believes Harry inflicted upon him) or perhaps passing down his murderous urges, Dexter panics and distances himself from Rita, unable to touch her stomach and be touched by his imminent fatherhood. After Astor is approached by a convicted pedophile in a supermarket and photographed by him at the beach, Dexter murders him, noting in 3.3 that: "nobody hurts my children" and thus seemingly accepts his paternal role. Ironically, however, pronouncing the baby news to Cody and Astor, Dexter fucks up, causing Astor to withdraw from Rita and him. The instability of Dexter and Rita's relationship is reinforced by Astor's questioning of why they are not married. The situation is, as Dexter narrates, "overwhelming" (3.5). Reflecting on his polarization, his performance as both the ideal father and the father who may "fuck up" the child, he laments: "Here I am, paradox personified. Taking life, creating life."

The real father is nominated by Lacan (in Evans 2003:63) as "the agent of castration, the one who performs the operation of symbolic castration." In Season 3, Miguel Prado can arguably be identified as the real father as he becomes an increasing threat to Dexter's mortality and freedom and continuing relationship with Rita by undertaking the act of murder (as taught by Dexter) while refusing to adhere to Harry's/Dexter's "code." Miguel purposefully and defiantly chooses to ignore the parable that Harry instilled in Dexter, opting instead to eradicate those who threaten his career progression and ability to do "what he wants, when he wants, to whom he wants" (3.10). While initially posing as an intimate friend to Dexter (a man who will accept him for what he truly is), Miguel progressively takes the knowledge passed down to him from Dexter and perverts the skills taught to satisfy his own murderous greed.

Harry's symbolic paternal function and admittance of the "responsibility," acceptance and channeling of another's murderous urges (notably Dexter's own), are addressed in episode eight, "The Damage a Man Can Do." This episode marks out the significance and intertwining nature of the three fathers, making visible the symbolic, imaginary, and real fathers and pointing out the links between them. Indeed, Harry's role in this episode is symbolic. He attempts to guide Dexter, warning him of the gamble he is taking by passing on his knowledge and legacy to others (Miguel and his unborn child): "It's a lot of responsibility teaching him [Miguel] that. You have a heavy burden. I hope you're a stronger man [than me]." This comment operates as an acknowledgment of Harry's weakness which of course leads the viewer to infer that Dexter did indeed "kill Harry," however unintentionally. Dexter's own role as the imaginary father, both ideal, the guide, and helper of Miguel (as well as Rita, Deb, Cody, and Astor) and as the man responsible for "fucking up" (allowing Miguel to kill Billy Fleeter and as such seeing from a different perspective the "butterfly effect"—the effect of such an act upon others and the disturbance caused in balance of nature) is highlighted here (3.8). Miguel also makes visible his role as the real father in this episode through increasingly disrespecting Dexter's boundaries, sitting in his chair, utilizing his computer without permission, and nominating Harry/Dexter's code as "bull-shit" (3.8). Episode nine ("About Last Night") sees Dexter's recognition of Miguel's real betrayal of the code—in which it is revealed that Miguel has acted alone to murder his working rival Ellen Wolf. On finding her body Dexter reflects that: "I told him how, guided him to this. I created . . . this" (3.9). Again in episode ten, "Go Your Own Way," Dexter notes: "I am responsible if Miguel takes another innocent life [. . .] Harry was right, he's always been right [. . .] Miguel has left me no choice" (3.10).

The season ends with Dexter's ultimate recognition of the role of the father: "the sins of the father go on and on and on, from kid, to kid, to kid" (3.12). Again, however, the scene is haunted and the conclusion is indeterminate. The truth that lies beneath the surface is then, perhaps, one based on interconnection. What this season reveals as the ultimate source of pain, is intimacy. The butterfly effect—the unexpected, unknowable effect of an occurrence on the "natural order"—in the most violent and poignant ways threatens to transform the life that Dexter has created for himself. At the end of the series two things occur: Dexter and Rita marry, and Deb is given the case file that may potentially reveal the relationship between the informant Laura (Dexter's mother) and Harry. While this file remains unread, it serves to reinforce the impossibility of secrets. Ultimately, again, the truth about Dexter lies "just beneath the surface" (1.2).

8.
Blood Brothers: Brian +
Dexter + Miguel

Fionna Boyle

> **Dexter:** Something Harry didn't teach me, something he didn't know—
> couldn't possibly know. The willful taking of life represents the ultimate
> disconnect from humanity. It leaves you an outsider, forever looking in
> . . . searching for company to keep.
>
> ("Popping Cherry," 1.3)

If we are judged by the company we keep, then what does that say
about Dexter Morgan? Typically, sociopathic serial killers don't keep
much company—other than, perhaps, their victims. However,
despite his protests to the contrary, Dexter is neither a typical
sociopath nor serial killer. A murderer with a conscience, an antisocial who subconsciously wants to connect with others and belong,
Dexter has been able to form lasting relationships with several
people, including his foster-sister Debra, his partner Rita, and her
children, Astor and Cody. Yet Dexter tells himself he doesn't really
have feelings; these interactions are simply roles he must play, part
of the code his foster-father Harry taught him to maintain a façade
of normalcy. He keeps a carefully constructed guard to ensure they
never find out his secret and discover the "real" Dexter. Because of
this, Dexter believes he can never know true acceptance or have a
genuine connection with anyone, until lightning strikes—twice
(three times, if you count Lila[1])—in the form of Brian Moser and
Miguel Prado. Though they have led radically different lives, Brian
and Miguel are actually quite alike and play similar roles in Dexter's
life, bonding with him in a way no one else has.

Brian (a.k.a. "Biney," a.k.a. prosthetician Rudy Cooper, a.k.a. the
Ice Truck Killer) is Dexter's biological brother, but the two share

more than parentage: they also enjoy the same extra-curricular activities—murder and dismemberment. Brian is the first person other than Harry to see behind Dexter's disguise, but unlike Harry, Brian is far from disturbed by what he finds. He embraces Dexter's true nature and encourages him to embrace it, too. For the first time, Dexter feels accepted for what and who he really is.

Of course, it can't last. Despite being kindred spirits, not to mention kin, Brian has violated the code Dexter lives his life by in the most egregious of ways by attempting to kill Debra, and so Dexter is compelled to kill him in turn. Once again, Dexter finds himself isolated, living his life in hiding, but now with the additional anguish of knowing what it feels like to have finally found—and lost—the only person who ever truly understood him.

It isn't until Dexter meets Assistant District Attorney Miguel Prado that he finds a true surrogate for Brian. Like Brian, Miguel is an upstanding citizen on the surface but harbors dark urges. Like Brian, Miguel doesn't subscribe to any code and kills innocent people without remorse. Like Brian, Miguel finds out Dexter's secret and creates a unique, powerful connection with him. Like Brian, Miguel not only encourages Dexter to be his real self but wants to be his partner in crime. If Brian is Dexter's blood brother, Miguel is his brother in blood.

Brotherhood means different things to Dexter, Brian, and Miguel, and the roots of the relationships between Dexter and his "brothers" can be traced back to the way each was raised—one in a loving, middle-class family, one isolated in an institution, and one as a refugee with a violent father. Their childhoods helped create the men they would become.

Until a combination of chopped-up doll parts, therapy, his biological father's death, and a bloody hotel room crime scene jogs his memory, Dexter has no recollection of life before the Morgans took him in. But Harry does, and knowing how the horrific circumstances in which he found Dexter would inevitably affect the boy, he teaches Dexter his infamous code in order to survive: be as "normal" as possible, so you won't get caught.

As such, Dexter considers his interactions as a brother (and friend, and boyfriend) part of the "costume collection" (1.4) he must wear—a necessary pretense with no emotional attachment:

"Human bonds always lead to messy complications . . . if I let someone get close, they'd see who I really am, and I can't let that happen. So, time to put on my mask" (1.4). Dexter insists he is empty inside and fakes human emotions, but is this really true, or just one more costume? Has being a killer made him completely inhuman, disconnected, and aloof, or is he both human and killer, repressing genuine sentiment because he thinks he should be disconnected and aloof? His behavior towards his sister indicates the latter.

While Dexter claims not to have feelings about anything, he admits "if I could have feelings at all, I'd have them for Deb" (1.1). The notion of brotherhood may have begun as a construct Harry taught him, but Dexter's relationship with Debra seems to be sincere. A typical brother, he is irritated by some of her behavior, doesn't notice her new hair cut, and doesn't want to hear about her sexual escapades. When Debra wants to know why they never discuss "brother-sister stuff," Dexter reminds her, "Our father was a cop. You're a cop. I work for the cops. For us, this is 'brother-sister stuff'" (1.2). But Dexter also supports Debra and boosts her confidence at work, giving her advice about how to better handle herself, and is genuinely proud when she is transferred from vice to homicide and gets her detective shield. When Debra insists Dexter meet her to celebrate her transfer, despite being moments away from killing habitual drunk driver Matt Chambers, he puts his sister's wants above his own needs and joins her. He is concerned about her safety, both as a teen when he catches her shooting tin cans with Harry's gun ("I had to tell him. . . . Dad was worried about you and so was I. Deb, you're my sister" (1.6)) and as an adult when she pursues Ramon Prado as a suspect in the Skinner case ("I don't want you getting hurt" (3.6)).

It is when Debra falls prey to Brian under the guise of the Ice Truck Killer that Dexter's brotherly love is most evident. In the first season finale, "Born Free," Brian presents Debra to Dexter as a gift they will kill together, but Dexter hesitates: "I can't. Not Deb. I'm actually quite . . . fond of her" (1.12). This is as close as Dexter has ever come to saying he loves her. Ultimately, he saves Debra's life, choosing the foster-sister he grew up with over the biological brother who understands him: "I drove away a brother who accepts me, sees me, for an adopted sister who would reject me if she knew" (1.12). Afterwards, Dexter lets Debra move in until she is ready to be on her own, which speaks volumes about what she means to him, considering how much of his secret life is hidden in his apartment (his blood slides and killing kit).

Dexter has spent his whole life being a brother to Debra, but only has several hours to be a brother to Brian. It's a profoundly different relationship, not only because the parents, shared history, and memories aren't the same, but because it is based on brutal honesty that results in violence, instead of carefully constructed lies that maintain a status quo. While Dexter is close to Debra, she can never know (and could never accept) the real him. Being a brother to her means keeping her at arm's length and hiding the truth to keep them both safe. Conversely, Brian knows Dexter's secret and embraces it. Being a brother to him means opening up and being truly free for the first time ever. Debra, the cop, and Brian, the killer, represent Dexter's dual nature—his adopted morality versus his natural instincts. When his two worlds collide, the confusion and uncertainty he feels—not to mention the emotional tug-of-war over his siblings—is overwhelming.

Like Dexter, there's a dichotomy to Brian: a cold-blooded serial killer and a caring, loving sibling. Both boys seemed happy and well-adjusted in their early years, despite their mother's undertakings as a drug dealer and police informant (more duality!). An affectionate and protective big brother, Brian tended to Dexter's scraped knees and taught him how to ride a skateboard. Even after witnessing the horror of their mother's murder in the blood-drenched shipping container, Brian held Dexter's hand and promised to look after him . . . until Harry arrived and carried Dexter away, leaving four-year-old Brian behind.

> You were three, a little bird with a broken wing. [Harry] wanted to make you all better. But me? . . . All he saw was a fucked-up kid. They all did. So they locked me up . . . While you were being raised by the Morgan family, I only had the memory of a family. Mom always told me to look after you. Imagine how I felt when I tracked you down and found out you were exactly like me. (1.12)

Instead of being adopted, Brian grew up in a mental institution. While Dexter was taught Harry's code and family values, Brian was diagnosed with antisocial personality disorder, his "family" consisting of doctors and therapists. Unlike Dexter, Brian grew up knowing he had a brother. When Dexter was learning how to be a brother to Debra, Brian was left with memories of the brother he loved and lost.

The trauma of seeing their mother slaughtered by a chainsaw and enduring the bloody aftermath had a chillingly identical effect on Brian and Dexter's psyches. Despite being raised in very different environments, they grew up to be the same—not only do they both kill, they dismember their victims with saws (Dexter for ease of disposal; Brian as an homage) and have issues with blood (Dexter analyses it; Brian drains it).

The difference between them is Dexter doesn't know what made him the way he is; all he knows is "it" left a hollow place inside (1.1). So when the Ice Truck Killer plays his macabre cat-and-mouse game, Dexter is curiously drawn to him in the hope a like-minded soul is reaching out to him in the darkness. As time goes on, Dexter's need to "connect with someone" (1.7) increases. His brother eventually presents him with the opportunity, in a way he never imagined.

When Brian re-enters Dexter's life disguised as Debra's boyfriend Rudy, he immediately slips back into his affectionate, protective, brotherly role. His first words to Dexter are "I've waited a long time to meet you" (1.9), and he bypasses a handshake in favor of a hug. After Dexter steals his (their?[2]) biological father's ashes from the morgue and almost gets caught, Brian is there to rescue him, just like a big brother helping a little brother out of a jam. Later, Brian shows up at Dexter's apartment with beer and steaks, ostensibly to discuss his argument with Debra, but his ulterior motive is to reconnect with his brother and to try to refresh his memory about their past.

Brian considers himself Dexter's real "blood" brother—"through birth and death . . . none of this foster bullshit"—and Debra his "fake sister" (1.12). Everything Brian does, from becoming the Ice Truck Killer to buying their childhood home to dating and nearly killing Debra, is motivated by the desire to reunite with Dexter and show him how alike they are. When Brian's identity is finally revealed, he tells his brother he understands him in a way no one else can: "You're trapped in a lie, little brother. The same lie they tried forcing me into. . . . I know what you've been going through all these years. The isolation, the otherness. The hunger that's never satisfied" (1.12). He goes on to say Dexter has been away from his "family" since he was three, but "I'm here now. I can help you. We can take this journey together" (1.12). In Brian's mind, he is still looking after his little brother.

Brian's purpose is not just to offer Dexter solidarity, but to provoke him to overturn the rules he lives by and kill simply for the sake of killing. Brian is evil in a way Dexter isn't; Harry's code means nothing to him. Dexter's latent humanity compels him to do the right thing, but he is tormented by the notion of severing the bond with the only person who ever accepted him. He dreams of "a life with no more secrets" (2.5), but knows there's no one left alive who can handle his truth—he's back to being alone and living a lie: "Sometimes I wonder what it would be like for everything that's inside me that's denied and unknown to be revealed. But I'll never know. I live my life in hiding. My survival depends on it" (1.12).

Enter Miguel Prado. From his humble beginnings as a refugee who escaped Castro's reign as a child, Miguel has become a pillar of Miami society. The top prosecutor in Florida for the past three years, he takes great pride in cleaning up the streets, and is respected and beloved by the Cuban community. As he tells Dexter, "People appreciate knowing I'm on their side" (3.3).

Part of the reason for Miguel's success is a desire to prove his father wrong. Despite his accomplishments, Miguel was "a failure who could never measure up" (3.3)—a sentiment Dexter can relate to since he discovered Harry committed suicide after witnessing the "evil" (2.11) manifested in his son. Dexter even tells Miguel that Harry was "disgusted" (3.3) by him, something he's never revealed to Debra or Rita. Miguel thinks they wouldn't understand anyway: "They don't know what it is to be a man, to be a son, with all the pressure" (3.3). Sensing Miguel can identify with him, Dexter agrees: "You grow up to be exactly the man your father molded you to be, and still . . . Not be good enough" (3.3). While this is a recent discovery for Dexter, it has been a lifelong burden for Miguel and presumably explains his increasingly dark behavior. Miguel claims when he finally fought back against his alcoholic father's abuse, it was the first time he ever felt in control. He has been trying to regain the feeling ever since, and says he understands the darkness inside Dexter because he has it as well: "I just want to let some of mine out, too" (3.8). Dexter is also trying to take back control of his life from the shadow of his father, by rebelling against his code. He and Miguel bond over carrying the weight of their fathers' disappointment and the need to become their own men.

Miguel's fraternal relationships are also strikingly similar to Dexter's—he has a dead brother, Oscar, who was involved in illegal activities (drugs instead of murder), and another sibling, Ramon, who works in law enforcement and is prone to impulsive outbursts. Like Dexter with Debra, Miguel often apologizes for Ramon's behavior: Miguel calls him his "gracious brother" (3.3) after Ramon insults the investigation into Oscar's murder; Dexter calls Debra his "loud sister" (3.1) in reference to her comment about Oscar being a junkie.

Despite their differences, the Prado brothers were close-knit. As Miguel tells Dexter, "We had each other . . . No matter what kind of horrible shit you would pull, they knew you inside out, the good and the bad, and they were there for you, no matter what" (3.3). When Dexter admits he's never had that, Miguel suggests he is lucky because that means he can't miss it if it disappears and won't be left with a hole in his life. He tells Dexter losing Oscar is "going to leave a pain in [his] heart [he doesn't] think is ever going to heal" (3.1) and asks if Dexter has a brother—a question which catches him off guard, and to which he has no answer. Of course, Dexter did have a brother, one who knew all about his "horrible shit" and whose death left a void, which Miguel himself will fill. In fact, Miguel and Dexter both replace the lost brother in each other's life.

Sibling rivalry plays a significant role in the relationships between Dexter, Brian, and Miguel, but in an unexpected way. Neither Brian nor Miguel are jealous of Dexter; in fact, they support and encourage his work. In "Born Free," Brian tells his brother, "You don't ever have to apologize to me, Dexter. Not for who you are, or anything you do" (1.12). Miguel echoes this after discovering Dexter killed

Ethan Turner: "You have nothing to explain to me, nothing to apologize for. Ever" (3.5). Instead, Brian's hostility is directed towards Dexter's other sibling, Debra, and his relationship with her. Any resentment pertaining to Dexter's relationships with Brian and Miguel comes from a different set of siblings—Debra and Ramon.

In a way, Brian should feel bitter toward his brother—after all, Dexter was rescued; Brian was not. But he is moved by their reunion and wants to reassure Dexter of their brotherhood: "You're not alone any more, Dexter. You can be yourself with me. Your real, genuine self" (1.12). It is Debra who bears the brunt of Brian's anger, because she represents everything he resents: she's a cop (society, the code, rules), the daughter of the man who left him behind (rejection, abandonment), and Dexter's sister (family, love, acceptance) . . . the perfect victim.

To Brian, Debra isn't Dexter's real family: "She's a stranger to you and she'll always be one" (1.12). He wants to share killing her with his brother to strengthen their bond and sever Dexter and Debra's ("bros before hos" taken to its extreme?). Brian even "prepares" Debra the way Dexter likes, saying "this time, we'll do it together" (1.12). However, Dexter's reaction is not how Brian "envisioned [their] family reunion" (1.12), and his frantic search for Debra shatters Brian's illusions about which sibling Dexter will choose.

For her part, Debra treats Dexter the way a sister typically treats a brother, with unconditional acceptance and equal parts exasperation and love. Yet, she also competes with him for attention, both professionally and personally. She is jealous of the time Dexter spent with Harry and, ironically, of his relationship with Brian. Debra is constantly exasperated by Dexter's aloofness, so when she discovers her brother and her boyfriend have been spending time together without her, she feels doubly resentful—towards Dexter for shutting her out but talking to Brian, and towards Brian for shunning her in favour of Dexter—and lashes out: "You don't talk to me, Dexter. You've spent our entire lives keeping me at a distance. . . . [Y]ou are all the family I have and I barely know you. . . . So if someone's going to break through your walls, I think it should be me. I think I have earned it" (1.10).

Similarly, Ramon is unhappy about Dexter's relationship with

Miguel. Concerned Miguel will tell his brother about Dexter killing Freebo, Dexter creates a situation where Miguel can see what a loose cannon Ramon is. Dexter knows he can't force Miguel to trust him over his own flesh and blood, so he drives a wedge in between the brothers instead, insinuating to Ramon that Miguel confides in him like a surrogate brother and turned to him when he needed someone to talk to. "What goes on between me and my brother is between me and my brother" (3.4), Ramon angrily responds, but the damage has been done. Ramon and Miguel's relationship is never quite the same—Dexter replaces him as Miguel's "brother" and Ramon's hatred of Dexter continues to escalate. The way Dexter manipulates the relationship between the Prado siblings to his advantage is similar to the way Brian manipulates the relationship between the Morgan siblings to his, only Dexter is successful while Brian is not.

Of all the sibling relationships, Dexter and Debra's is the only successful one. They are each other's only family and have a long, shared history. Harry encouraged Dexter to lean on his sister for support if he felt like he was "slipping" (1.3), and Debra tells Dexter after what happened with Brian, she thanked God she had her brother: "Every time I started to spin out of control, I had you to grab on to" (2.11). While Dexter is layered and closed, Debra is an open book—what you see is what you get. So, although Dexter has to keep up his façade, he doesn't have to worry about Debra having a hidden agenda or ulterior motives. Despite the fact Debra is a cop, Dexter trusts her more than anyone else—she's never let him down and is "loyal to a fault" (3.11)—which is why he ultimately chooses her to be best man at his wedding.

Prior to Debra, Miguel was Dexter's best man (and best friend). Miguel befriends Dexter during the investigation into Oscar's murder—not knowing Dexter unintentionally killed Oscar and framed Freebo, Dexter's intended victim. But their friendship doesn't really flourish until Miguel catches Dexter red-handed (literally) after he murders Freebo, something Miguel intended to do himself. Miguel mistakenly thinks Dexter was avenging Oscar, so instead of turning him in, he whispers his thanks with tear-filled eyes. He promises they will get rid of the evidence and even gives Dexter his blood-stained shirt as a symbol of his loyalty.

When Dexter questions why Miguel is trying so hard to be his "new bestest friend" (3.3), Miguel explains Dexter gave him peace by taking care of his brother's murderer and he wants to return the favor. He wants Dexter to understand he is not in this alone: "It's you and me. Together" (3.3). Like Brian, Miguel connects with Dexter by suggesting they are allies, a team of two against the world.

For Dexter, friendship is a new experience fraught with uncertainty. Angel and Vince consider him their friend and assume they are his (to the point where they argue over who will be his best man), but Dexter cannot truly connect with them. Having always been a loner leading a secret-filled life, the prospect of Miguel as a brother-in-arms (so to speak) is intriguing. "Is it possible I've actually made a friend? Someone I can trust with my dark secrets? Or am I being foolish for even asking these questions?" (3.3). Dexter thought he quashed his search for connection following his brother's death, but, clearly, something in him responds to Miguel the way he responded to Brian.

For Miguel, friendship is "a sacred bond built on trust" (3.11), tantamount to brotherhood. Dexter takes the place of Oscar, whom Miguel lost to drugs long before he was murdered, and Ramon, whom Miguel is losing to grief, violence, and instability in the wake of Oscar's death. Dexter becomes the only person Miguel can trust, something Miguel knows he has difficulty reciprocating: "I can see you're used to carrying your secrets yourself. . . . [I]t's a hell of a burden. I'm used to having a brother to share the load. I'm hoping maybe you'll get used to it, too" (3.4). Another echo of Brian—this time, the desire for Dexter to share his hidden life with a trusted "brother."

Following a late-night visit to Dexter's apartment, alcohol in hand (yet another similarity to Brian), Miguel ingratiates himself to Dexter through the "simple joys of male bonding" (3.6), including golfing, fishing, and lunch dates. Having no frame of reference, Dexter is initially bemused by Miguel's attention ("Showing up late at night . . . is it creepy, or just what friends do?" (3.3)), but to his own surprise, grows to enjoy their friendship: "It seems so mundane, but it's oddly . . . soothing. Maybe this is what belonging feels like" (3.7). For the first time, Dexter begins to question the pretense and detachment on which he has built his existence: "To be a brother.

To have a friend. . . . [I]f you play a role long enough, really commit, does it ever become real? Could I become real?" (3.4).

Miguel and Dexter's relationship evolves from drinking beer to plotting murder, which affords Dexter a different sense of belonging: Miguel discovers the true nature of Dexter's lifelong hobby and becomes an enthusiastic protégé: "When Harry saw what I really was, he was repulsed. It destroyed my brother . . . but not Miguel. Somehow, he looks at me and he's . . . proud" (3.5). As was the case when Miguel befriended him, Dexter is bewildered at first: "Is this the beginning of a whole new level of friendship? Is it the end of life as I know it?" (3.8). His uncertainty ultimately gives way to acceptance, and he not only teaches Miguel Harry's code, something Brian had no time for (though, in the end, neither does Miguel), but assembles a killing "starter kit" for him (3.8).

With Miguel's newfound knowledge comes an ever-increasing desire to apply it: he goes from simply being grateful Dexter killed Freebo, to helping capture Clemson Galt, to killing Billy Fleeter with Dexter, to actually killing Ellen Wolf by himself, an act that causes a permanent rift in his relationship with Dexter. Like Brian with Debra, Miguel's chosen victim is an innocent, something Dexter cannot condone.

It would be easy to dismiss Miguel as Brian 2.0, given their similar roles in Dexter's life. However, while Brian and Dexter's relationship unfolds over a matter of hours, Miguel and Dexter's relationship has much more time to develop. It involves different experiences which offer new insights into Dexter. Though Brian and Miguel both share a special camaraderie with Dexter, Brian's death ends any possibility of a real partnership. Miguel, on the other hand, is the only person to see Dexter with blood on his hands (other than Harry). His friendship makes Dexter feel alive—and vulnerable—for the first time.

When Dexter prepares to capture Clemson Galt with Miguel, he notes it feels different: "I won't be alone. Uncharted territory for me. Not without risk . . . and strangely exhilarating" (3.6). Later, after they kill Billy Fleeter, Miguel says he feels real "maybe for the first time in [his] life" (3.9), and Dexter agrees. For Miguel, this feeling is connected to the kill, but for Dexter, who is certainly not new to killing, it is more to do with the validation he feels after letting someone bear witness to his secret. Letting Miguel into his inner world authenticates that world, and by extension, Dexter himself: "Miguel and I took a life together. And today, someone knows my truth. Shares my reality" (3.9). It's a heady new sentiment for Dexter, who is normally meticulous about keeping his guard up.

Sharing such an intimate bond is not without risk, however. Trusting someone implies a certain amount of vulnerability and requires a belief they have no hidden agenda. Dexter is a masterful liar who spends his life deceiving people, yet, as Miguel illustrates, he can also be deceived. His suspicions are raised when Rita inadvertently describes a conversation where Miguel repeats the same flattering things he said to Dexter, but they are confirmed when Dexter discovers the blood on the shirt Miguel gave him, as a "symbol of trust" (3.3), is not from Freebo, but a cow: "He's been using me the whole time. I didn't create a monster, I was used by one" (3.9). Miguel's deceit marks the first time Dexter has truly been manipulated.

Miguel is like Brian, though, with respect to urging Dexter to abandon his ethics (such that they are) and dispense with the code. Brian insists it is not even Dexter's code but Harry's (1.12), while Miguel compares it to wearing a straitjacket (3.8). Their influence appears to be limited, though; any experimentation with the code is more a result of Dexter's anger with Harry than anything his "brothers" say.

Harry's primary concern has always been Dexter's safety, and he views both Brian and Miguel as threats to this. He went to great lengths to keep Brian's existence hidden from Dexter because he sensed Brian was unstable—Brian even says he could "see it in [Harry's] eyes" (1.12)—and he didn't want Dexter corrupted by his brother's influence. With Miguel, Harry makes his feelings known through Dexter's subconscious. He cautions that Dexter doesn't realise what he's done and urges him to stay away from Miguel: "I didn't teach you the code to share with your buddies. I taught you the code to keep you alive. You don't get to have any friends, Dexter. Nothing good can come of this" (3.8). Harry insists Miguel and Dexter aren't as alike as Dexter thinks: "You think Miguel's a pal? Your wingman? Put that notion to the test. . . . Every time you let someone get close, it ends badly" (3.6).

As usual, Harry is right. Or, as Dexter puts it, "My search for connection always ends in blood" (3.10). Though he forges a special bond with Brian and Miguel, Dexter comes to the realization he has no choice but to kill them to stop their violence, even if it means he will be alone again. Understandably, these two murders—his brother and his best friend—mean more than any others he commits.

Brian tells Dexter he "can't be a killer and a hero" (1.12), referring to Dexter's double life, but Dexter is, in fact, both: he takes his brother's life and saves his sister's. However, Dexter is not without compassion for Brian. Even though he knows Brian needs to be "put down" (1.12), Dexter considers his death a "special occasion" (1.12). He tries to kill him as humanely as possible, intending to do it while Brian is unconscious, and offering him more tranquilizers when he wakes up. He even bypasses taking a blood sample for his collection because Brian is not a "trophy" (1.12) to him.

The brothers' last moments together are heart-breaking. In tears, with foreheads touching, Dexter confesses how difficult this is for him: "You've done more to deserve my knife than anyone . . . and you're the only one I ever wanted to set free" (1.12). As he slits Brian's throat, Dexter's face is full of anguish and guilt. For someone who claims to have no feelings, he is clearly emotional. Killing Brian means killing part of himself, literally (his own flesh and blood) and figuratively (the freedom to kill indiscriminately).

But there's another part of himself Dexter seems to have killed along with his brother—his self-confidence. Brian's death haunts him for months, and his grief makes Dexter uneasy, anxious, and impotent. Killing is almost like sexual release for him (in "Dexter," he becomes aroused when demonstrating the Ice Truck Killer's technique to Rita), so it's no surprise he suffers from performance anxiety on a variety of fronts: he's unable to perform sexually and professionally (he compromises the integrity of a crime scene), and unable to kill new victims ("When I picked up the knife, it's like I didn't know who I was" (2.1)). He can't even bring Astor and Cody the right donuts.

Dexter acknowledges he is a "little rusty since killing [his] brother" (2.1) and wonders how he lost the "orderly, controlled, effective Dexter" (2.2). More importantly, he wonders how to get him back: "I feel like a jigsaw puzzle missing a piece and I'm not even sure what the picture should be" (2.2). He starts having hallucinations of Brian and flashbacks to their time in the shipping container as children. When Brian asks if Dexter misses him, Dexter replies that he killed him. Brian disagrees: "You just took my life" (2.2). His presence is still there, affecting everything Dexter does, because of the guilt Dexter feels for killing him. Still the protective big brother, Brian says what Dexter did to him isn't his fault, even though he knows Dexter feels it is because "it's human nature" (2.2).

Dexter realizes the only way to get closure is to sever the tie and let his brother go, so he symbolically drops the doll's head Brian gave him into the ocean: "I had to say goodbye in order to reconnect with what's really important. With who I was. With who I have to be" (2.2). Dexter tells his brother to rest in peace: "I am" (2.2).

Interestingly, when Dexter daydreams about the shipping container in "The Dark Defender," he only sees himself and his mother, as if Brian has been excised from his memory. Additionally, Dexter doesn't mention Brian when he confesses to Rita that he saw his mother's murder as a child. Obviously, he wouldn't say his brother was the Ice Truck Killer, but he doesn't even mention his existence in passing.

Brian's death is a departure from Jeff Lindsay's *Darkly Dreaming Dexter*, where Brian escapes and is never heard from again. Both instances feature Dexter making and losing the connection with his brother; however, having Dexter kill Brian creates much more emotional impact than simply having him disappear and leaving his story open-ended. *Dexter* Executive Producer Sara Colleton says, "It would have been a cheat to have put in the time through the season to have no resolution" ("DVD Commentary," 1.12).

Brian seems more sympathetic dead, yet this wouldn't be true if it were LaGuerta, Doakes, or even Debra who killed him. Dying at the hands of the police would be typical, at the hands of Debra would be fitting, but at the hands of the brother he wanted to connect with for so long, his death seems almost tragic.

Says Co-Executive Producer Daniel Cerone: "At the end of the book, the Ice Truck Killer gets away, but [having Dexter kill him] felt much more honest . . . Plus, what do you do after this? Where do you go with that character? Are you going to keep chasing [him] next year?" ("DVD Commentary," 1.12). RIP, Biney.

As history demonstrates, anyone who finds out Dexter's secret is inevitably killed: Brian and therapist Dr Emmett Meridian in Season 1; Lila and Doakes in Season 2. In a way, the endgame for Season 3 was set up from the beginning when Miguel realized Dexter killed Freebo. Although Miguel didn't try to turn him in, become his soulmate, or murder his sister as a result of what he discovered, in the end, his fate was the same as that of the others.

Like Brian, Miguel is a rare emotional kill for Dexter, but rather than sorrow and regret, he feels anger and betrayal. Dexter let Miguel come closer than anyone else in his life, sharing his darkest secrets and sacred code: "I had higher hopes for you, for us. But I finally just have to accept it—I'll always be alone . . . You actually had me believing I could have a friend" (3.11). Miguel's murder signifies the end of Dexter's rebellion against Harry, the realization that he "[doesn't] get to have friends" (3.11) and can really only trust himself. There's no compassion or humanity this time around, only brutal truth. When Miguel tells Dexter he accepts him like a brother, Dexter bluntly states he killed his brother . . . and Miguel's, too—the final nail in the coffin of their relationship. Dexter concludes, "You can tell a lot about a person by the friends he keeps. And this . . . is my best friend. Good-bye, Miguel" (3.12).

When Miguel screams, "You think this ends here? It doesn't!" (3.11), as Dexter strangles him, he isn't kidding. While Brian's death was an intimate affair, Miguel's comes with an entourage, in the form of Ramon and George Washington King (a.k.a. the Skinner), both of whom threaten Dexter's life. There were lingering emotional repercussions for Dexter to deal with after killing his brother, but Miguel's death requires a more immediate and tangible kind of closure. It is not until Dexter sets things right with Ramon and disposes of the Skinner that he can fully put Miguel behind him.

Any lingering misgivings Dexter may have felt about killing his best friend are snuffed out after his conversation with Ramon, which reveals the full extent of Miguel's lies: it was Ramon who pushed their father down the stairs to protect his brothers, not Miguel, and Ramon who constantly put himself at risk to clean up Miguel's problems. Dexter says he "know[s] the frustration, the disappoint-

ment of wanting to help your brother and not being able to" (3.12)
... but is he talking about Miguel, or Brian? Or both?

Dexter's rationale for killing Brian and Miguel is that they killed
innocent people and didn't follow Harry's code. (Dexter himself
plays "fast and loose" (2.2) with these rules at times, as in the case
of Little Chino, Oscar, the pedophile Nathan Marten, and the
terminally ill Camilla, although these exceptions can all be justified.) Nevertheless, his "brothers" do accept and approve of what
Dexter is, and claim to understand him better than he understands
himself. There is some truth to this—both see through the arti-
fice of his life and urge him to embrace his real self. However,
Brian and Miguel fail to understand the dichotomy between
Dexter's life and self isn't as black-and-white as they assume; both
halves co-exist in shades of gray Dexter understands better than
they ever could.

Brian has never forgotten his mother's murder, something Dexter
was too young to remember. Consequently, he recognizes this trauma
was responsible for Dexter's behavior long before Dexter discovers
it himself. Brian's entire relationship with his brother is spent trying
to reconcile Dexter with what Brian perceives to be his true self,
causing Dexter to question the foundations of his identity.

> He's not corrupting the happy Hallmark images of my youth. He's reveal-
> ing the ugly truth behind them. ... Everything about him is brazen,
> authentic. What does that make me? ... If I'm just a collection of learned
> behaviors, bits and pieces of Harry, maybe my new friend is right. Maybe
> I am a fraud. (1.4)

When Brian finally confronts Dexter, he contends Dexter's carefully constructed life is nothing but a lie from which he needs to
be extricated. He begins to tell Dexter what he will "never be" (1.12),
but Dexter, thinking his brother is right, doesn't want to listen.

Except Brian isn't right and doesn't know Dexter as well as he
presumes—when he leaves Tony Tucci "gift-wrapped and begging
for death" (1.4), Dexter won't kill him because it doesn't fit Harry's
code: "My new friend doesn't see me as clearly as he thinks. ...
[He] thought I wouldn't be able to resist the kill he left me, but I
did. I'm not the monster he wants me to be" (1.4). Brian may have

unique insight into Dexter's past, but he doesn't understand who Dexter has become since then. Camilla underscores this on her deathbed; after confessing she knows the truth about his brother's identity, she says Dexter "could never be like [Brian]" (3.7).

If Brian's insight into Dexter is because of their shared experiences as children, Miguel's is due to their shared experiences as adults. Dexter's vigilante justice appeals to Miguel, who must wade through an "ocean of bureaucracy" (3.6) before the death-row killers he convicts are executed. However, he correctly perceives Freebo wasn't Dexter's first victim and senses there are more sinister motivations behind his actions. When Dexter confronts Miguel about wrongfully killing Ellen Wolf and demands, "Whatever happened to serving justice?," Miguel fires back with "Is that really why you do this, Dex? To serve justice? We don't have to pretend with each other" (3.9). Like Brian, Miguel sees through Dexter's subterfuge and claims to understand who he really is, because they are "like-minded" (3.6).

Though Miguel insists he knows Dexter "better than anyone else" (3.11), when things spiral out of control following Ellen's murder, it becomes clear he doesn't understand who (or what) he is dealing with. After threatening to tell Rita, get a search warrant, and investigate Debra in an ethics probe, Miguel vows, "I'll do what I want, when I want, to whomever I want—count on it!" (3.10). Not only does he grossly underestimate Dexter's prowess and survival skills, he cannot grasp the fundamental difference between Dexter and himself, of which Dexter is well aware: "I'm like you!" Miguel declares at the end. "No," Dexter replies. "I know I'm a monster" (3.11).

Though Brian and Miguel understand Dexter unlike anyone else, by the close of Season 3, Dexter has put the ghosts of his "brothers" to rest. While Dexter acknowledges the possibility he may be "drawn to the safety of belonging or being part of something bigger than [himself]" (3.12), he no longer feels the need to search for this connection with fellow Dark Passengers. His need for brotherhood has given way to an anticipation of fatherhood, and he has replaced the fractured family ties he has to his mother and Harry with new ones he and Rita will create. Rita may never understand Dexter the way Brian and Miguel did, but by marrying him, she has given him security, acceptance, and a renewed blood bond in a way they never could. He has replaced his partners in crime with a partner in life.

Of course, getting married won't negate Dexter's true nature. On his wedding day, Dexter contemplates his life thus far: "I'm still who I was, who I am. Question is, what do I become? There are so many blanks left to fill in" (3.12). If Brian showed Dexter his past and Miguel helped him define his present, it is now up to Dexter to take what he has learned from them and create his own future.

Part Four.
A View to a Kill: Politics, Ethics, and *Dexter*

9.
The Ethics of a Serial Killer: Dexter's Moral Character and the Justification of Murder

Simon Riches and Craig French

I. Dexter and the Code

Dexter Morgan is a forensics expert, specializing in blood-splatter analysis, who works in the homicide division of the Miami Metro Police Department. On the surface, he is a law-abiding—and law-*enforcing*—citizen. But, unbeknown to his colleagues, sister, girlfriend, and friends, he conceals a dark secret: he is a serial killer with an overwhelming desire to commit murder.

And yet Dexter is an interesting kind of serial killer, in at least two ways. Firstly, each murder that Dexter commits is carefully planned to the very last detail. Dexter's killings are executed with meticulous care. The murder scenes are cautiously prepared beforehand and, utilizing his forensics expertise and years of experience, Dexter leaves no traces. The bodies are dissected and efficiently disposed of into the sea, as if he is doing no more than taking out the trash. So, although Dexter's *desire* to kill is very much animalistic, in *satisfying the desire*, Dexter is perfectly ratiocinative.

There is a second way in which Dexter is an interesting kind of serial killer, and a further sense in which his killing is ratiocinative. Throughout the series, Dexter believes his actions to be in some way *justified*. In Dexter's view, his killings are *reason based* since he adheres to what we will call a *code of killing*. We might think of a "code" as a set of action-guiding principles and standards and so therefore *a code of killing* is a set of principles and standards, which guide, control, and restrict a subset of Dexter's actions, namely, his killings.

The code of killing was instilled in Dexter as a young boy by his adoptive father Harry. The content of the code—that is, what the principles and standards *are*—is revealed throughout the show by a combination of a voice-over, where Dexter expresses his inner thoughts about his plans and actions, and flashback scenes, which give us an insight into Dexter's childhood and his relationship with Harry. The voice-overs and flashbacks reveal a great deal about Dexter's character and how this was affected by childhood experiences. This fact, coupled with the code that he adheres to as an adult, raises the question that we will consider in this essay: what is the nature of Dexter's *moral character?*

The kind of moral philosophy we will engage in will make no judgments as to the correctness or otherwise of Dexter's actions and intentions. (We will not offer a judgment as to whether or not Dexter is, say, a *good person*, or whether he *does the right thing*.) However, by analysing certain key scenes, and by relating our observations to issues in moral philosophy, we shall offer reflections that will put one in a better position to make such judgments about Dexter's moral character.

Perhaps the most obvious way to gain an understanding of Dexter's moral character is by attempting to decipher the content of his *code of killing*, since this code, it seems, is, in a certain sense, a *moral code*. This is a crucial aspect of the series, but it is also an aspect that is philosophically delicate. In even calling the code *moral*, certain eyebrows might be raised. We shall clarify this point shortly, but first it is necessary to discuss the provenance of the code.

II. The Provenance of the Code

Dexter's adoptive Harry—himself a police officer—initially instilled the code in the young Dexter in order to provide some kind of control and direction for his irresistible desire to kill. Later on, it is revealed, or at least insinuated, that Dexter's desire to kill and his lust for blood originates in a traumatic childhood experience in which he witnessed his mother being chainsawed to death in a shipping yard crate. We later find out that Harry rescued him from this disturbing situation.

In a flashback scene in episode one of Season 1, Harry talks to

Dexter about his urge to kill. After having discovered that Dexter had killed a dog, Harry also discovered other bones among the dog's remains, suggesting that Dexter's killing of the dog was not an isolated incident—a fact that Dexter does not deny. Harry's reaction to this discovery is striking. He does not appear overawed with shock, and he does not express disgust; rather, Harry's reaction is one of love and concern for a troubled son.

In response, Harry did not look outside the family for help, but instead finds a way to control or restrict Dexter's urge. One assumes that he believed that Dexter's urge to kill could not be eliminated; and perhaps Harry's reaction of understanding, rather than condemnation, derives from an appreciation of the severity of Dexter's childhood experience of his mother's murder.

There is a sense in which Dexter's code of killing originates as a means of his survival: it is something his father instills in him so he can survive as a killer, so that he can satisfy his urge without getting caught (either by a victim or by the police). Harry has an obvious expertise here since he is a police officer who has dealt with murder many times before. In a voice-over in episode one, Dexter claims that Harry "taught him how to think like [a cop and . . .] cover [his] tracks" (1.1).

Given its provenance, one might think that all there is to Dexter's code of killing is a certain practical utility. One might think it is merely a practical code of killing. Although the practical utility that the code has for Dexter is undeniable and very important (he *does* survive, he *does not get caught*), it seems that the code is *also morally contentful* and *purposeful*.

This claim accords with another aspect of the code's provenance. When contemplating Dexter's predicament, Harry suggests that Dexter's urge might be used "for *good*" (1.1), and that it might be used to kill people who *deserve* it. So it seems that Harry had morally substantive considerations in mind when instilling the code in Dexter—that is, considerations of the *good* and *desert*.

To many viewers of *Dexter*, his code of killing will seem, in some sense, to be a *moral code*. We shall now discuss what this means, and what its content might be.

III. A Moral Code

What is it for a code to be moral? If one describes a code as moral, one is thereby appraising it as, in some sense, *right*. This is similar to the case where one might say of a particular action that it is *moral* (say, Joan might give to charity and have her action appraised, by a friend, as *moral*). But it is not this sense that we intend by saying that Dexter's code of killing is moral. Nor do we claim that it is *wrong*, since, in this essay, we adopt a neutral stance with respect to the *moral evaluation* of Dexter.

What we mean in saying that the code is moral is to *classify it* as being of a particular sort: we mean to say that the code is something which *aims* to represent moral reality—the facts about what is right and wrong, good and bad. The code could, therefore, be a *false moral code*, which is to say that it does not accurately represent moral reality (this would, in effect, be to claim that a particular moral principle, or set of moral principles, which partially constitutes the code is *false*—it is not supported by the moral facts). On the other hand, it could be a *true moral code* if it represents moral reality. So what defines Dexter's code as *moral* is that its subject matter is in some sense *morality*. It is a code that is *about* the moral territory, in the way that a map is about the geographic territory. The analogy extends further: there can be good maps and bad maps; similarly, there can be good moral codes and bad moral codes. Whether Dexter's moral code is good or bad, it is nonetheless a *moral* code in our intended sense.

There are related complex philosophical issues that should be noted. One issue is how exactly to characterize the moral territory that moral codes—and hence actions guided by those codes—are answerable to. That is, what does the moral territory concern? This is not clear, but whatever it is, a moral code counts as moral (in our intended sense) insofar as it is answerable to the moral territory. So, Dexter's set of action-guiding principles, his code of killing, is moral insofar as it is about morally substantive issues. It is answerable to the moral facts, regardless of what they are. Later in this essay, we will return to the question of how to characterize the moral territory.

Another related issue concerns what one might call the *status* or *robustness* of moral reality. Are the demands of morality *real*? Are they *objective*? There is a philosophical tradition known as *moral realism*. Broadly characterized, this position holds that facts about what is right or wrong, and other facts about morality, are in some sense *independent of us*. They are *there anyway*. Historically, the ancient Greek philosopher Plato is the champion of an extreme version of this view. According to an alternative *anti-realist* tradition, moral facts are in some sense dependent on us—perhaps, for instance, they are dependent upon, or relative to, societies or cultures. Properly understood, this is a highly complex distinction—there are many *varieties* of realism and anti-realism—and, in some cases, it is hard to see a distinction at all. For present purposes, however, we can remain fairly neutral. We merely claim that Dexter's moral code purports to represent moral reality and be neutral on both whether it does that and how we are to understand the status or robustness of that moral reality.

Our concern is the *content* of Dexter's moral code. On the assumption that Dexter himself *takes his code* to be a moral code, to ask the question of what its content is, is, in effect, to ask what Dexter believes the moral facts to *be*. If we can discover this, we will have advanced our understanding of Dexter's moral character. Furthermore, by relating Dexter's moral beliefs to themes and theories in moral philosophy, we will be in a better position to morally evaluate Dexter.

Dexter's moral code is not a code like the Ten Commandments. The Ten Commandments is a very precise, stringent and determinate moral code. It is hard to take Dexter's code to be *as* precise and determinate. That is not to deny that Dexter's code is principled, but it is just to say that its principles have some degree of flexibility and adaptability—they are less determinate. Dexter may adapt a given principle in accordance with the specific details of a given situation: this is why it is sometimes hard for him to decide whether a person meets his criteria for murder.

Given the nature of his moral code, we will not here try to characterize it according to a precise and determinate set of principles. Instead we will look at some of Dexter's killings and extrapolate from them, and Dexter's commentary on them, the underlying reasoning by which Dexter is guided. This will provide some insight into the content of Dexter's moral code, and hence into the nature of his moral character.

IV. The Killing of Children

Episode one of Season 1 opens with Dexter killing Mike Donovan, a man in his forties. Mike is initially portrayed as a happy family man, but he is later revealed to be a *child killer*. As the leader of a boys' choir, Mike abused and killed three young boys. Dexter does not take kindly to this and so stalks and eventually murders Mike.

As we would expect from the general features of Dexter's character outlined above, Dexter's killing of Mike is executed with care and precision. The pre-killing stalking consists of Dexter gathering evidence about Mike's crimes so as to provide for himself a basis on which to justify his killing of Mike. It seems that there are key truths about Mike which enter into Dexter's decision to kill him which reveal what Dexter values morally. This gives us an insight into Dexter's moral code.

What are the relevant features of this case which motivate Dexter to kill? The most fundamental feature seems to be that Mike is himself a killer. Obviously, it is not this feature *alone* which is decisive, since, if it were, then Dexter would, by the same reasoning, kill himself. So although Dexter is, in a clear sense, a killer of killers, he is a killer of only a restricted class of killers. What restricts that class gives us some insight into what Dexter takes to be morally acceptable killings.

Dexter thinks that if an individual has the property of *being a killer*, then that fact *combined with other features* is decisive in Dexter taking that individual to be deserving of murder. But what are those other features? That is, what, in Dexter's view, makes it the case that an individual who is a killer deserves to be killed, and thus, differentiates them from one who is a killer yet does not deserve to be killed (such as, in Dexter's view, himself)? One relevant aspect in Mike's case is that he had killed (and perhaps abused) *children*. So if an individual is a killer of *children*, then Dexter takes that individual to be deserving of murder. This key aspect of Dexter's moral character is revealed when Dexter expresses strong disapproval of Mike's *child* killing, just before killing him.

V. The Killing of Innocents

Season 1 is dominated by the search for and the exploits of a serial killer other than Dexter himself – a killer who is dubbed by the police and media as the "Ice Truck Killer." The Ice Truck Killer is eventually revealed to be a man named Rudy Cooper—a prosthetics expert involved in a relationship with Dexter's adoptive sister Debra. Later, Rudy Cooper is revealed as Dexter's biological brother.

There is an interesting parallel between Dexter and his brother. Not only are they both serial killers, but their urges to kill seem to have the same origin; Dexter's brother also witnessed the slaughter of their mother. Unlike Dexter, however, his brother was not rescued and adopted by Harry; he did not, therefore, receive the same *mode of controlling* his urge to kill that Dexter did by way of the moral code. It is interesting to note that, in this regard, the show appears to want to display a distinction between a serial killer who is utterly immoral, and a serial killer who—whether or not he, too, is utterly immoral—at least *tries* to be moral.

The Ice Truck Killer displays, as one might expect, certain similarities in his killing to Dexter: both are highly intelligent and meticulous in their killing procedures with respect to both the planning and execution of the killings. When Dexter first encounters the Ice Truck Killer's victims, he is even *impressed* by the precision and attention to detail. Yet in the final episode of Season 1, Dexter kills the Ice Truck Killer. So why does he do this? That is, why does Dexter take it that the Ice Truck Killer fits the code and deserves to be murdered?

Although the Ice Truck Killer is a killer, he is not, it seems, a killer of *children*. So what else is it about his killing that motivates Dexter to kill him? It cannot be that he is a *serial* killer because, again, by the same reasoning, Dexter would kill himself.

Other than the fact that he is a serial killer, various features of the Ice Truck Killer's character and actions make him deserving, in Dexter's view, of murder. For a start, the Ice Truck Killer's victims do not seem to deserve to die. They are, in a sense, innocent—he murders seemingly innocent prostitutes and attempts to murder Dexter's sister Debra, a law-abiding citizen. This fact reveals an interesting aspect of Dexter's moral character, since he appears to believe that one should not kill innocent people, and that if one does, then one deserves to die.

There are other contributing factors that might not themselves constitute, for Dexter, reasons for him to kill the Ice Truck Killer, but might, in combination with the fact that the Ice Truck Killer kills innocent people, supplement Dexter's view that he is worthy of death. For instance, despite his methodical nature, there is a clear sense in which the Ice Truck Killer is out of control. First, the Ice Truck Killer does not seem to follow a moral code. Second, he is willing to let his instincts get the better of him in particular circumstances. In this sense, the Ice Truck Killer is quite unlike the more ratiocinative Dexter.

There is an interesting parallel here with Dexter's treatment of district attorney Miguel Prado in Season 3. Dexter teaches Miguel how to kill in accordance with the *code of killing*. Having learned Dexter's killing method and code, in episode eight of Season 3, Miguel decides to kill someone on his own, albeit with the prior assistance of Dexter. Of course, according to Dexter's code, merely being guilty of murder is not sufficient to make one deserving of being murdered. The victim, in this case, however, is murdered for what is, in Dexter's view, the wrong reason: to pay off his gambling debts. With this evidence, Miguel is *allowed* to proceed. Here we see Dexter trying to instill the code into Miguel. In many ways, Dexter is to Miguel what Harry was to him. Dexter appears to have an excellent student.

However, Miguel eventually breaks Dexter's moral code when he kills Ellen Wolf, a fellow lawyer who gets in his way professionally. For Dexter, Ellen is not deserving of murder since she does not "fit the code." She is not herself a murderer. But having expressed his desire to kill Ellen, Miguel is angered by Dexter's disapproval and kills her anyway. Dexter realizes what has happened and exposes this killing to the police and the public. Miguel buries Ellen in a graveyard; Dexter uncovers her and leaves her to be found. Although he does not name Miguel as the culprit, these actions constitute an attempt to teach Miguel a lesson.

Dexter then proceeds to break off his friendship with Miguel, but does so carefully as Miguel knows too much about him. However, Dexter's boss Maria LaGuerta (who was previously romantically involved with Miguel and who became friends with Ellen just before Miguel murdered her) discovers that Miguel murdered Ellen. Eventually, Miguel realizes that Maria knows his secret and plans to kill her. Once Dexter knows that Miguel wants to kill Maria, this is a step too far. So, in episode eleven of Season 3, before Miguel can kill Maria, Dexter kills Miguel—of course, by this stage, such a murder more than fits Dexter's code.

The parallel with the Ice Truck Killer is that Dexter kills Miguel seemingly for two reasons: firstly, Miguel kills innocent people, and, secondly, Miguel is *out of control*—revealing to Dexter, and to the audience, that it is possible to be *taught* the code, yet still not adhere to it.

This final point reveals how Dexter values a certain kind of moral sensitivity—or, at least, sensitivity to what one takes to be the demands of morality. Such sensitivity is lacking in both the Ice Truck Killer and Miguel Prado. For instance, by way of contrast to both these killers, Dexter recoils at the idea of killing innocent people, even when it places him in danger. In episode twelve of Season 3, Miguel's brother Ramon suspects that Dexter is involved in Miguel's murder. Dexter considers killing Ramon, but decides to reason with him instead, convincing him that he has nothing to do with Miguel's murder. After all, murdering him would not fit his moral code since Ramon is not guilty of murder. Here we see Dexter as not only a *ratiocinative* killer but also one who is morally sensitive. In the next section, we shall explore this idea further.

VI. Emotional and Familial Connections

It seems that emotional and familial connections are vital in shaping Dexter's moral code and character. One might be struck by this claim, given that, in Dexter's reflections upon himself, it is quite clear that he views himself as emotionally *empty*. Dexter takes himself to be merely *acting out* feelings for so-called friends and family; there is, in his view, no real substance to his relationships. Dexter *thinks* that he does not *really* feel love for his sister, that he does not *really* love his girlfriend and her children. How, then, can it be that emotional and familial connections shape his moral character, if—as Dexter claims—they are not even *real*?

The answer is that Dexter is *self-deceived* about his emotions. The voice-over reveals the beliefs he has about himself and his emotional make-up, but those beliefs are clearly *false*. This is a bold claim so we want to defend it in the following way. First, we will say why we take those beliefs to be false, and, second, we will say why Dexter nonetheless has them—that is, we will explain what function they serve for him.

First of all, his beliefs are false because they are inconsistent with his actions, and his emotions are manifest in his actions. Dexter's actions are not the actions of an unemotional man. Consider Dexter's response in Season 1, when Rita's ex-husband—a violent drunkard of a man—returns and attempts to force himself back into the lives of Rita and the children. Dexter acts in such a way as to exhibit protectiveness and concern for the welfare of the family of which he is part. This can be taken as nothing but a manifestation of *love*.

A second example is when, in the first episode, the Ice Truck Killer drops a decapitated *head* of one of his victims onto Dexter's car. It is clear that Dexter's instinctual reaction is one of *fear*—again, expressing fear is inconsistent with being properly unemotional.

A third example is when the Ice Truck Killer captures and attempts to murder Debra. Dexter's reaction is anything but unemotional. Dexter displays signs of distress, worry, and panic—and other emotional reactions that one might expect of a brother (who loves his sister) in response to his sister being endangered. With respect to this example, Dexter is motivated to kill the Ice Truck Killer, not because he fits the code, but because he wants to *save his sister*. Again, this is an emotionally charged desire.

One might protest at the claim that Dexter is, despite his claims to the contrary, a deeply emotional man. One might think that we can explain his actions as *mere pretense*. But this is highly implausible. After all, most of what we are taking to be his emotional actions are indeed *instinctive reactions*, which it is hard to *pretend* to have.

More significantly, it seems to us that we might be able to explain the tension between Dexter's expressed beliefs about his *lack of* emotionality and his actions, which manifestly *display* his emotionality. The explanation is that Dexter is not only self-deceived, but that this self-deception serves an important function with respect to how he can cope with the killings his moral code compels him to perform.

In our view, if Dexter had *recognizable surface feelings* then he would—being human—recognize himself as feeling a certain degree of empathy and concern for his victims and their families. But if he recognized himself to have *those* feelings, then that may well just prevent him from carrying out what in his view *must be done*—that is, *must be done in the interests of what he takes to be what is morally required of him.* So, by *telling himself* that he is some emotionless monster, he prevents himself from having to deal with the feelings and manifest horror that killing brings, and thereby enables himself to do what is, in his view, the right thing—that is, sustain a deep commitment to the moral code that he lives by. Deceiving himself about his own emotional capacities and the feelings that he has serves as what one might call a *detachment mechanism*—a mechanism which is a condition of the possibility of him following his code. So Dexter *does feel*, and he is emotional. It is just that he has to hide this fact from himself, by self-deception, in order that he can still engage in what he views as his moral purpose.

A further, more fundamental, philosophical point, to one who is still not convinced that Dexter really is an emotionally engaged individual, is that emotional engagement is a condition of the possibility of having a moral code at all. That is to say, if one is to be in a position to recognize what one takes to be moral demands—which one needs to be if one is to have a moral code—then one must be emotionally capable.

This follows from the nature of the kind of territory that morality covers. It seems that morality is concerned with, in some sense, other people or perhaps, more specifically, what the contemporary American philosopher T.M. Scanlon regards as "what we owe to each other" (although one should note that Scanlon thinks there are also other realms of moral concern). In our view, if one is to properly appreciate that this is what morality is about, then one needs an appropriate connection to, and an understanding of, others—an appropriate *emotional* connection to others. One needs to be able to *care* for others, and *feel* for others.

That Dexter's *apparent* emotional and familial ties are indeed *real* and *substantive* is significant with respect to considering his moral character. This is because Dexter displays certain tendencies to offer preferential treatment to his loved ones, especially Debra, Rita, and her children; and also, as a young child, Dexter was concerned about doing right by his parents and arguably *still is*, insofar as he displays a kind of loyalty to Harry by following "Harry's code." However, although Dexter does have preferences for family and friends, there are two examples where, *despite* ties of friendship and family, Dexter *still kills*. Dexter kills his brother and Miguel Prado, despite his feelings for both men. This shows that Dexter's code is very strong and overrides preferences he might have for certain people.

VII. Justice, Law Enforcement, and Consequentialism

It seems that Dexter values justice, albeit his own particular brand of it. Part of his moral purpose lies in picking up the slack from his colleagues at the Miami Police Department. In episode one of Season 1, we learn, through Dexter's commentary, that in Miami there is only a 20 per cent solve-rate for murders. It seems, then, that Dexter feels it is his duty to solve the unsolved murders. This is why he gathers evidence about the perpetrators of the crimes. But Dexter also *punishes* and, in a sense, *convicts* the perpetrators of the crimes. Dexter thus plays cop, judge, and jury.

Dexter understands justice in a certain legalistic way. It seems that, for Dexter, justice is done if one who is guilty of a serious crime like murder is sentenced to death. Death is what Dexter takes the law to demand for murderers: he enforces that law where the police department fails. One might question, of course, whether Dexter has understood justice correctly or whether his actions are the best way of realizing justice. For instance, *even if* the law demands that murderers are put to death, it does not follow that this is what is *morally required* (although it seems that Dexter *does* think it is morally required). Furthermore, if it *is* morally required, it does not follow that *Dexter* is morally required to put the criminals to death.

Dexter's whole world involves law enforcement. He works for the Miami Police Department and all his friendships involve his colleagues. Dexter's sister is a cop, as was his adoptive father Harry, and Miguel, who eventually becomes Dexter's best friend, also works in law enforcement. His relationship with Rita and the artist Lila, in Season 2, are perhaps two exceptions.

Being part of such a world serves two functions for Dexter. Firstly, it clearly aids him in his killings—he has access to inside information on the criminals he pursues, and the technical knowledge involved in his work enables him to conceal his crimes. Secondly, one might argue that it serves a psychological function. Although Dexter is involved in law enforcement as a forensics expert for the Miami Police Department, he might feel that he is entitled to enforce the law in a further sense, as an *extension* of his role in the law-enforcing team. If he was not already in that team, then it might seem to him that his actions have less validity.

Given that Dexter is contributing to law enforcement in Miami in this way, perhaps he takes himself to be *maximizing some kind of good such that the morality of his actions depends on the good that is thereby maximized by performing those actions.* One might argue that this would make Dexter a kind of *ethical consequentialist.* This brings us back to the issue of how to characterize the moral territory.

Broadly characterized, the idea behind ethical consequentialism is that the morality of actions depends on the value of the consequences they bring about. So, if say *happiness* or *pleasure* is what is most valuable, then the morality of actions will depend upon whether or not those actions maximize happiness or pleasure. This kind of view is to be found in the British nineteenth-century philosopher J.S. Mill's *Utilitarianism.* In Chapter 2 of *Utilitarianism*, Mill says: "The creed which accepts as the foundation of morals, Utility, or the Greatest-Happiness Principle, holds that actions are right in proportion as they tend to promote happiness, wrong as they tend to produce the reverse of happiness. By happiness is intended pleasure, and the absence of pain; by unhappiness, pain, and the privation of pleasure" (7). This *utilitarian* brand of consequentialism is not the only kind of consequentialism. For instance, if it is *welfare* that is most valuable, then the morality of actions will depend upon whether or not those actions maximize welfare. And so on for other candidates for what it is that is most valuable.

For a more thorough understanding of consequentialism, one must also take into consideration further issues such as what the relevant consequences are consequences of. In the characterization just provided, we are taking it to be the consequences of *actions* that are relevant, but others would take the consequences of *rules* to be the real moral issue.

However, the broad characterization enables us to give some thought to the question of whether or not Dexter is a consequentialist. The first thing to note is that there are two senses to this question: a *third-personal* and a *first-personal* sense.

With respect to the third-personal sense, one might wonder whether we can take Dexter's actions as being *morally justified*. This is clearly a difficult question to decide. One might think that Dexter's actions maximize overall happiness (or welfare), since he reduces the number of murderers in Miami. And yet, on the other hand, one might think that, by *being a serial killer*, Dexter somehow contributes a certain unease to the city—the kind of unease which one has knowing that one lives in a city that has a serial killer at large. As such, Dexter would be contributing to unhappiness in some sense. So the *calculation* of whether or not Dexter maximizes some good (happiness, welfare, and so on) is a difficult matter to decide.

With respect to the first-personal sense, one might wonder whether Dexter takes himself to be an ethical consequentialist. This is, in effect, to ask whether Dexter himself endorses or uses consequentialism as a decision procedure for his actions. Again, this is a delicate question. Insofar as he follows a moral code, Dexter is concerned with what he takes to be the demands of morality. In this sense, it seems that Dexter wants to *do good*. However, it is unclear that he wants to *maximize the good for the greatest number*. Part of the reason for this is that it is unclear *what* good Dexter has in mind. For instance, he shows no particular privileged concern for merely the happiness or pleasure of the greatest number. However, it might be that Dexter is motivated by maximizing *a number of goods* for the greatest number, say, justice, peace, pleasure, happiness, welfare, and so on. His reflections on the code do not provide us with a clear answer as to the particular brand of consequentialism he might be adopting, and yet, in a very general sense, he does seem to be motivated by consequentialism.

VIII. Conclusion

In this essay, we have attempted to put one in a better position to understand Dexter's moral character and moral psychology as a serial killer. In particular, we have focused on his code of killing, and explained how it appears to be morally contentful. We have attempted to spell out certain aspects to the content of the code, such as Dexter's hatred of child killers and killers of innocent people, and then shown how his own self-deception about his emotional make-up serves to provide a deeper explanation of how he is able to follow the code. Finally, we have raised the issue of justice and of moral justification and shown how this is a pertinent and difficult question with regard to Dexter. Hopefully, this discussion has clarified some of the ethical questions related to Dexter's actions, and puts us in a better position to consider whether he really is morally justified in all the murders he commits.

10.
The Devil You Know: *Dexter* and the "Goodness" of American Serial Killing

David Schmid

Fans of *Dexter* with disposable income have many ways to express their love for the show. On the official Showtime *Dexter* website, one can buy such items as glass-printed Dexter coasters in a commemorative box, bobblehead dolls of the main characters, body parts earrings, and a "Vote for Dexter" t-shirt. The more discriminating consumer will be thrilled to learn that, in the summer of 2008, a group of top designers transformed a New York City townhouse into what one article described as "a luxurious beacon of modernism inspired by the top six original hit series from Showtime" ("Showtime's"). The Dexter dining room designed by Amy Lau and Johnny Grey's Dexter-inspired kitchen produced such limited edition items for purchase as dining chairs apparently spattered with blood, dinner plates with bloodstains, and "dismembered flatware," where each knife, fork, or spoon consists of pieces of several styles of flatware—a real steal at only $500 per place setting.

Such phenomena illustrate not only the extraordinary popularity of the *Dexter* series, but also the way in which the show has solved spectacularly well the puzzle that has baffled the vast majority of serial killer-related popular culture that has come before it: how to have the audience identify with serial killers in a relatively unconflicted way. Finding the answer to this problem has enabled *Dexter* to become not only a successful television show and marketing and merchandizing bonanza, but also a cultural phenomenon in its own right. Never before has serial killer pop culture been so mainstream, so accepted in American society as with *Dexter*; as such, *Dexter* represents a turning point in the willingness of

Americans to embrace the serial killer as one of their own, as the personification of essentially American values. In the epilog to my 2005 book, *Natural Born Celebrities: Serial Killers in American Culture,* I argue that in the aftermath of 9/11, serial killers were not, as one might expect, replaced in American pop culture by the figure of the terrorist. Instead, serial killers continued to play a prominent role in a variety of media, including books, movies, websites, and television series. For the most part, post-9/11 representations of serial killers shared marked similarities with their pre-9/11 counterparts, but, in some respects, the function of serial killers changed after the terrorist attacks. If serial killers had previously been the personification of random, terrifying evil, now they were on their way to being rehabilitated, or, at least, familiarized. Despite the seeming unlikeliness of this claim, the argument of this essay is that the fondness with which American culture can sometimes regard the figure of the serial murderer is borne out and exemplified by the eponymous title character of *Dexter.* Dexter Morgan is the quintessential American serial killer of the post-9/11 era in that he is provided with an abundance of characteristics that make him a sympathetic, even identificatory, figure to the audience.

The purpose of this essay is to explain exactly how *Dexter* was able to achieve this extraordinary outcome, and the first step in doing so is to emphasize the extent to which the show is merely the latest episode in a long history of American engagement with criminality and violence, an engagement that has helped to define what it means to be American. Popular culture has always been an integral feature of this engagement, ever since the Puritan era. Most people would obviously not associate the Puritans with violent popular culture, but, in fact, they were just as obsessed with the acts, trials, and executions of criminals as we are today. It's just that their interest necessarily took different forms, and one of these forms was not only reading about crimes but also attending executions. Public hangings aroused tremendous popular interest during the Puritan period, and ministers seized the opportunity of being able to address such large numbers of people to instruct the crowds attending these events about the proper way to view the criminal's demise. Clergymen typically delivered sermons on capital cases on the Sunday before the sentence was to be carried out, or very often on the day of the execution itself. By all accounts, these sermons were often as well attended as the executions themselves, and the fact of their subsequent publication and distribution made them extremely influential and well-known documents.

These sermons did not present the criminal as some type of monstrous outsider; rather, the criminal was seen as a representative member of his/her community, precisely because s/he had sinned. In fact, one could argue that criminals were model citizens of the Puritan community because by sinning, confessing that sin, and then asking for God's forgiveness, they dramatized the process of conversion and redemption. This tension around the issue of whether the criminal should be considered as either integral to or mutually exclusive from forms of American community is obviously highly relevant to our understanding of a figure like Dexter, but equally relevant is a shift that started to take place in these popular cultural narratives about murder in the latter half of the eighteenth century, a shift that showed itself in an interest in the lives of the criminals themselves, an interest that goes beyond the earlier Puritan emphasis on the representativeness of these individuals. Instead, the emphasis now falls on the exceptional nature of the criminal, and they are exceptional not only in the sense of being uniquely wicked or evil, but also in the sense of being uniquely entertaining, dashing, even admirable. This shift indicates that American attitudes toward killers have never consisted simply of condemnation and revulsion but also of fascination and even sympathy. Precisely because Puritan crime narratives presented the criminal as a typical, fallible member of the community, that criminal was as much an object of sympathy and compassion as of revulsion and punishment.

But whereas Puritans made great efforts to keep criminals integrated into Puritan society, later forms of American popular culture organized around violent criminals tend to present the criminal as a distinctly asocial creature. I want to emphasize, however, that the concept of monstrosity did not simply replace the concept of representativeness as an explanation of criminality. Rather, monstrosity and representativeness coexist as a way of addressing the public ambivalence about criminals, an ambivalence that comes from our sense that murderers are, in an obvious sense, so very different from ordinary people and yet in another sense they seem disturbingly like us. Representations of homicidal violence in American popular culture consistently try to make sense of this duality at the heart of our feelings about those who kill by changing and adapting as our society as a whole changes. This is a key reason for the enduring popularity of American popular culture about homicide.

Such popular culture has developed a range of ways to handle the complexities of our feelings about homicide. To some extent, of course, the techniques vary according to what kind of criminal we are dealing with. While it might be a relatively uncomplicated matter to have audiences identify with figures such as Bonnie and Clyde, gangsters who can easily be portrayed as victimizing the rich to benefit the poor, getting readers to side with serial killers is much more difficult. As Paul Kooistra has argued, "While we undoubtedly find psychological release by vicariously experiencing the rebellious deeds of the lawbreakers, we choose to undergo this experience with a very limited number of criminals" (21). Tellingly, Kooistra explicitly excludes serial killers from this select group. Although, Kooistra argues, we may find serial killers such as Albert Fish and Ed Gein fascinating, "we do not make heroes of them" (21).

While Kooistra is undoubtedly correct to say that serial killers cannot be turned into heroes in any straightforward sense, the cultural omnipresence of serial killers both factual and fictional such as Jeffrey Dahmer, Ted Bundy, Hannibal Lecter, and Dexter indicates that the unstable structures of identification generated among the audiences of the various forms of pop culture that feature these figures can, in fact, be disciplined. But how? The answer, in short, is through disavowal. The most successful forms of serial killer-related popular culture give audiences a way to disavow their involvement and identification with serial killer characters; indeed, such disavowal is the key to the success of such pop culture. Thomas M. Leitch has argued that the disavowal of violence has become an increasingly influential feature of American film, especially as those films have become more and more violent: "For as representations of violence grow more clinical or shocking or disgusting or threatening, American films have developed an immensely sophisticated battery of techniques to disavow the power of the very images they are displaying onscreen." Leitch provides a detailed discussion of the techniques of disavowal used by contemporary American films, and summarizes them in the following terms: "Violence can be rendered acceptable to a sensitive audience by being ascribed to an evil Other, or by being justified in rational terms, or by being limited in its effects, or by being stylized through narrative conventions or rituals that deny its consequences, or by being rendered pleasurable through appeals to aestheticism or masochism or eroticism" ("Nobody Here"). Film uses these techniques, according to Leitch, to deny personal responsibility—both the responsibility of the agents of violence and the responsibility of those who watch and enjoy the representations of violence.

I would like to extend Leitch's thought-provoking argument about film by claiming that disavowal is, to a greater or lesser extent, a structural and necessary feature of all forms of popular culture about serial killers, and *Dexter* is a particularly significant example of that fact. By using many of the techniques described by Leitch, the makers of *Dexter* let their audience members off the hook by enabling them to enjoy their relationship with Dexter through placing that relationship within a moralistic framework that relieves them of pursuing the implications of that enjoyment. The remainder of this essay will describe these techniques, and then conclude by pursuing the larger implications of their use and their role in the success of *Dexter*.

The most fundamental disavowal technique used by *Dexter*, and certainly the one that has attracted the most comment, is the series' characterization of its eponymous protagonist. The guiding premise of the show, that Dexter only kills other killers, in other words, people who deserve to be murdered, is both the most audacious and original aspect of the series, and the most important factor in the show's success because it defines what Leitch describes as the justification of violence "in rational terms." While Dexter's need to kill obviously possesses a deep emotional dimension, his devotion to the "Code of Harry" taught to him by his adoptive father both keeps Dexter a "moral" killer and also encourages the audience to support and identify with Dexter's acts of homicide.

There are a number of reasons why this gamble pays off in *Dexter*. The first is that it draws upon and references the long-standing popularity of vigilante narratives in American pop culture, most notably the *Death Wish* series of movies featuring Charles Bronson. Fear of rising levels of violent crime, a perception that violent criminals routinely go uncaught and unpunished, and a more general level of skepticism about the effectiveness of the legal apparatus have all been long-standing features of American public discourse about law and order, and all of these factors play a role in the success of *Dexter* the series and the popularity of Dexter the character.

The second reason for the success of this characterization of Dexter is the fact that the television series places far greater emphasis on the positive outcomes of his vigilantism than the novels by Jeff Lindsay that provide the inspiration for the series.[1] I have in mind here such stand-alone episodes as "Love American Style" (Season 1, episode five) and "Shrink Wrap" (Season 1, episode eight), both of which feature storylines not present in Lindsay. In "Shrink Wrap," Dexter pursues and kills Dr Emmett Meridian, an unscrupulous therapist who victimizes powerful women by addicting them to antidepressants and then encouraging them to commit suicide. In this context, Dexter's murder of Meridian becomes available for rehabilitation as a proto-feminist gesture. In a similar vein, "Love American Style" presents Dexter as a defender of immigrant rights as he kills a husband-and-wife team responsible for the exploitation and murder of illegal Cuban immigrants. Both of these examples demonstrate the ways in which *Dexter* presents the protagonist's homicidal acts as moral, even progressive, responses to unscrupulous and unethical behavior. Interestingly, this aspect of the show actually requires Dexter to kill even more frequently in the television series (especially in Season 1) than in Lindsay's novels. Although one might assume that the frequency of Dexter's murders would jeopardize the audience's identification with him, the success of the series suggests otherwise, and it is worth underlining the point that such identification comes about not *in spite of* Dexter's murders, but *because of* them.

Equally important to the success of *Dexter*, however, is not only whom he kills, but whom he does not kill, or refuses to kill. This aspect of Dexter's character becomes especially prominent in Season 3 when his friendship with Miguel Prado places Dexter in the difficult position of having to turn down candidates for murder suggested by Prado because they do not meet the strict conditions established by the Code of Harry. The disagreements between Dexter and Miguel give the audience another opportunity to appreciate Dexter's morality and the extent to which that morality is defined both by whom he targets and whom he lets live. Leonard Cassuto has also drawn attention to the importance of victim selection to the success of *Dexter*. In the context of explaining the appeal of Dexter the character, Cassuto argues that:

> Dexter's secret source of sympathy is children. He has a special affection for kids. "One of the few character traits that genuinely mystifies me," he says in Lindsay's *Darkly Dreaming Dexter*, "is my attitude toward children. . . . They are important to me. They matter." It's not just that "kids are different" and (as Dexter says in the opening episode of the television show) he has "standards" that don't permit him to kill them. Avoiding child victims is much more than professional ethics for Dexter. "I like them," he says—and he shows it. If children were among Dexter's victims, there could be no story. ("Rooting")

Dexter the series drives this point about the role of children home right at the start of the pilot episode by having Dexter's first victim be Mike Donovan, a boys' choir leader responsible for the deaths of at least several children. Although this incident is based fairly closely on the opening episode of Lindsay's first Dexter novel, *Darkly Dreaming Dexter*, it is interesting to note that the television show departs decisively from Lindsay in its characterization of Cody and Astor, the children of Dexter's girlfriend, Rita. Whereas in Lindsay's novels, these children turn out to be miniature Dexters in the sense that they are possessed by the need to kill others because of their traumatic childhood experiences, in the television series they remain the innocent victims of their father Paul's brutality.

This difference between Lindsay and *Dexter* the television show is significant for several reasons. It suggests, for example, that the show's much-vaunted blurring of the line between good and evil, a line that other television crime dramas have been criticized for drawing too neatly, only extends so far.[2] Although it is obviously extremely difficult to say definitively whether Dexter is good or evil, a difficulty that is crucial to the success of the show, it is also obvious that the ambiguity surrounding Dexter is purchased at the price of a complete lack of ambiguity regarding the victims. Victims in *Dexter* are either guilty (and are subsequently killed by Dexter) or innocent (as with Cody and Astor and those victimized by Dexter's victims); there is no gray area between.

But the innocence of Cody and Astor is also structurally necessary for *Dexter* the television show for another reason: to highlight the guilt, the evil, and the violence all personified by Paul, their abusive father. Paul is a relatively minor character in Lindsay's novels, but he plays a major role in Season 1 of *Dexter* because he is just one instance of another disavowal technique used extensively by the show, a technique that Leitch describes as violence being "rendered acceptable to a sensitive audience by being ascribed to an evil Other." Dexter's violence, in other words, is contextualized, rationalized, and thus made more or less palatable for the viewers of *Dexter* not only by the fact that he kills other killers, but also by the fact that Dexter is also usually accompanied by other aggressive, even homicidal characters who, relatively speaking, make Dexter's violence look quite benign. Although the viewer may feel some residual discomfort about identifying with someone like Dexter, Paul is such an aggressive, unpleasant, and inconvenient character that such discomfort is likely to be minimized when he is finally disposed of by Dexter, thus enabling Rita and Dexter to be together, and freeing Cody and Astor from an unwholesome and dangerous influence on their lives.

Paul is also important for the way that he establishes a metonymic link between Dexter and Rita's children. Although this link in Lindsay's novels takes the form of a shared lust to kill, in *Dexter* the series, Dexter, Cody, and Astor are instead linked by their shared victim status, the fact that all three of them have been through intense childhood trauma and survived. This fact also highlights the extent to which the success of *Dexter* depends upon establishing a back story for Dexter in order to encourage audience sympathy and identification for him. Rather than having the origin of his "evil" remain inexplicable and mysterious, the series goes out of its way to emphasize that Dexter was turned into a killer through no fault of his own, and so, when Harry takes pity on him, raises him as a member of his family, and insists repeatedly that Dexter is

139

fundamentally a "good kid," the audience is alerted to the fact that it is permissible for us to support him, too.

The themes of Dexter's back story and the series' use of the "evil Other" as a way to disavow the violent acts committed by Dexter come together in Season 1 in the guise of Rudy Cooper, aka Biney, aka Dexter's long-lost brother, Brian Moser. In a technique borrowed from Thomas Harris's *The Silence of the Lambs, Dexter* creates audience sympathy for the "good" serial killer by contrasting him with a "bad" serial killer. Just as Buffalo Bill allows readers to maintain their attachment to Hannibal Lecter in a relatively untroubled form, so the Ice Truck Killer, despite his family resemblance to Dexter, enables us to continue rooting for the "hero" of the series.

Moreover, I would argue that we stay on Dexter's side partly because Brian represents everything we have come to associate with the "pre-9/11" serial killer. In "Born Free," the Season 1 finale, Rudy/Brian asks Dexter, "Who am I?" Dexter replies, "A killer without reason or regret" (1.12). In contrast to Dexter's murders, in other words, the Ice Truck Killer's homicidal activities are random, unmotivated, malevolent, and vicious. In short, he is everything that Dexter is not. As such, Brian has to die, and Dexter's killing of him, precisely because it is the most difficult thing he has ever done, succeeds in making the audience feel an unparalleled degree of sympathy for him. Indeed, we know that this point must have been considered especially important by the makers of *Dexter*, because it is such a dramatic departure from Lindsay's *Darkly Dreaming Dexter*, in which Dexter lets Brian go free. Dexter's willingness to sacrifice his blood brother and choose his "real family" of Deborah and Harry instead both ratifies and cements the audience's feelings of sympathy for and identification with Dexter; after Brian's death, we feel closer to Dexter than ever.[3]

The presence of the "evil Other" is such an integral part of the success of *Dexter* that we can find a representative of this figure in all three seasons. In Season 3, Dexter gives in to feelings of isolation and the desire for a friend by taking on Miguel Prado as a kind of protégé. Although this relationship is initially quite satisfying to Dexter, things go badly wrong when Prado starts working on his own and kills people who do not meet the exacting standards of Harry's code. When Dexter kills Prado in order to stop him from killing more innocent people, we are encouraged to feel that he had no choice, and even to sympathize with him to the extent that his initial decision to befriend Prado was apparently inspired by two very human emotions: guilt over the fact that he had murdered Prado's younger brother, Oscar, and loneliness, a loneliness that Dexter tries to address by finding a friend, and then finally comes to terms with at the end of Season 3.[4]

For the purposes of this essay, however, by far the most interesting example of the "evil Other" archetype in *Dexter* is the true villain of Season 2, Lila Tournay. At first glance, the most important aspect of Lila's character is her gender. Her emotional and sexual involvement with Dexter enables the audience to see sides of Dexter that have previously been hidden, and to some extent, at least initially, we hope that Dexter is indeed successful in finding a soul mate, someone with whom he can share his deepest, darkest self, especially as that possibility is so obviously ruled out in Dexter's relationship with the insistently anodyne Rita. Ultimately, however, the makers of *Dexter* understand that the audience wants to be the only one with intimate access to Dexter, and so once Lila becomes aggressive, controlling, and threatening, it is almost a relief to see Dexter turn upon her, especially when she starts to threaten Cody and Astor, reminding us of the metonymic link between Dexter and the children.

It is at this point of Season 2 that another aspect of Lila's character arguably becomes even more important than her gender; namely, her Britishness. Although Lila's national identity is obvious from the moment of her first appearance in *Dexter*, thanks to Jaime Murray's accent, initially the series does not make much of this difference, which makes the title of the Season 2 finale, "The British Invasion," even more striking. When Deb finds out that Lila is apparently in the country illegally, and threatens her with deportation unless she leaves Dexter alone and gets out of Miami immediately, Lila's national identity becomes both more visible and more prominent than ever before. The purpose of Lila's national otherness, I want to argue, is to highlight the representative function of Dexter's American-ness, thus underlining the extent to which *Dexter* the series represents a perfect example of how American culture can learn to embrace serial killers as native sons. The fact that Dexter eventually kills Lila after she has escaped to France, and does so quickly so that he can immediately fly back to the US, emphasizes even more strongly Dexter's status as an "American in Paris" (with apologies to Vincente Minnelli!), a distinctively American phenomenon out of place outside the borders of the United States.

As I explained at the start of this essay, the merchandizing that has accompanied the success of *Dexter* is one very important indication of the extent to which identification with serial killers is now an apparently accepted part of mainstream American culture, but perhaps an even more symptomatic example of the same phenomenon is the rebroadcast of *Dexter* episodes on CBS rather than Showtime in 2008. As one might expect, this rebroadcast attracted significant opposition from such groups as the Parents Television Council, who objected to the way in which *Dexter* encourages its viewers to empathize with a serial killer (Hibberd). The fact that the CBS broadcasts went ahead despite this opposition, along with the fact that they were able to do so with a minimum of cutting (no pun intended), suggests both the extent to which the gap between broadcast and cable television standards has closed in recent years, and the extent to which *Dexter* and its vision of sympathetic serial killers really has been embraced as part of the American mainstream, something that was unimaginable just a few years ago. This is the real achievement of *Dexter*.

11.
Neoliberal *Dexter*?

Michele Byers

This chapter explores the way that *Dexter* is produced at the intersection of a set of ambivalent discourses about criminality, identity, and citizenship. I am especially interested in the way that the series grapples with these issues within the particular socio-cultural context of its production and how, while attempting to offer critiques of various forms, social relations, and modes of governance, it ends up trapped in the neoliberal and neoconserv-ative discourses that form the nexus of their (and its) emergence. That is, I'm interested in the circular way in which *Dexter*'s stories arc towards a neoliberal/conservative narrative about the relation-ship between criminality and identity in contemporary America, even as the series appears to try to critique that relationship.

Television and Neoliberalism

In a discussion of representations of criminality, we must take various discursive, political, spatial (that is, locational or perhaps national), and technological frames, and the shifts that have engen-dered them into consideration. In much US TV programming, even on series like *Dexter* that exist outside the network mainstream, what we primarily see are two discourses about criminality: criminology of the self, associated with neoliberal discourses of rational selfhood, and a criminology of the other wherein criminals are imagined as monsters inherently different from the bourgeois citizenry (Garland in Bonnycastle, 154). This isn't to suggest that there is a unified way in which American TV programming represents crime and criminality. Certainly, there are series that diverge from this type of representation. *The Wire* (HBO 2002–8), for example, positions its narratives quite emphatically within a space which critiques the dominance of neoliberal and neoconservative discourses and practices—particularly of law, policing, journalism, education, and politics—in the social construction of contemporary American spaces and (racialized, gendered, and classed) identities. But *The Wire* is somewhat anomalous in the consistency of its critique. More often, in my experience, series become trapped in their own attempts to critique "the system." In so doing, they end up entangled, producing narratives that ultimately reify the very systems they purport to critique.[1]

Dexter is and yet is not so different from popular contemporary crime fare produced for network TV. *CSI* (CBS 2000–), for example, has dominated the televisual landscape for most of the decade at least in part because of the vision of risk it offers while effectively erasing the social and political landscape in which most risk is constituted (poverty, racism, addiction) and repackaging it within a neoliberal language of rational choice in which the criminal as a white, middle-class social actor has no need of the state (Byers and Johnson, xx). *CSI* promises a form of governance that appeals to a post-9/11 society in which mitigating factors of social life are rendered irrelevant. On *CSI*, the state has or will fail the citizen, but science cannot:

> *CSI* not only depoliticizes policing by fashioning white, rational choice bourgeois criminals who are one hundred percent responsible for their crimes, but sanitizes punishment as a logical and just response undertaken for the greater good of all society. . . .
>
> This narrative strategy effectively screens the criminogenic effects of a neoliberal political economy on poor, racialized, and other working-class communities by normalizing purposive acts of violence and portraying predatory killings as rational choices made by autonomous and free subjects whose punishment can be deemed by *CSI* viewers as legitimate, rational, and civil. (Bonnycastle, 166)

Does *Dexter* differ from this description significantly?

In his reading of Andy Sipowicz, the central character from the long-running series *NYPD Blue* (FOX 1993—2005), Kenneth Meeks notes a certain growth in the character vis-à-vis racism and issues of racialization over the series' twelve-year run. Meeks begins by noting that, in the early years of the series, Sipowicz is, "[I]n essence, a racist," which is, as he is essentially the hero of the show, deeply problematic. And yet, Meeks acknowledges, "Sipowicz grows" (49, 50). Could we say the same of Dexter and of *Dexter*? I'm not sure, as will become clearer in the discussion that follows. I'm not sure because—and acknowledging *Dexter* has only had three, not twelve years to evolve thus far—the series is deeply ambivalent about its position vis-à-vis crime, criminality, and the dispensing of justice. It is deeply, if not wholly, embroiled in a neoliberal political ration-ality—one which produces "[a] form of governmentality . . . [which] convenes a "free" subject who rationally deliberates about alternative courses of action, makes choices, and bears responsibil-ity for the consequences of those choices" (Brown, "Neoliberalism" par. 17)—entrenched in a neoconservative ideal in which "the possi-bility of linking power and morality" has been operationalized (Fukuyama in Brown, "Neoliberalism, Neoconservativism" 697).

In *Dexter*, as elsewhere, these two intertwined strands enable the idea of a moral subject whose "autonomy is measured by their capacity for 'self-care'—their ability to provide for their own needs, and service their own ambitions" (Brown, "Neoliberalism, Neocon-servativism" 694). This isn't as simple as it seems, because the ability to care for the self and the ability to be "moral" are not achievable by all. As Wendy Brown describes in *Regulating Aversion*, the discourse of tolerance works as a "domestic discourse of ethnic, racial, and sexual regulation" (7). A tolerant neoliberal society suggests meritocratic values in which all persons who can show a capacity for self-care and a willingness to stay within the moral guideposts (such that they are) of the day are all that is needed for success. But this is itself a lie, and it's the lie at the centre of *Dexter*. The lie is that only certain figures can occupy this space of moral self-care, just as only certain (and the same) figures are seen within this discursive frame as rightfully occupying traditional spaces of social power. And with each trespass by Other figures (take your pick, women, racialized and ethnicized "minorities," homosexuals, children, immigrants, the poor) into spaces of moral self-care and social power, those who had previously had absolute claim on those spaces—white or Anglo middle-class, straight men—become the apparati of their reclamation by any means. This, again, is the story of *Dexter*, the story of how one man whose life has been devoted to the learning of self-care, cleanses and/or neutralizes the public sphere of not only criminals but of those Others who have usurped spaces that rightly belong to him.

On *Dexter*, the story is framed in such a way (and by framed here, I refer to its choice of location and the way the series is cast) that an obvious or surface reading of racism and misogyny are rendered problematic. As Yasmin Jiwani acknowledges in reference to very different circumstances, the production or reminder of the presence of social difference is often a useful tool in the dismissal of claims of racism, sexism, and white supremacy (78). So on *Dexter*, the presence of men and women, and men and women with various claims on white, Latin, and African-American identities—as well as different statuses in terms of class, education, and citizenship—creates a mythic space that appears not only tolerant, but both amnesiac to the historical legacies of social hierarchy and blind to their contemporary incarnations. Here it is all about the individual and the code; this is where the buck stops. At times, the series' self-reflexivity seems to look critically at "race,"[2] but whiteness remains inscrutable, especially white masculinity dressed up straight and middle-class (and increasingly so as the *Dexter* seasons move on). Ultimately, the sociopathic vigilante is simply a white, Anglo-Protestant male pumped up to cartoon (hence superheroic) proportions. It is not surprising in light of this that his foils are less, ultimately, the failed state or the criminals who, having slipped through its fingers, are its greatest failures. Rather, his foils are primarily women and African and Latin American men.

Dexter is, on some level, a warning that taking the law into one's own hands is—as the Bush government so often demonstrated—the prerogative of privileged white masculinity. In reading the series not only through its seasonal arcs, but as a continuing macro-arc, what becomes discernible is a narrative about the victory of Anglo masculinity, not just over other forms of masculinity and femininity, but over the "law" and "justice/order" as spaces corrupted by the present Others who are blind

(LaGuerta), corrupt (the Prados), or who refuse to allow Dexter to follow his code (Doakes).

The Neoliberal Impulse in Seasons 1–3

The neoliberal discourses that construct the *Dexter* narrative are actually articulated within a broader neoconservative narrative, in which various characters are not reformable, in the sense that they are not malleable and will not allow themselves to be made to play Dexter's game or see the world within the specific—although evolving—framework or code as it is articulated by Dexter Morgan. This is not only true of the various killers Dexter dispatches within the episodic aspect of the narrative, but, as I've said, within the larger serial playing field as well (no pun intended). If we look at the arc that forms the entirety of the series' three seasons to date, this neoliberal/conservative score becomes more visible. *Dexter* becomes a parable about the incursion of Others into the domains of power which were previously the (almost) exclusive jurisdiction of white, middle-class masculinity: the law, policing, politics. This incursion, on *Dexter*, marks also the failure of the state to live up to its role as a protector of "the people," a role which can now only be filled by the vigilante, the middle-class, white male who has presumably lost his power within the formal spaces of the system. As much as Dexter sees his role as tidying up after the state's failures, his doppel-gänger role is of mitigating the incursion of Others within the system itself. *Dexter* is thus, in large measure, about freedom, about who has the right to be free and to act with impunity to protect themselves, their loved ones, and their moral code.

In the first season of *Dexter*, we are introduced to an interesting array of core characters, centering on Dexter himself, a forensic expert who moonlights as a serial killer. We learn that Dexter was adopted in childhood into a "normal" Miami family, his police officer father schooling him in the art of pretense and teaching him how to channel his violent tendencies in the "right" direction, thereby establishing a code that ensures both Dexter's survival and his sense of moral righteousness. His day job as a blood-splatter expert allows Dexter to use the system and its regimes of truth and knowledge to find and torture criminals whom he believes have escaped formal justice. The job, and his relationship with his adopted sister Deb—a cop herself and the one person Dexter seems to have "real" feelings for—root his performance of middle-class white Anglo masculinity in a certain kind of legitimacy. These roots are further entrenched through Dexter's involvement with Rita, a tightly wound, pretty, blonde single mother who has escaped a violent and drug-addicted ex-husband. Although Dexter's voice-over reminds us constantly that he is performing a role that he doesn't understand (because he doesn't "feel"), what comes through in the subtext of these ruminations is the importance of the performing body. Dexter is strange, but it's difficult to understand his strangeness in the context of the body performing it. That is, Dexter's particular type of strangeness is irreconcilable (as criminality) with his white, middle-class identity—although it isn't at all irreconcilable with his identity as a neoliberal subject who both makes moral choices and can give a very clear accounting of these and of himself. In a sense, Dexter's crimes—and his identity as a serial killer—"are not comprehensible to the white middle class that bred" him (Faith and Jiwani 84). But in their reframing as vigilante justice that serves the people (and saves them from the failures of the state), Dexter and his crimes become not only comprehensible, but somehow laudatory. That's what makes him "work" as a hero in the narrative: ostensibly he does what *we* understand needs to be done.

Season 1—Blood and Brotherhood

The first season of *Dexter* has a couple of big reveals. The first involves Dexter's having to come face to face with that part of himself that he can give no account of (Butler). For Dexter, this means recalling the circumstances prior to and which led to his adoption into the Morgan family. What he remembers is shocking: being found in a warehouse ankle deep in his mother's blood after she had been butchered by chainsaw-wielding drug dealers. Later, we learn that Dexter has an older brother—Brian/Rudy—who was also in the warehouse on the night of their mother's murder. This brother is also a serial killer, but not having been schooled by someone like father Morgan, his rage is directed at women, prostitutes, whom he bleeds and butchers, leaving their pristine body parts for Dexter to marvel over. What this sets up is a series of binaries around nature/nurture and good/evil, binaries that are intrinsic to neoliberal and neoconservative conceptions of identity and criminality. Since Dexter and his brother are both killers, maybe this impulse is genetic. Since they both witnessed their mother's brutal murder, maybe it was created by that event. Dexter's "training" to control or to give moral structure to his murderous impulses—to give in to the law of (the) his father if not those the state imposes—is engendered it seems by his ability to repress these crucial events. He exemplifies what Judith Butler describes as a life narrative that "begins *in media res*, when many things have already taken place to make me and my story possible" (39). Because of this schooling, Dexter appears to develop a narrative capacity necessary "for giving an account" of himself "and assuming responsibility for [his] actions through that means" (12). The father's code is thus delivered in the first season as the anchor, the moral language through which Dexter can tell his story and take responsibility for his actions, a feat set against his brother's inability. Ultimately, Dexter chooses the moral code of the father over the temptations of self-knowledge Brian/Rudy—his "blood" brother—offers. In killing off his brother, he enacts a moral cleansing through which he demonstrates his own ability to make moral choices and to take care of himself.

Season 2—Emancipation

The only person who seems to see through Dexter's performance in the first season is Sergeant Doakes, an African-American Homicide Detective and former Special Forces operative. Doakes is as erratic as Dexter is controlled, which makes him Dexter's perfect foil. The second season opens with the discovery of the dismembered bodies Dexter has been dumping into the Miami harbor, prompting a manhunt for the newly named Bay Harbor Butcher. Throughout the season, Doakes pushes to discover and reveal the truth about Dexter. He ultimately stumbles on Dexter's other life, but he knows he needs tangible proof before anyone will believe him. As his frustration grows, Doakes becomes an easy target, almost setting himself up to take the fall for Dexter's crimes. Concurrently, Dexter fabricates a drug addiction to try to throw Doakes off his trail. He meets and is sponsored by Lila, a strange woman to whom he feels, for the first time since meeting his brother, he can reveal his "true" face. Like Brian/Rudy, Lila refuses to follow father Morgan's code. But before Dexter can get rid of her, she has an important role to play.

The central problem for Dexter in Season 2 is how to reconcile framing Doakes for murder within the moral framework provided by his father. Doakes may be an asshole, but he's "innocent." Dexter can't kill him, but can he send him to jail for life? The answer is clearly yes. And this works for a number reasons. First, as I said before, the community within which Dexter operates cannot read him as a killer. "Killer" as operationalized within mainstream discourse has very specific attributes, and middle-class white masculinity—ironically those very attributes that are the supposed calling card of the serial killer—are not among them. No matter what Doakes tries to say about Dexter, he cannot be heard and the more he pushes his view, in fact, the guiltier he himself appears to be. Second, the importance of Dexter as a moral subject performing a moral purpose, one that's even more important than that of a police officer like Doakes, is at stake. Dexter is more important in maintaining a sanitized and just state than Doakes. Third, Dexter's performance of white masculinity, of a masculinity upon which others depend, that they need, is set in contrast to the bankrupt and empty life of his African-American colleague. For all these reasons, Dexter *has* to frame Doakes rather than take responsibility for his own actions. But we don't have to go there. Lila, in an effort to win Dexter back, intervenes by killing Doakes herself—in a scene of incredible violence reminiscent for this viewer of a lynching. Lila's moral failing allows her to "fit" into the structure of father Morgan's moral code; Dexter is liberated from the threat of exposure emanating from a masculinity which isn't invested and thus can see him as the murderous product of white middle-class America, and, in return for this liberation, he is also able to liberate himself from a femininity which refuses to act in the service of masculine desires and needs.

At the beginning of Season 2, Dexter asks himself: "Where is the orderly, controlled, effective Dexter? How did I lose him? How do I find him again?" (2.2). At the end of the season, he (and we) have the answer: he is found through the proclamation of self which requires the repudiation of Others and the reclamation of spaces they would inhabit and overrun. These may be abstract or moral spaces, but they are also literal spaces: the police station, the home, the city. Dexter ends the season by saying: "The code is mine now and mine alone . . . They're not just disguises anymore . . . My father might not approve, but I'm no longer his disciple. I'm a master now. An idea transcended into life" (2.12). Dexter has become a master by learning to care for and narrate himself as the true neoliberal/conservative subject he always was. He has surpassed his father's vision because his father belonged to another time, another way of imagining and being in the world. Dexter needs no disguise because his best disguise was always what he performed, white, middle-class masculinity, now dressed up with a heterosexual family in tow. To get there, he needed to get rid of those Others—in this season women, Black men, and poor/addicted men—who could see through this performance; those who understood that there's no such thing as no disguise. As he himself offers at the end of the final episode: "I've never been one to put much weight into the idea of a higher power, but if I didn't know better I'd have to believe that some force out there wants me to keep doing what I'm doing." Here we see the neoconservative moral/ethico-religious voice come explicitly into articulation, and it will become even more explicit in Season 3.

Season 3—Friends and Fathers

Season 2 closes with the following rumination: ". . . this is my new path. It's a lot like the old one, only harder. To stay on the new path I must explore new rituals, evolve. Am I evil? Am I good? I'm done asking those questions. I don't have the answers. Does anyone?" (2.12). Here Dexter tries to articulate himself as a subject finally free of his father and his father's old views of the failed state and the public good. He dispenses, seemingly forever, with his father's dichotomous view of identity. He sees himself as a particular type of neoliberal subject, one that can finally act in service of himself;

but he is, in fact, exactly the sort of subject long theorized as "available to political tyranny and authoritarianism precisely *because* they are absorbed in a province of choice and need-satisfaction that they mistake for freedom" (Brown, "Neoliberalism, Neoconservativism" 705, emphasis in the original; Zizek). Dexter's sense of his own ability to choose a satisfying life (a performance) completely separate from authority, to choose his own ideas about good and evil, is presented as a radical emergence of identity. But, in fact, it glosses the heavily regulated/governed space that Dexter inhabits and which forms the framework through which all his decisions are made (Foucault). As we shall see over the course of the third season, Dexter not only mistakes this space for freedom, he fails to note the way in which his entrance into this space marks his return to an earlier self.

By the end of Season 2, Dexter has rid himself of Lila, Doakes, and Paul. He's successfully averted being tapped as the Bay Harbor Butcher, and has firmly linked himself to Rita and her children, establishing himself even more firmly as an average white, middle-class family man. And he's shed his father's code—or so he insists—and is ready to be his own man. In Season 3, as before, new characters are introduced as foils for the dichotomous valorizing of Dexter, and, by extension, white middle-class masculinity. The first is Miguel Prado, a Cuban-American ADA who becomes Dexter's friend, a real friend whom Dexter slowly invites into the most secret spaces of his life, shocked to learn that Miguel has appetites similar to his own. The second is a serial killer known as "the Skinner." The Skinner is eventually revealed to be George King, also known as Jorge Orozco, a former Nicaraguan Army interrogator accused of acts of torture.

Although Miguel and George King represent very different spaces within the socio-culture of Miami—one being a highly visible member of the upper class and the other a virtually invisible immigrant tree trimmer—they are both Latin men in a city increasingly identified with Latin rather than white cultures. Both refuse to live, not only by the "law," but by the code established by Dexter via his father, a code of morality that seems "true" and "natural" but that also scripts and privileges white, middle-class masculinities. Their immorality is presented as inherently different and more transgressive than Dexter's own. This differentiation helps to obscure the reasons Dexter needs to get rid of both men. Yes, they go against the code, but Dexter really wants both men dead for reasons beyond the code's most obvious parameters. These reasons have to do first, with their ability—like Doakes before them—they "see" and thus expose Dexter and put him (and thus his ability to do his "work") at risk, and second, with the threat they pose to those with whom Dexter has relationships that give him an air of normative masculinity, particularly Deb and Rita.

Miguel appears to be Dexter's ally—which means his accomplice and being willing to allow Dexter to call all the shots—but is then revealed to have set Dexter up in order to further his own agenda. When Miguel suggests they kill Ellen Wolf, a prominent prosecutor with whom he has a conflict, Dexter is unsure. He decides that, although Ellen's work has set many murderers free, although, that is, she is an important cog in the failed system he sees himself as supplementing, she is "just doing her job." Killing her would go against the code, he tells Miguel. When Miguel goes ahead and kills her anyway, this begins to give Dexter a legitimate reason to kill him. Thus via Miguel, the *Dexter* Miami landscape is purified of a powerful woman—Miguel's murder of Ellen Wolf, much like Lila's murder of Doakes, ironically consolidates Dexter as an unambiguously moral subject even as it frees him up to kill again and again, including to kill Miguel (and Lila)—and deals another blow to Ellen's friend LaGuerta, already beleaguered after the death of Doakes and gentling towards Deb. Dexter can feel virtuous in his murders of Miguel—his destruction of the whole trio of Prado brothers, in fact—and George King.

Throughout Season 3, Dexter has been seeing his dead father who cautions him against his deviation from the code and his friendship with Miguel. Dexter, only too late, realizes how right his father has been. Thus Season 3 ends with a return of the law of the father, a return to the original code in a sense. This is not only a return to the father's code, but signals Dexter's return to a code of normativity that belongs to him, that is his legacy as a white, middle-class, heterosexual man. His attempt to reach out to the "wrong" type of Others, to Brian, to Lila, to Miguel, has been revealed as inexperienced foolishness. Now he knows better.

He now knows that he needs to consolidate his performance of normative masculinity by keeping himself close to people whose identities warrant his protection. As has been true throughout the series' three seasons—now that we can look back on them as a whole—this means, in particular, white women, Deb and Rita, whose virtue and protection have been the "real" catalyst for the eradication of the Others discussed in this chapter.

The idea that life is good anchors the third season. Dexter thinks this to himself in episode 3.1 ("Our Father"); after we see him making love with Rita, he ruminates that she "is the scaffolding" holding his performance of normalcy together. And the "truth" of this comes full circle in the season's last episode: "Either way I'm a married man, soon to be a father. But what do I have to offer a child? Just me. Demented Daddy Dexter . . . Sure I'm still who I was. Who I am. Question is who do I become. There're so many blanks left to fill in. But right now, at this moment, I'm content. Maybe even, happy. I have to admit that when all is said and done, life is good" (3.12). Marrying Rita, adopting her children, and creating one of his own, enables and necessitates several things in/from Dexter. To get to this point, he needs to fully incorporate the law of the father, to enter fully into this subject position. To get there, he has to believe that the murders—whether he has committed them himself or merely set the stage for their commission—of Brian, Paul, Doakes, Rita, Ellen, and Miguel are not only necessary to his ability to care for himself, but for his development as a moral masculine subject. His choice of Rita is telling. He suggests in the first season that she is a good choice because she is damaged—like he is—and thus cannot see, does not push and demand that he be a "normal" man. Rita becomes more than the scaffolding; she is, in her unambiguous white blondeness, the innocence Dexter has the moral obligation to protect from the moral failings of the state and from the incursion of Others (Rajiva).

Conclusion

The questions left unasked and unanswered at the end of Season 3 are: at whose and at what expense comes Dexter's happiness? What constitutes the goodness of his life? What right does he have to it? How are we, as viewers, to feel about Dexter and this statement that closes the series (to date)? It seems to me that Dexter's happiness comes at a high price. His life is good, not because he is cleaning up the messes of the state, but because he has found a way to survive and keep on killing. He has done this, he has been able to, because he has at his disposal not only the cunning and the knowledge granted by family and education, but because he carries with him, nay he embodies, the most traditional and accepted version of privilege. Dexter's life is good because he's safe: a married man, an educated man, an employed man, a family man, a home-owner, a white man. His privilege comes at the expense of Others who must be dispatched or tamed in some way, to keep them compliant with Dexter's view of the world, with his moral code. This way of imaging self is very much in tune with Wendy Brown's description of discourses of tolerance, which "gloss[es] the ways in which certain cultures and religions[3] are marked in advance as ineligible for tolerance while others are so hegemonic as to not even register *as* cultures or religions" (*Regulating* 7, emphasis in the original). These discourses are so mundane in their circulation within American culture that it's not surprising that they operate on an intrinsic level, organizing *Dexter* "from a conceit of neutrality that is actually thick with bourgeois Protestant norms" (7).

As a cable access series, *Dexter* appears to specifically seek out the liberal, at times critical viewer and to offer a space of critique of mainstream discourses about crime, punishment, and evil. *Dexter* is drawn extensively from neoliberal and neoconservative discourses. It's deeply moralistic; it presents the state as ineffectual, dangerous, and dead, but offers no real options for change. At the same time, Dexter as criminal is rendered as a neoliberal subject who is able to make rational choices and to be able to care for himself. In fact, a criminal like Dexter can hardly be figured as a criminal at all, but must, rather, be hailed as a neoconservative hero.

Dexter, as a crime drama, labors in the production of mediated discourses about crime and citizenship. The series tries to critique a world that it continually participates in producing, imagines a world where there is freedom and democracy and yet one in which subjects are increasingly governed. Wendy Brown, drawing on Foucault, argues that there is indeed a link between "individual choice and political domination" (705) even if this seems illogical. Zizek concurs via Kant: "the only way to secure social servitude is through freedom of thought" (and hence, the opposite "the struggle for freedom needs some reference to some unquestionable dogma" (3)). In an increasingly neoliberal world, people are seen as resources, "individual entrepreneurs and consumers whose moral autonomy is measured by their capacity for 'self-care'" (Brown, "Neoliberalism, Neoconservativism" 694). They are bound by neoconservative images of citizenship as moral subjecthood. Citizens like Dexter now have responsibilities, including cleaning up the state's mistakes, on one level by filling its holes—by dispensing vigilante forms of justice—but also by cleaning up the broader problems created by the erosion of traditional systems of privilege and power—by purifying the public sphere of Others. In the space where TV dreams of criminality, the death of the state is legitimated by the presence of monsters who now look very much like the rulers of yesterday.

12.
Dexter's German Reception: Why are German Networks so Obsessed (and Troubled) with US Shows?
Vladislav Tinchev

The German TV Landscape

Germany was awaiting USA Pay TV broadcaster Showtime's new show with both impatience and fear. The fans were excited. Some experts, however, were already wearing grim faces. Sources that wish to remain anonymous have reported to me that *Dexter* has been considered morally dangerous to the German public. Regarding television in general, censorship seems to be the only thing Germany and America have in common at present. But their aims are different. In Germany, everything related to violence and self-justice is thoroughly attacked—crime shows find themselves in a gray area because the victims are already found dead. Nudity and everything else connected with sexuality, on the other hand, are freely admitted to public broadcast. In the United States, things are exactly the opposite. The reasons for this lie in the political history of both countries.[1] And there is a fundamental difference between the two nations as far as ratings are concerned.

Before *Dexter* debuted on Free TV on the private German broadcaster RTL2, the Pay TV station Premiere aired it in the fall of 2008. Premiere, as usual, absolutely refused to make their ratings known to the public, so we can only guess as to *Dexter*'s success. Unfortunately, however, we do know the RTL2 ratings much better than we'd like to: they are cruelly disappointing.

Let me give you an overview:

On the average, only 0.46 millions viewers over the age of three watched *Dexter*, which means a 3.7 per cent share of the market.

In the target zone of the 14– to 49–year-olds, 0.35 millions watched—that is to say, a 6 per cent share of the market (*Thomson Media Control*). This failure was neither due to the fact that *Dexter* was shown in an abridged version, nor to the negative reviews written by German critics. *Dexter*'s failure on German television is, in my opinion, the result of a number of factors I would like to point out in this article—even more so because these circumstances set the tone of how US serials are handled by German broadcasters in general.

In short, *Dexter*'s negative reception in Germany was largely the result of the following factors:

- The German debut happened more than a year too late—the target audience knew Dexter already from US or UK DVDs or Internet streaming.
- *Dexter* was given to the wrong network, and, therefore, presented to the wrong audience.
- Unsuitable time slots were chosen.
- The advertising was poor.
- The dubbing of the product turned out to be of poor quality.

All these aspects are, of course, closely related to each other. The weak ratings in the key demographic are caused by *Dexter*'s availability on DVD as well as by the poor dubbing and the time slot (22:55 or 10:55 p.m.). Most target viewers are working, so they cannot stay up late on a Monday night to watch television. In addition to this, it must be considered that those viewers who record the show to watch it later are not included in the ratings, which skews them significantly. The evaluation of ratings is problematic in Germany, and not only for this reason.

The main goal is to reach the key demographic, which, in Germany, consists of the 14– to 49–year-olds. This group of people is most sought after, especially by commercial broadcasters. The public ones are rather inclined to go after the whole population, although it is a well-known fact that mainly elderly people watch their programs. We also must not forget that the average German viewer is 50 years old, i.e. ahead of the key demographic; elderly people make a higher percentage of the whole audience than the latter.

German commercial broadcasters are financed mainly through advertising fees, whereas public ones are subsidized by the state. Advertising during a primetime program is forbidden to them; they are then obliged to advertise only during clearly defined slots between two different programs. But this, too, makes extra money.

The government money is mainly drawn from GEZ (Gebührenein-zugszentrale or Fee Collection Center) fees. Every household in Germany that owns some broadcasting device—radio, a personal computer with internet access, a television—is legally obligated to pay those fees (a monthly amount up to 18 Euro), unless one is too poor to afford it and can prove it. Whether the viewers watch public or commercial programs is of no consequence here. Even traders are forced to pay certain fees for any device they have in stock, no matter whether they have unpacked them or not (Eick 140). This means that ratings serve the public broadcasters mainly to defend their fee income.

Unlike in America, the measurement of ratings in Germany is basically organized by the broadcasters themselves. The ratings of programs and channels established by the AGF/GfK TV panel are the standard tool used in media planning and program research in Germany. After ARD and ZDF had measured ratings on their own through decades, the AGF was founded in 1988 by public and commercial broadcasters (ARD, ZDF, RTL, and Sat.1). Pro7, Kabel1, RTL2, and Tele5 (DSF) soon came aboard. The AGF panel is supposed to represent all those private German households that own at least one TV device and whose head is a citizen either of Germany or of another European Union state. It includes 5,640 households with about 13,000 persons at present; 5,500 households have a German, 140 a European Union head. One household represents 6,000 others, which means that 73.42 million people are television users in Germany.

This simple calculation covers a serious problem as far as non-EU foreign citizens are concerned. All those persons who form the major part of Germany's foreign population—Turks, Russians, Asians, Africans, Serbs, Croats—are not included in the ratings, but they are forced to pay GEZ fees. This situation is made even more puzzling by the fact that the recipients of the fees, the public broadcasters, traditionally regard their purpose not only as entertainment,

159

but mainly as the fulfillment of a "social mission." This means not only culture and education, but to make the rights and troubles of the foreign inhabitants a key topic—inhabitants who, in sum, must pay for watching TV and are unable to influence the quality of its products. We are talking about 7,255,949 people (8.8 per cent of the population) here who absolutely affect the ratings (Statistisches Bundesamt). Not to take them into account is to enter a severe loss in the commercial broadcasters' books. Foreign families are a good deal younger on average than German ones.

Public and commercial German TV stations are entangled in a pillow fight as they court the viewers' favor. In fact, the German TV landscape is determined by three "powers." The first one is ARD/ZDF, the two big publics, between whom competition is made unnecessary by several agreements. The commercial RTL Group is a close second, having been the market leader of the key demographic for years. It consists of RTL itself, RTL2, Super RTL, VOX, n-tv, and the Disney Channel. Third comes the second big commercial group, ProSiebenSat.1; Kabel1 and the news channel N24 also belong to them.

RTL and Pro7 are trying hard to establish a monopoly on the advertising market. This has caused a little scandal lately. It became public that the two commercial groups used their leading position improperly, secretly agreeing on the administering of advertising slots. This led to great disadvantages for the smaller broadcasters. The Federal Cartel Office has sentenced both groups to pay fines of 96 million Euro (RTL) and 120 million Euro (Pro7/Sat.1). RTL2 is currently thinking of suing both groups to pay another 60 million, explaining that they have missed this amount of advertising income through illegal agreements. We must consider that RTL owns 35.9 per cent of RTL2![2]

A "productive" competition, as it is known in the United States, fails to develop between German TV broadcasters. Schedules are developed by avoiding strong shows on other channels instead of taking the offensive and placing strong shows at the same time. It is only too obvious that this does not increase the quality of German television. Closely related to this problem is another one: the dependence of smaller commercial broadcasters on the big ones. In the RTL group, for example, RTL's concerns take precedence over all the others. RTL's programs come first; RTL decides which license products are to be bought and which broadcasters from the group are to get them. Only VOX was allowed to acquire programs on its own—until *CSI* was licensed a few years ago, and until Anke Schäferkordt, ex-directrice of VOX, became the directrice of RTL. The German rights for *Dexter* were bought by the Tele München Group, based on an agreement with RTL, which has now given the show to smaller RTL2.

Made in Germany? No, Thank You!

If God is in the details and if I believed in God, then He is in this room with me. I just wish He brought an extension cord.

("Crocodile," 1.2)

US shows are German broadcasters' only joy—and their biggest problem. They transport quality into German television—at a level which is completely out of reach for any German fictional show. The constant failure of self-made products takes a toll on the nervous systems of those who are responsible. Even the public broadcasters ARD/ZDF, though independent of ratings and aiming at elderly viewers, often arrive at nothing with their own products in the key demographic. Praised and cherished "home-grown" shows are, in some cases, dropped after one episode.

Broadcasters lack both courage and patience. One would love to establish their own products successfully, but, however hard one tries, the viewers continue to ignore all those attempts mercilessly.[3] The latest examples—*R.I.S., Deadline, Post Mortem, Die Anwälte*— all had one thing in common: lousy ratings. But they also have something else in common. All of them are adaptations of successful US shows: *R.I.S.* and *Post Mortem* were attempts at a German *CSI, Deadline* was a cover version of *24*, and *Die Anwälte* (dropped after one episode) copied *Boston Legal*. The similarities cannot be overlooked in either of these cases, though the broadcasters would argue the opposite—in their press reports as well as in personal interviews, like RTL's Fiction Director Barbara Thielen recently did during an interview with the author of this article. There is, of course, nothing to be said against quoting from and alluding to

other shows. But viewers feel taken for a ride when they find themselves watching complete scenes that have been copied almost word
for word, when a whole dramaturgy has been lifted.

After numerous flops during the last few years, none of the
broadcasters want to sink more money into the production of shows
for the following reasons: the overwhelming rival shows from the
US, the lack of interest from German viewers, the long and expensive production processes, and the financial risk that is so much
larger here than in the case of a cheap reality show. In addition,
the costs of US productions have risen to such a level that one has
to consider with care where to cut down. In Great Britain, the
purchase of foreign programs has slowed down, and they have
instead invested money in home-made shows, whereas the only
"big" investments German broadcasters have made are in US shows.
(The website *Serienjunkies* ("Series Junkies"), developed by key
demographic persons and becoming exceedingly popular in
Germany, leaves no doubt as to what their likings are.) Not only
are new mainstream shows like *CSI* and *Desperate Housewives* being
requested by viewers, but also almost forgotten TV treasures like
Buffy, Angel, Firefly, etc., that had been long dropped or concluded.[4]

In the nineties, *ER, The Simpsons, The X-Files*, and *Sex and the
City* dominated the international television landscape (again: we
are speaking of the key demographic here!), in Germany no less
than elsewhere. Towards the turn of the millennium, the demand
subsided; German viewers showed a major interest in home-made
reality shows (as they still do). But then, seven years ago, the *CSI*-
franchise caused an avalanche of enthusiasm: the fervent interest
in the label "Quality Television" was born. These programs became
the utter desire of any foreign broadcaster; no one could miss these
shows. In Germany, it seemed as if a series became more idolized
the more it experimented with narration and visual style. Warner
Bros President Jeff Schlesinger explained this phenomenon similarly: "European audiences are more open to experimenting with
storytelling and dramatic exposition. And they are responsive when
they see something produced by us that has production values
greater than what can be made locally" (Guider).

A specific (German?) irony lies in the fact that the same people
who are loudly criticizing US American politics and values also

show an unrestrained greed for US television shows. When German broadcasters present their new schedules, there is only one important question everybody's asking: Which US shows have been purchased, and when are they to be shown? Never before has there been such a gap between political and "private" opinions and attitudes. In Germany especially, US shows have never been this popular since the 1980s, when viewers were ecstatic about *Miami Vice*, *Dallas*, and *Magnum PI*. Then, too, the US government—that is to say, Reagan—was anything but popular in Europe. But we are speaking of single shows concerning that period, exceptions that were preferred by German viewers—whereas today, a broadcaster is put at the bottom of the scale when it has *only* three US shows to offer.

The German Television—A Serials Killer?

Large sums are spent on US shows. German broadcasters have specialized in delivering the death blow to high-quality programs. In many cases, a commercial broadcaster is completely at sea about what to do with a show once it has been bought—not only small stations like RTL2 and Kabel1, but also the market leaders RTL and Pro7—and must consider a number of factors in scheduling it. On which weekday should the show be placed, i.e. when does it *not* compete with the programs of the other stations in the group? At what time of day or night can a series in demand be shown—or, even more difficult, one with questionable moral contents? Where would a strong program be most helpful to a weaker home-made show? It is no wonder that even the best shows are wasted when so many second-rate questions are hiding the one that should come first: What kind of show have we bought, and how can we make the best out of it?

I would like to give a detailed example here: In 2003, *24* was given to RTL2, two years after the show started in America. This successful series was impossible to handle for the small commercial broadcaster, which showed *24* irregularly between 2003 and 2006 and profoundly confused viewers as a result. The first season was aired in double episodes three nights a week, the second and fourth in double or triple episodes one night a week, the third in between, mostly in single units. The fifth season could be watched in triple episodes every Wednesday night during January and February 2007. The ratings remained at the bottom (at an average of 800,000 viewers). The Pro7/Sat.1 group secured the rights for the sixth season and broadcast it in 2008. The Pay TV station Premiere, which is in close touch with Pro7/Sat.1, owns the rights to the seventh season and has been broadcasting it for paying customers, but Kabel 1 (also a part of the Pro7/Sat.1 group) will show it on Free TV this year starting in September. One show, four stations, bad ratings, huge fan club!

Some shows exchange their time slots several times; others are moved from one broadcaster to the other. The most recent example of this strange strategy is *Without a Trace*. This Jerry Bruckheimer production was shown at first by Pro7 and then given to Kabel1 because of low ratings. After having recovered a little there, it was transferred to Sat.1, which constantly produced flops during that period (January 2007). The ratings went back down, and *Without a Trace* was sent back home to Kabel1.

An even more famous example is the change of *CSI: Las Vegas* from VOX to RTL in 2006. Noticing that the show was gaining more and more ground on VOX, RTL decided to swallow it up into their own schedule, pretending that it would reach an even bigger audience there. The show was really used to establish RTL's own *CSI*-clone *Post Mortem*, placing the latter at 20:15 (8:15 p.m.) as a lead-in for *CSI* at 21:15 (9:15 p.m.). But *Post Mortem* turned out to be of exceedingly poor quality; moreover, the viewers refused to accept their favorite show at a new slot and on a different weekday with a new broadcaster. So *CSI: Las Vegas* suffered a severe loss of viewers. It took the show six months to recover from this crash. It has remained with RTL, but with no better ratings than it used to have at VOX.

Expensive shows are often kept in stock for years because no one dares to broadcast them, and, if one station finally does, they are often placed and treated so carelessly that they are eventually dropped after a few weeks. Pro7 is famous for that (*Dr Who, Alias, Angel*). German broadcasters tend to withdraw to their home territory, concentrating on reality shows—easily and cheaply made, but a threat to their image. RTL, for example, is currently the main target of any critic just because of the permanent program changes and the loyalty towards reality shows. And then there are stations like Sat.1, which have been in free fall for years. Week after week, Sat.1, whose management is constantly changing, tries out new programs, only to drop them immediately, thus doing great damage to their US shows, like *NCIS, Criminal Minds,* and *Without a Trace* (as long as Sat.1 chooses to keep them, that is). The strength of the series format is in its very regularity: of time slot, of weekday, of station, of theme. When this rhythm goes astray, no watching habits can develop on the viewers' side. As most US shows are now available on US DVDs or British DVDs, and every season is broadcast at least one year later in Germany than in America, most people no longer rely on the ever-changing TV program, but rather on Amazon and ebay. The German broadcasters are lucky enough, considering the fact that their US colleagues have refused so far to make their shows available also to foreign customers on the internet. Otherwise, there would be no one left to watch the German programs. US broadcasters, however, point out that they would lose large sums if they offered their shows to foreign internet users. Foreign broadcasters would never pay as much for the license contracts if that were the case. Being thus "protected," US shows remain hits on German TV schedules. In spite of all that, there have been some examples recently as to how to succeed in securing good ratings by means of programming cleverly and in a clear-cut manner. The small commercial broadcaster VOX (which belongs to the RTL group) is the only one to report steady and rising ratings on the German TV market. This development is mainly based on US shows. Three nights a week, VOX exclusively offers American shows during primetime: Monday (*CSI: NY, Shark, The District*), Tuesday (*Criminal Intent, The Closer, Boston Legal, Close to Home*), and Friday (*Crossing Jordan, Gilmore Girls, Men in Trees*). These shows have managed to tie a faithful fan club to themselves who keep watching them week after week, as the ratings show: *Boston Legal,* for instance, constantly nets about 8 per cent of the key demographic viewers, *Criminal Intent* 14 per cent, *Crossing Jordan* 8 per cent during the first two seasons and 14 per cent for seasons 3–6, *CSI: NY* 14.5 per cent, etc. VOX has managed for years to form interesting and entertaining TV evenings, like the *Krimi-Montag* in 2006/2007. Every Monday night was "Crime Time" on VOX, with

CSI: NY, Criminal Intent, and *Crossing Jordan.* All three shows brought in their top German ratings during that time.

The current Tuesday night on RTL, with *CSI: Miami, House,* and either *Psych* or *Monk,* has also had great success. Each of these procedurals produces sensational ratings up to more than 30 per cent of the key demographic. I mention "procedurals" on purpose here: it seems that this type of show functions better than serials on German TV. Even *Lost* and *Grey's Anatomy* are permanently lagging behind the ratings of the procedurals. One could very well go so far as to claim that procedurals make up the mainstream of the German TV landscape, whereas primetime serials are being watched by smaller niche groups. Another criterion that decides the issue of being a favorite with German viewers is whether the program has to do with crime. Germany loves crime shows. Every show that constantly brings in high ratings in Germany is a crime show. For this reason, about 90 per cent of the shows made in Germany are crime shows—and the most successful German export product ever is a crime show, too: *Derrick.*

RTL2: I Love *Dexter*?

Looking at German internet forums or the German ebay, it is evident that mystery and sci-fi shows are leading the lists of favorites. Prices for old *Buffy* or *Battlestar Galactica* seasons remain high, and thousands of fans are discussing them. This, however, is not reflected in TV ratings. Shows that are somewhat "special" or "demanding," like *Six Feet Under, The Shield, Battlestar Galactica,* or *24,* are usually distributed between the smaller stations to try them out, i.e. to save the big broadcasters from being damaged by bad ratings. This way of proceeding has been practised since the foundation of the commercial broadcasters; they are still indecisive or even nervous about putting more experimental shows on the schedule.

In the case of *Dexter,* which has been given to RTL2, this is exactly the problem. I have pointed out that the station's programming depends on the decisions RTL and the Tele München Group make, which shows they buy, and which ones they turn over to RTL2. RTL itself would not dare to try such shows like *Rome* and

Dexter because they are too violent. One fears the damage they might do to the station's image. This fear seems paradoxical, considering the fact that reality shows and self-made productions have turned out to be far more disastrous to the viewers, as far as education and entertainment are concerned. Be that as it may: RTL2 is the one that gets shows like *Dexter*.

One could be of the opinion that it does not matter to a good show where and when it is broadcast. I have shown already that this is far from true. RTL2 has no great audience, and usually the broadcaster's image does have a strong influence on the series it shows—and not the other way around. As a result, *Dexter*'s critics have been outspoken, stressing the fact that RTL2 has *Dexter* just because the show consists mainly of violence and dirty language and is therefore morally reprehensible. RTL2 is viewed as the station devoted to any kind of TV trash, like *Big Brother* and any other kind of morally questionable programming. The network has been trying to polish itself up a little, with the help of quality shows from the United States. It has also taken advantage of the interest—even in scientific circles!—in sci-fi series: those programs are considered "cult" series now, and they make up the biggest part of RTL2's program: *Battlestar Galactica, Andromeda, Stargate, Hercules, Xena Rome* and *24* were supposed to be the next step up the ladder, but this plan was thwarted by their own image and incapacity. I have already discussed the fate of *24*—and the most expensive show ever, *Rome*, was unable to convince viewers either. (It was severely edited, of course.)

RTL2's current flagship series is *Heroes*; the show started with strong ratings in October 2007. Since then, the ratings have gone down 50 per cent; nevertheless, the station has managed to stop its free fall. In 2008, two more "special" programs were scheduled to air: *Dexter* and *Californication*. The hype about *Dexter* had assumed proportions so alarming at that time that a counter-discussion of its moral dubiousness began. The show had become a problem in Germany even before the first episode was broadcast. But all the wailing about self-justice, the making of a hero out of a serial killer, and so on was incapable of weakening the enthusiasm on both the viewers' and the critics' parts. When I mentioned that I was going to show some *Dexter* excerpts during a lecture at Hamburg

University in the summer of 2008, the whole hall buzzed with excitement.

The TV stations who own the rights to *Dexter* do not seem to share this enthusiasm—or are they just unable to communicate it, for example via advertising? RTL2 had announced a huge campaign, which ended up in some underground station billboards. This would not have been so bad if it had not been for the rather absurd slogan: "Keine Angst, der will nur töten"—"Don't be afraid, he just wants to kill," written in huge letters above Dexter's grinning and blood-spattered face. The German phrase alludes to what dog owners cry out when their pet is running up to someone: "Keine Angst, der will nur spielen"—"Don't be afraid, he just wants to play." (There are lots of dog owners in Germany, and almost as many SIGNS referring to dogs, of course.) In sum, this advertising not only made a desperately stupid impression, but confounded the two main prejudices against *Dexter*: blood-thirst and a glorification of self-justice. And when a broadcaster like RTL2 headlines its Monday night schedule—*Californication* and *Dexter*—as "Der unmoralische Montag" ("The immoral Monday"), one feels a stale taste creeping into one's mouth.

The Pay TV broadcaster Premiere, which started *Dexter* on 25 February 2008, made but one move to promote their new show: a "day of the serial killer" with documentaries about this abnormal human (?) species. Premiere, being in urgent need of additional subscribers, rather surprised us by making absolutely no effort to whet the appetite of potential new customers for the new show—even more so when we take into account that Premiere had only two other new shows to offer in 2008: *K-Ville* and *Terminator: The Sarah Connor Chronicles*. The last crowd-pleaser, the seventh season of *24*, had to be put off anyway because of the Writers' Strike in Hollywood. *Dexter* turned out to be the only trump Premiere could play—but the Pay TV station seems so preoccupied with soccer and Formula 1 racing that neither time nor money was left to promote the show.

Most Premiere subscribers mention soccer games and blue movies as their main reasons for the subscription. Premiere makes the impression of being unwilling to change that—just like they will not change their unwillingness to produce their own shows.

During the presentation of their 2008 schedule, Program Director Hans Seger pointed out that Premiere would, of course, love to be the German HBO, but received only bad scripts. Are we supposed to believe in earnest that a whole country is unable to bring forth one good script? Premiere simply refuses to take any risk whatsoever—because its own position in the German market is unstable.

Still in 2008, Hans Seger left Premiere—of his own free will, or so they say. So did RTL2's Program Director Axel Kühn at the end of the same year. *Dexter* turns out to be a pretty good serial killer after all . . .

What was that, Morgan?

Quite often, the German delay in broadcasting new US products is explained by the necessity of dubbing, a process which is supposed to take a lot of time. Considering the remarkably poor results in some cases, one cannot help wondering why it takes so long to ruin a good show. Especially those viewers who have seen (and heard) the original version of some episodes can hardly bear the dubbed one. As Germany is one of the biggest buyers of licensed products worldwide, a large number of dubbing companies exist here that are instructed by the broadcasters to do the dubbing completely—only the final editorial control is kept by the stations themselves. The dialogues are first translated "roughly," focusing on thematic correctness and consistency. After that, the text is worked into a version that can be spoken simultaneously with the original dialogues, without leaving out any subjects or themes. The author of the dubbing script rewrites the dialogues while watching the actors' mouth movements, pauses, and breathing; these dialogues are recorded afterwards. Then, the recorded dialogues are newly mixed with the music and sound atmosphere of the original program. In most cases, producers deliver an International Tone-(IT) or Music-and-Effects-Track (M&E) which contains music and noises, but no spoken dialogues. Sometimes, however, some IT elements must be produced anew (Schütte and Karstens 238). Despite all the efforts to create a dubbed version as close to the original as possible, many things are changed on purpose. Some political, cultural, or decency-related contents seem intolerable to the broadcasters and are therefore toned down, extenuated or even replaced. In addition, terminology is often handled too negligently. The American version of *CSI*, for example, deals skillfully and carefully with scientific terms; the German version cannot cope with that: the GC/MS of the American original regularly turns out to be a simple "Spektrometer," whereas the FT-IR spectrometer becomes a "Spektroskop" (3.17). German translators also have problems with chemical substances. On the visual level, certain issues are "post-produced"—mainly for FSF[5] reasons and often in a very rude manner, cutting out parts or even whole scenes and neglecting the narrative context. Recently, RTL2 came under attack for their dreadful dubbing of *Heroes*. RTL2's German version of *Dexter* comes pretty close to the bottom. In general, it can be said already from the few German episodes I have watched that the synchronization of *Dexter*, produced by the second cheapest dubbing company in Germany, has failed horribly. I am not even alluding to semantic aspects—contents that have been translated incorrectly or insufficiently or have been changed, like Dexter's statement about "Dahmerland," which is translated as "Serienmörderland" ("serial killer's land") in German. (Well—probably a German audience cannot be expected to know the name of one of the most famous serial killers worldwide, Jeffrey Dahmer.) The missing rhythm and the monotony of voices in the dubbed version, especially where male characters are concerned, are not going to add much to the show's fame, personally speaking. It is particularly deplorable that Dexter's German voice is wide of the mark; the charisma of the voice-over is lost that way. It is, of course, not too easy to copy Michael C. Hall's remarkably theatrical voice, but this voice is so utterly important to the whole show. Too much uninspired dramatization, too little irony and subtlety in the German voice—it simply does not match at all! We must consider that *Dexter* is a speaking show; it lives out of dialogue and monologue. The variety of voices should also have been considered. Was it really impossible to find a "black" German voice for Doakes? And was it really necessary to water down Deb's cynical way of speaking until the profile of her character cannot be shaped out any more? The German *Dexter* episodes have a strangely dumb or blurry sound over them, as if one had forgotten to switch on the background noises. The dubbing voices babble out their lines; listening to them, you cannot help imagining some folks sitting around in the studio, holding sheets of paper in their hands and simply reading aloud. The rhythm of the dialogues has been changed or eliminated; the voices are generally too soft and lose themselves in the soundtrack. Premiere, at least, offers the original version as an alternative.

Unfortunately, we must assume that *Dexter* is to be the next victim of German television. He has not yet been treated dexterously in Germany. Nevertheless, thousands of German viewers are willingly sacrificing themselves to *Dexter*—but not on the tables of German broadcasters.

Part Five.
Dexterity: *Dexter* and Genre

13.
The Lighter Side of Death: *Dexter* as Comedy
James Francis, Jr

> **Dee Dee:** Dexter, what's wrong?
> **Dexter:** I have no friends, and I am totally unpopular.
> **Dee Dee:** Duh.
>
> (*Dexter's Laboratory*)

Before 2006, the name Dexter we all knew and loved belonged to an animated character in a series for children. Oddly enough, this young scientific madboy isn't so different from the title character in the Showtime original series *Dexter*. He's methodical, likes his alone time, and is constantly irritated by his sister Dee Dee (whose name also starts with "D" and is truncated from a proper name like Deb on *Dexter*). And the comparisons don't stop there. Cartoon Dexter keeps his secret lab hidden behind a bookshelf, his nemesis (Mandark) has a crush on Dee Dee, and he has to plot against a man driving an ice-cream truck. Showtime's Dexter hides bloody keepsakes in his air-conditioning unit, and his first season rival, the Ice Truck Killer, is also the same man who starts a relationship with Deb. But the animated Dexter is no killer. Michael C. Hall, on the other hand, is just as cute and cuddly as he was on *Six Feet Under* in that morbid undertaker manner, constantly surrounded by death, but, in this role, he is more often than not the one who brings about death by murdering degenerates of society. It's no secret, at least not to the audience, that Dexter Morgan is a cold-blooded serial killer. But to classify him as such stereotypes too easily and takes away from his complete embodiment as a member of and outsider to society. As odd as it may seem to say, *Dexter* is a funny show, and the title character's dark, brooding nature captures and evokes comedic effect throughout the series. There is no laugh track present and no one is being pied in the face; the humor of *Dexter* is subtle and psychologically geared toward audience identification. Serial killers are traditionally no laughing matter, but it is important to examine Dexter's character with regard to other notable fictionalized presentations; the comedy and drama of other filmic serial killers helps us better understand our morbid love for *Dexter*.

Whether it is believed that serial killers are born or made, Dexter is one. Dexter kills only criminals who have escaped justice, but he is a killer nonetheless. What we choose to examine here is how such a killer can be classified as comedic in a series concerning murder, deception, pedophilia, kidnapping, prostitution, and more of life's unpleasant occurrences. The audience is provided flashbacks into Dexter's past dealing with the horrors he witnessed as a child, the teachings he gleaned from his adoptive father Harry, and present-time situations of stalking his victims to show how he became and continues to evolve into a sociopathic ideal. The show uses flashbacks, Memorex references showcasing Dexter's serial-killer beginnings, in order to provide reasoning for his current murders. The framework of a televised series, however, offers but one true beginning—the opening credit sequence. This filmic and serialized TV convention, along with Dexter's persona during kill mode or his position in life that attempts to define normalcy, and the show's mix of dialogue (conversation and inner monologue), provide definite context through which the series showcases drama with a playful reveal of comedy and dramatic irony.

Comedy starts with introductions. Comics take the stage, tell the audience who they are through witty conversation, slapstick action, deadpan delivery, and so forth. Dexter is introduced by the series opening sequence, and, from that beginning, the viewer is able to discern dark, murderous events about to take place with an underlying tone or companionship of levity.

The credit sequence opens with the depiction of a mosquito, the blood seeker. And the irony is the bug attempts to feed upon Dexter's arm, a fellow blood tracker; its ploy is cut short when it is swatted into nonexistence. Maybe the same will have to happen to Dexter in the "end" in order to correct his actions. The viewer then sees Dexter go through his entire morning routine—shaving, flossing, dressing—but it is the breakfast sequence that offers the most comedic intrigue.

No morning is complete without a healthy, hearty breakfast. Dexter slices through wrapping to get at the meat he tosses into the pan. The dexterous (it had to be said) cuts he makes here are the same given to his victims before tossing them to their final resting places with altered existences; the meat goes from raw to cooked just as the victims change from living to dead. In his precision of cuts and meat devouring, Dexter is meticulous and technically skilled in his actions; he embodies part of what the "bad guys" were in their own actions, impulses, desires, and compulsions. Meat preparation and eating are simply symbolic of a general consumption, that of viewer to the series, and how Dexter is consumed by his work, family worries, and killings.

The next three elements of the sequence offer a delightful play on horror and comedy, as well as provide the audience with a hankering for the local breakfast pit stop. Dexter cracks an egg, cooks it sunny side up, and slices through it on his plate; however, blood splatters onto the stove burner and plate. He brews coffee by grinding his own beans, and he cuts a blood orange in half before juicing it. It's easy to see the relevance of these depictions: blood mixes with his everyday doings, stainless-steel products (pan, grinder, eating utensils) are incorporated into his breakfast routine and ritualistic killings, and pink mist flies from the orange, much like that of the seemingly now popular way to describe shooting or explosive deaths in other series such as *Law & Order* and *Grey's Anatomy* or a film like *Jarhead*. And let's not forget the flying teddy-bear stuffing in *Supernatural* (Bobbitt).

Professor Rebecca Bobbitt, pop culture expert and avid *Dexter* viewer, offers astute commentary about the act and filming of *Dexter's* breakfast sequence. She explains, "The way the credits are filmed turns the everyday, quotidian action of making breakfast into an act of violence. We're supposed to see the credits as darkly humorous because we recognize the horror conventions used in the filming—that are applied to actions that aren't related to murder (unless you're really hardcore about ham)." The breakfast routine is also more than reminiscent of horror content; the technical filming aspect conveys meaning, as well. Bobbitt continues:

The close-ups are reminiscent of horror porn. Lingering shots of gore, but instead of bodies being mangled, we see an orange mutilated on a juicer, coffee beans in a grinder. And the jump cuts are meant to unsettle, to keep the eye and mind from relaxing while watching because they break up the action. But then the editing is so playful when the actions occur on beat—the blood hitting the sink on the ding, the dejuiced orange shot cut into sections that change on beat. Cutting on the beat isn't scary, especially when the score is so jaunty. ("RE: dexter's lab")

Again, *Dexter's* form *and* content provide the audience with demonstrations of fear and killing, but the lighter side of death is always present when those elements of the series toy around with convention and link fiction to reality.

As Dexter crosses the final screen setting from right to left, against conventional eye movement, he slightly nods; he bows to the camera and viewer with a tinge of a smirk on his face. He knows that we know. And although his facial expression does not convey it, the sequence score ends with a musical chime, the symbolic wink he physically denies those watching. Dexter has been released, the monster from its cage, and we watch with our own intended winks in return because we want him out there. And with every episode that hooks the audience, each opening sequence the viewer gazes upon, he is continually released and given the freedom to kill again. This is no *Dexter's Laboratory*, but we watch with the same childlike innocence, curiosity, and hint of laughter at this series, with its horrific narrative we turn comedic to make ourselves feel better about the permanent smirks affixed to our own faces.

Dexter's strongest portrayal of the dramatic crime drama/thriller, and its biggest attempt to remove our smiles, is when its title character is in kill mode. In a way, Dexter is always in this state; he doesn't have an on-and-off switch, but when night falls and he is on the prowl for his next victim, the focus is keen and single-minded. In Season 1, Dexter faces the Ice Truck Killer who is later revealed to be his brother Brian; Season 2 brings about a host of problems for the anti-hero, like coping with killing his brother, Deb moving in to feel safe after falling for the killer, his victims' bodies being discovered, and Sgt Doakes finding out the truth; and Season 3 incorporates the Skinner, Dexter mentoring Miguel, and a marriage to Rita. These are all poignant events that Dexter has to deal with throughout the series, and they are certainly not all of the intricate situations the character confronts. But if Dexter is to be a serial killer, it is important to uncover just what kind of serial killer he is through his actions, and comparing him to other notable madmen makes for an easy investigation toward classification.

Dexter has the intelligence of Hannibal Lecter, the comedic bravura of Patrick Bateman, and the moral outrage of John Doe from *The Silence of the Lambs*, *American Psycho*, and *Se7en* respectively. These serial killers' pollution of the moral environment marks them as genre monsters (Simpson 10), and, although Dexter has much in common with his forefathers of serial killing, his monstrosity is tempered. As he works as a blood-splatter analyst, it is only fitting that Dexter's keepsakes of his victims are blood samples on microscopic slides. He is able to keep his victims categorized like a taxonomy of death. Each victim's demise is dutifully planned and executed to the best of his ability, barring any unforeseen circumstances that change procedure. Dexter prepares a safe room to house the victim, and he secures the wrongdoer like a sandwich saran-wrapped to a constructed deathbed. There usually follows light conversation to explain to the victim why the death sentence is about to be pronounced just before he takes his blood sample and provides the swift death strike. Dexter cleans his crime scene with diligence, leaving no trace of himself behind, and he delivers the body to his special dumping grounds in the ocean. This is, of course, not the way that Dexter was able to conduct all of his murders, but it was the routine he set up for himself in Season 1 of the series.

This presentation of his intelligence has much to do with control—control over his victims, adherence to the Code of Harry, the strategic and patient stalk and kill, and the concealment of the crimes from Deb, his family with Rita, and the law enforcers he works with in the department. Dexter is also simply a man of science. His study of blood-splatter patterns turns crime scenes into art installations at times, and his expert analysis befuddles even the smartest detectives and officers on the squad. He is no novice when it comes to his job, but he further excels in his knowledge of the body. Dexter's technical and practical expertise mimics that of Lecter, ever so strong in his comprehension of how the body functions (organs, blood flow, the human mind). He remains composed (at least outwardly) in the most stressful of situations until the time comes to confront a victim and then the emotions are released in a mesmerizing soliloquy to which the victim doesn't get much time to respond before death.

Dexter uses his professional know-how to study a crime scene and throw off the police at the same time, if it's a crime he's trying to conceal for himself or get ahead of the detectives for his own investigation. In *The Silence of the Lambs*, Lecter offers Clarice clues about the serial killer she is tracking, but he never gives outright information that would solve the case; he likes watching others think and work to solve a mystery that has taken him no time at all to uncover. Dexter's actions play on the same intellect; he dare not give all that he knows about a crime-scene investigation away to the police. He might give Deb a hint to help with her career ambitions or throw the police off the trail completely, but he wants others to discover the truth through their own brain processes; he would rather not be the kid everyone copies exam answers from in class. In another light, his intelligence can be a detriment to his serial-killer lifestyle.

Dexter's intellect of control can sometimes be too exacting and too precise where the overabundant planning simply seems comical. His night-time stalks, plastic-wrap tombs, and inner monologues about crime-scene analysis attempt so much perfection that the viewer has no escape but laughter in reaction to such a display of obsessive compulsive disorder behavior. Bateman springs to mind when his murder of Paul Allen in *American Psycho* is considered. He rambles on and on about Huey Lewis and the News—the band's early work, sound, and political statement about society—while playing "Hip to be Square." Bateman is unlike Dexter in that his violence with the ax is somewhat uncontrollable, although he does wear a plastic raincoat and cover the floor with newspaper to keep things tidy. His attempt to relate the history of a band to his murder victim is yet another display of a serial killer's compulsion for order; historicizing the band's success chronologically is similar to Dexter's taxonomy of victims. Both illustrate there is a place for everything and everything is in its place. This orchestration of actions is so grand and over the top, it almost approaches camp in the way that camp is art that proposes itself seriously, but cannot be taken altogether seriously because it is "too much" (Sontag 59). The absurd nature of serial killers being tidy and teaching their victims about life before killing them is as dark as comedy can be exposed.

The lighter side is revealed after Bateman finishes his death blows to Paul. He is covered in blood, but still manages to slick back his hair and compose himself; order absolves chaos. Although Bateman sees this as a return to civility, he is clearly mistaken. This is the blood-smeared mask the viewer sees through even in the calmest demeanor he attempts to project. Dexter's break occurs in the same vein; he is the picture of sanity until he has to wiggle out of a situation that could reveal his true nature and crimes. In the isolated room he constructs to kill Freebo in Season 3 ("Finding Freebo"), Dexter has everything in order as usual until Miguel interrupts the full proceedings. As Dexter attempts to sneak out of the scene, Miguel confronts him and he has no option but to express disarray on his face in a classic *I Love Lucy* "uh oh" moment. And this isn't the first time followers of the series encounter this situation; in Season 1's "Seeing Red," Dexter hits Rita's ex (Paul) with a frying pan in the kitchen. His body falls limp to the floor, and although he was asking for it by enraging Dexter when he was only trying to do the dishes, the problem is that Rita and the kids are in the next room. Dexter allows his emotions to get the best of him, and, of course, breaks a code of Harry. He stands over Paul's motionless body with a grimace reminiscent of a child caught spilling milk on the kitchen floor. Dexter unravels before our eyes in a moment of dire consequences; the only thing missing is a sound bite of "Eek!" But laughter rings through because the audience knows Dexter will pull through somehow so there is no salient fear present, or at least none that lasts too long before he manages to squeak by danger or luck out of the situation.

Bateman's introduction is also similar to that of Dexter. It's a sequence of his morning routine—exercise, shower, pore-minimizing mask he leaves on for ten minutes, and other product-driven cleaning applications. He is a neat freak, but what stands out the most is the scene where he peels off his herb-mint facial mask and describes himself. Bateman says, "There is an idea of a Patrick Bateman, some kind of abstraction but there is no real me, only an entity, only something illusory. And though I can hide my cold gaze, and you can shake my hand and feel flesh gripping yours, and maybe you can even sense our lifestyles are probably comparable, I simply am not there" (Harron). This is the same mirrored confrontation the viewer sees (or doesn't see) of Dexter. Both killers have faces they don't fully recognize, and the audience is unsure of the identities within, as well. The irony present is that of serial killers knowing everything there is to know about the human condition, but they have no clue about their own identities. In a quirky moment of intertextuality, Season 1's "Return to Sender" lets the viewer know that Dexter uses an alias, Dr Patrick Bateman, in order to secure the animal tranquilizer he uses on his victims. He is forced to erase this alter persona when his lab mate (Vince Masuka) includes him in a compiled listing of local doctors who could be responsible for one of the murders. The alias disappears but Dexter and his plight are not quelled.

Dexter has seasons to go before the series comes to an end, so it's not possible to predict what will happen to the title character and supporting cast; however, the end of *American Psycho* may provide a clue. Bateman declares that nothing has changed for him; he remains an outsider looking in, but not really wanting to be a part of the society he despises. He declares, "My pain is constant and sharp, and I do not hope for a better world for anyone. In fact, I want my pain to be inflicted on others; I want no one to escape" (Harron). Dexter's current outlook on life isn't as bleak; he does hope for good things to come to Deb, Rita, and the kids. But he continues to inflict pain on those who do wrong in his judge-and-jury eyes. As of now, the question cannot be answered whether he will find further fulfillment in life or become more of a hollow void like Bateman.

What does remain is Dexter's aforementioned judgment on low-life members of society; he has zero tolerance for anyone causing harm to others. In some ways, Dexter's life is like a morality play where he gets to be the embodiment of Death, Knowledge, and Confession (*Everyman*). These allegorical names are reminiscent of the cardinal sins John Doe kills for in *Se7en*. His fascination with the way people adhere to these sins ties directly to the way Dexter is repulsed by those who commit them.

Serial killers are typically ordinary outcasts from society by choice and/or social nonconformity. By their designation as "others," they are afforded a unique vantage point from which to observe; they oscillate between the public and private spheres like the French flâneur. And this is exactly what John Doe and Dexter have in common; they observe human behavior enough to know who can be pronounced guilty of sinful crimes against others and therefore supply swift judgment. Of course, John Doe's very ordinariness is the means by which he can escape suspicion. Killing for Doe represents a profession that bestows on him an identity that he lacks but desperately craves. Dexter's formal profession as a blood-splatter analyst does not supply him with a meaningful identity. He is constantly berated by Sgt Doakes and not considered an integral part of investigation teams, although he is typically a few steps ahead of anything the detectives have uncovered. Dexter, like Doe, is defined by his killings; they provide him a profession or moral hobby of which he can be proud, but he still has to keep that life a secret.

Se7en has a catch; the film revolves around the Seven Deadly Sins and culminates with an ending that brings John Doe to Envy and Det. Mills to Wrath. Doe envies the life of the detective—his normal civil servant job, beautiful wife, and possibility of fatherhood. Along those same lines, Dexter once thought the idea of Rita and the kids was simply a good cover for normalcy, but he evolves this belief into an enviable ideal of standard living. Doe realizes he is a threat to the detective's promise of a good life, so much so that he kills his wife and unborn child with one beheading. This action of interrupting a happy home forces the detective to kill Doe and eliminate any further threat to his life. Mills shoots the serial killer to right the wrong, although it has already been committed, of family injustice.

This storyline carries through to Dexter in mutated form. In the Season 3 episode "The Lion Sleeps Tonight," Dexter is forced to protect his new family when a child predator (Nathan Marten) takes a liking to Rita's daughter, Astor. He is displeased to see the man talking to Astor in the grocery store, but he ignores the situation until Marten begins stalking and taking photos of the girl; he cannot allow the sin of Lust to flourish. Unlike Dexter's old staple set-up

183

for killing, he breaks into Marten's home and strangles him in front of the computer where he was going through photos of Astor. Dexter's actions are against the Code of Harry because Marten is a child predator, not a killer. But the threat to his family, his beard of normalcy turned wish fulfillment, is strong enough for him to pass judgment on the man for his sinful thoughts and actions. Dexter protects his family the way Det. Mills would have wanted to before his wife and unborn child were murdered. His own envy of familial commonality provides enough fuel to exact Wrath upon an impending hazard to the family unit. In Dexter's own words, "Nobody hurts my children" (3.3).

Dexter's words are certainly to be taken seriously as Marten finds out, but the comedic aspect of the series should never be overlooked. He protects his family like a lion to cubs, but can also find time to darkly dream about killing Rita's yoga instructor and reject such a form of normalcy. Okay, so the humor in *Dexter* isn't exactly slapstick, laugh-out-loud funny. It's dark, brooding, and a bit maniacal. It sounds strange to say but death is funny to a degree; it can be cartoonish in television and film, and because we know it is only a fictitious depiction, the fear we have for our own mortality can be relieved through the amusement of such scripted situations. The viewer comes so close to death s/he has no escape other than that of laughter. It is not because Dexter is killing someone deemed bad that makes it okay to laugh; the situation calls for laughter to ease the nervousness and fear of death that a fictional televised series brings so close to home.

The televised format of the series extends the content, message, psychology of fear, and underlying comedy more than is possible in a theatrical release; the audience has more time to digest and adjust to any fear the series purports. *Dexter's* comedic factor becomes easier to understand and participate in because viewers can watch with all the lights on, TiVo an episode for later, watch during the daytime, and a host of other variables not available in the dark setting of a movie theater. The fearful experience of watching things go bump in the night in a theater setting is lessened by the Showtime presentation. In this manner, *Dexter* may not be too far removed from *Dexter's Laboratory*; the brother and sister relationships are evident, both Dexters are geniuses of their craft, and the storylines provide the viewing audience with the single question, "How's he going to get out of this one?" Much of the audience has the same family issues, concerns about work proficiency, and tough situations to manage in life. Dexter is simply a hyper-realization of any man or woman, along with the added fact of being a serial killer.

Dexter *is* that one steely-faced, non-toothy grinning "pinup-boy serial killer" (Alston) photograph of himself used in the series promotional ads. His eyes are piercing, smile tight-lipped, neck tense, face all aglow, and yet the right side of his face is splattered with blood. He is desperately trying to portray happiness through the obvious red spray, daring us to believe his guy-next-door looks and not see the blood. And we buy it wholeheartedly. Maybe it's ketchup, or paint, or soda. This is the comedy of *Dexter*. In the face of murderous honesty, the viewer sees nothing more than a guy s/he would do anything to have as a friend. Audiences understand fictional characters like Hannibal Lecter to be intelligent and persuasive, Patrick Bateman as neurotic and obsessive compulsive, and John Doe as exacting and morally repulsed by life. Dexter is just one of the guys, a face in the crowd, an unclear reflection in a mirror. His everyday life of going to work, dealing with a sibling, managing a new family, and staying busy with a personal hobby is no different than that of a viewer tuning in to watch the show. But Dexter's assumption of the role of Regular Guy sits uncomfortably on his broad shoulders (Dean). The fear that he generates as a serial killer is assuaged because the closer we get to an element of fear that typically cannot physically or mentally harm us (i.e. fear depicted in television and film), the more apt we are to laugh about it, just like the violence showcased in a cartoon; it relieves the tension of real-life identification. Dexter's kill-mode personae and the opening credits often force viewers to go below surface presentations to make the connection to humor, but such is not the case with regard to dialogue.

Dexter's inner monologue is where stand-up resides; it is as strong as JD's self-banter in *Scrubs*. It was previously mentioned that Dexter has to erase his alias as Dr Patrick Bateman because Masuka includes him in a suspect list (1.6); he's terribly proud of his accomplishment. Before this happens, when Masuka points out that he has uncovered the animal tranquilizer and requested a list of doctors who could secure the drug, Dexter jokes to himself, "That's it. No more donuts for Masuka" (1.6). In the same episode, Dexter worries his cover will be blown by a child who may have witnessed his murderous actions. He finds it amusing and disappointing at the same time that his life's work might all be undone by a child. He internally remarks, "I usually like kids" (1.6). It is this type of self-reflection and inner monologue that puts comedy on the surface in *Dexter*. The material is witty and sharp, but the conversational dialogue is just as powerful in nature.

Dexter tackles therapy in Season 1's "Shrink Wrap" (1.8). He investigates the mysterious deaths of Dr Meridian's patients, played by Tony Goldwyn who also directed the episode. There's an element of *Analyze This* or *The Sopranos* any time a therapist attempts to provide an outlet for a killer to reflect upon life, and *Dexter* matches that dark comedy perfectly. During the first session Meridian says, "So tell me about Harry. What kind of stuff did you guys do together?" Dexter replies, "You know, normal father-son stuff," and then we see a flashback of young Dexter attacking Harry in a night-game trial run of what could only be described as "ambushing the victim" (1.8). The conversation is hilarious because the viewer knows what dark secrets reside in Dexter's memories; it's situational comedy with a terribly sinister atmosphere.

Dexter tolerates a couple of therapy sessions before coming back after hours to check out the doctor's office. With perfect timing Rita sends a text message that questions, "Where are you?" Dexter replies aloud, "Breaking and entering," moments after finding a way into the office. As he examines Meridian's recorded sessions, Dexter invokes cartoon merriment when he says to himself, "You're a mean one, Mr Shrink." And even in his serious moment of discovery as he realizes the control Meridian has been exacting over his female patients, Dexter muses, "I think I've had a breakthrough in therapy" (1.8). The light and dark of narrative mix effortlessly in these moments of texting and monologues, and with two more sessions the dark comedy never stops.

Dexter refrains from killing the doctor in his second-to-last session. He mentally quips, "This is ridiculous; I could be killing him right now," as he sits on the sofa and allows Meridian to try a deep-breathing technique on him. The procedure works; Meridian gets Dexter to think about moments of powerlessness, and this moment unlocks his struggle for control, memories of Harry, and a flashback of being left amid a bloodbath as a child. The session provides an awakening for Dexter's intimacy issues, and when he returns for his last session he comes out of the serial-killer closet. He says, "I'm gonna tell you something, and I've never told anyone before." After a long pause Dexter admits, "I'm a serial killer." He continues, "That feels so amazing to say out loud." It's a funny revelation, but the humor is heightened when Meridian thinks Dexter is just feeling better and in a jovial mood. Dexter assures him, "I'm not joking. I kill people" (1.8). The viewer laughs somewhat nervously at the entire situation because now that the secret is out the doctor must die.

In the kill room Dexter is almost remorseful about the situation, because Meridian helps him realize that he can control his killing; therapy works. But as soon as he puts on his helmet with splatter guard it's back to business as usual. He tells the doctor, "You helped me to accept what I really am. I'm grateful for that, but I was raised with a certain set of principles" (1.8), and those principles will not allow him to overlook the murder of innocents. As funny as the series can be at times in dialogue and action, it never fails to remind viewers that Dexter is a serial killer.

In the Season 1 finale ("Born Free"), Dexter talks about the tragedy he and Deb face in their lives post-Ice Truck Killer. Rita comments, "Poor thing [Deb] must be a mess, falling for a serial killer." Without missing a beat Dexter responds, "What are the odds?" Aside from this funny moment, tragedy is an important element to mention for a television drama. Like the masks of theater and Greek narrative, comedy cannot exist without tragedy and vice versa. *Dexter* is a terribly dramatic series; at times it can be horrifying, but the comedy is never too far away to keep the balance and remind the viewer that life (and death) is a twisted mix of joy and sorrow. Dexter's inner monologue reports, "I live my life in hiding; my survival depends on it" (1.12), and, in this manner, no one in the series is ever who they truly claim or appear.

Deb wears a smile on her face to hide the suffering within from falling in love with a serial killer; Dexter keeps a stoic countenance but is secretly grinning ear to ear when someone references a kill of his that has made the world somewhat safer; and even Rita attempts to put on a happy face for her children before allowing feelings of regret and fear to reveal the worry she greets each day. They, and other characters in the series, wear these interchangeable faces like theatrical masks, only letting happiness express itself in the comforting arms of grief. Season 1 presents all of this material but the same patterns follow as the show progresses.

Dexter remains a horrific comedy because the viewer has come as close as possible to the terror of a serial killer as s/he would like before realizing how much in common is shared with the character. Clearly as much as someone can identify with the "normal" parts of Dexter's life, s/he can only live vicariously through a fictional character to express a related personal sinister side; the Dark Passenger within the viewer is subdued by dramatic irony and comedic moments of the series. We fear and laugh at the opening sequence to *Dexter* because of its comedic wit in matching everyday life with a serial killer's action. No other current series correctly identifies how easily the approach to killing links to waking up, following a prescribed bathroom routine, eating breakfast, and heading off to professional job duties or hobbyist activities. As the old adage from *Freaks* declares, Dexter is "one of us" (Browning). At the end of Season 1, he floats through a daydream ticker-tape parade held in his honor where crowd members shout, "You sliced him up good," "Way to take out the trash—Thanks, buddy," and "Alright Dexter, protecting our children!" But in his words Dexter simply reminds us, "Yeah they see me; I'm one of them . . . in their darkest dreams" (1.12). Wink (chime).

14.
In a Lonely Place? *Dexter* and Film Noir

Alison Peirse

The title of this essay references *In a Lonely Place* (1950), considered one of the best and bleakest of film noirs. The film stars Humphrey Bogart as struggling screenwriter Dixon Steele, a dangerous anti-hero who regularly succumbs to apparently murderous rages. The film explores Steele's world as he stalks the streets of Los Angeles, accused of the murder of Mildred Atkinson (Martha Stewart). The themes and atmosphere of *In a Lonely Place* are symptomatic of classic film noir, which Andrew Spicer characterizes as "dark, malign and unstable where individuals are trapped through fear and paranoia, or overwhelmed by the power of sexual desire. Noir's principal protagonists consist of the alienated, often psychologically disturbed, male anti-hero and the hard, deceitful femme fatale he encounters" (4–5). This essay explores the film noir qualities of *Dexter*, a series described by its cinematographer Romeo Tirone as a "film noir graphic novel" (Tyree 82). While a study of the visual appearance of the show would be instructive in terms of film noir, especially in relation to lighting, framing, and music, this essay has chosen to offer a structural analysis of the first three seasons. It is argued that *Dexter* draws on some of the central tropes of film noir, including the male anti-hero, detection narratives, flashbacks, voice-overs, and the femme fatale. As such, the essay title speaks both to *Dexter*'s film noir origins while also signaling the protagonist's role in the series: by his very nature, Dexter is destined to be alone.

Film noir is characterized by crime films, thrillers, gangster films, and dark melodramas. The term can be traced back to film critic

Nino Frank, writing in Paris in 1946. In his article "Un nouveau genre 'policier': l'aventure criminelle," published in *L'Ecran Français* (Frank), Frank coined the term film noir (translated as "dark film"), as a play on the Série noire, a popular series of black-covered paperbacks published in the crime-thriller genre. Frank conceptualized film noir in response to viewing a number of psychologically complex American thrillers that significantly departed from the crime cinema of the pre-war years. These films included *The Maltese Falcon* (1941), *Murder My Sweet* (1944), *Double Indemnity* (1944), *Laura* (1944), *The Woman in the Window* (1944) and *The Lost Weekend* (1945) (Spicer 2; Krutnik 15; Naremore 13). The first film noirs are debated to be *Stranger on the Third Floor* (1940) and *Among the Living* (1941) (Spicer 49; Krutnik 22), but *The Maltese Falcon* is the most famous early entry in the canon. In her entry on film noir in *The Cinema Book*, Jane Root claims that "the major period of noir production is usually taken to run from *The Maltese Falcon* in 1941 to *Touch of Evil* in 1958" (305).

Film noir emerges from a number of movements, genres, and literary sources. The fast-talking, wisecracking anti-heroes of American hard-boiled fiction, characterized by Sam Spade in Dashiell Hammett's *The Maltese Falcon* (1930), have a significant impact on noir. In addition, the contributions of Raymond Chandler, Dorothy B. Hughes and Cornell Woolrich are not to be underestimated, while James M. Cain wrote *The Postman Always Rings Twice* (1934), *Mildred Pierce* (1941), and *Double Indemnity* (1943), all of which were remade as successful film noirs. The American gangster films of the 1930s are also an important influence, featuring iconic actors such as James Cagney and Edward G. Robinson in *The Public Enemy* (1931) and *The Roaring Twenties* (1939). European influences can also be discerned in German Expressionism of the 1920s. The distorted, anti-realistic backgrounds, unstable protagonists, and intense chiaroscuro lighting demonstrated in *Das Cabinet Des Dr Caligari* (1919), *Der Golem* (1920), and *Der Müde Tod* (1921) impacted upon the visual style and atmosphere of film noir. Furthermore, Mark Bould argues that its origins can also be traced back to French Poetic Realism (2), while Spicer cites the Gothic Romance, the Weimar Street film, the work of Val Lewton at RKO Studios, and Orson Welles' *Citizen Kane* (1941) as important stimuli for noir (10–19).

A central debate in the study of film noir is whether it should be considered as a genre or a movement. Susan Hayward suggests that film noir "is often referred to as a sub-genre of the crime thriller or gangster movie—although as a style it can also be found in other genres (for example, melodrama, western). This is why other critics see film noir as a movement, rather than a genre" (128). So, rather than functioning like the western, science-fiction, or gangster film, Hayward argues that noir is predicated upon visual style, its cinematography composed of "high-contrast lighting, occasional low-key lighting, deep shadows and oblique angles to create a sense of dread and anxiety" (129). Paul Schrader also believes that film noir is not a genre, and that it should be categorized as "a specific period of film history, like German Expressionism or the French New Wave" (230). Bould asserts that film noir is more than a visual style, suggesting that it can also be defined according to narrative, thematic, and stylistic considerations (12), while Spicer argues against definitive interpretation, pointing out that "any attempt at defining film noir solely through its 'essential' formal components proves to be reductive and unsatisfactory because film noir, as the French critics asserted from the beginning, also involves a sensibility, a particular way of looking at the world" (25). For the purposes of this essay, noir is interpreted in a structural manner: in terms of its gendered character types (the conflicted and alienated male protagonist and the femme fatale), its themes (detection of crimes and preoccupation with violent death), and modes of narration (flashbacks and voice-overs).

"The Dark Defender": Dexter as Noir Detective

Harry (to Dexter): There are people out there who do really bad things. Terrible people. And the police can't catch them all. Do you understand what I'm saying?

("Dexter," 1.1)

Dexter Morgan is the archetypal noir protagonist: solitary, unstable, and dangerous, a city-dweller who solves crimes beyond the remit of the law. As such, parallels can be made between Dexter and the protagonists of hard-boiled fiction and film noir. These characters are epitomized by Hammett's Sam Spade in *The Maltese Falcon* and Chandler's tough private eye Philip Marlowe, created in *The Big Sleep* (1939) and recurring in other novels including *Farewell My Lovely* (1940). Dick Powell played Marlowe in the film adaptation of *Farewell My Lovely*, entitled *Murder My Sweet*, and Robert Montgomery played Marlowe in *Lady in the Lake* (1947). However, Humphrey Bogart is the star most closely associated with the noir protagonist, playing Spade in the film adaptation of *The Maltese Falcon*, Marlowe in *The Big Sleep* (1946), war veteran Frank McCloud in *Key Largo* (1948), and Steele in *In a Lonely Place*. James Naremore comments that "Bogart's persona was tough, introspective, emotionally repressed, and fond of whisky and cigarettes; within certain limits, he suggested a liberal intellectual . . ." (27). Bogart's characters possess the ability to talk or fight their way out of any situation while simultaneously charming the "dames" and planning their next moves. All of these qualities (minus the cigarettes) can be seen in Dexter, an intelligent and maverick anti-hero who moves beyond the law in a dystopian city, seeking out truth and dispensing violence where he feels it is justified.

While Dexter's dark, anti-heroic detective status is cemented in season-long story arcs, a number of episodes reinforce it within specific storylines. In "The Dark Defender" (2.5), Dexter is called to a crime scene at a comic-book shop. The manager Denny Foster has been murdered, his head caved in with a snow globe. Dexter notices a graphic art poster on the wall entitled "The Dark Defender." Dexter discovers that "The Dark Defender" is Foster's personal spin on the Bay Harbor Butcher. The Dark Defender poster configures Dexter's role within the series. The image suggests darkness (with the attendant noir resonance), while also reinforcing Dexter's protagonist role, moving beyond the law and into the underworld, where the police cannot or will not go.

Film noir is characterized by its complex modes of narration based on detection. Indeed, the famous literary/cinematic antecedent is when Howard Hawks, director of *The Big Sleep*, asked Raymond Chandler, the author of the novel, who killed the chauffeur, and Chandler replied, "Dammit, I don't know" (Sutherland 5). *Dexter* moves through multiple interconnected levels of narration in its first two seasons. In Season 1, *Dexter* has three inter-dependent lines of narrative action. The first is based on the Miami Police Department's search for the Ice Truck Killer. The second level relates specifically to Dexter: while being involved in the Miami PD investigation, Dexter is privy to information that the police do not have and is tracking the Killer independently. Dexter's extra-curricular investigations have an intensely personal quality, as the Killer increasingly engages directly with Dexter in his crime scenes. The third level of detection relates to Dexter's "projects," his sepa-rate and private investigation of numerous murderers who have evaded justice. When he has proof that they have committed crimes, he then kills them himself (this mode of narration is discussed in more depth in the "Dexter and Clues" section, below).

Dexter and Clues

My friend left this. He's showing me where to go.
(Dexter's voice-over in "Let's Give the Boy a Hand," 1.4)

In her analysis of the "Road Hill House" murder, taking place in the English county of Somerset in 1860, Kate Summerscale writes, "the word 'clue' derives from 'clew,' meaning a ball of thread or yarn. It had come to mean 'that which points the way' because of the Greek myth in which Theseus uses a ball of yarn, given to him by Ariadne, to find his way out of the Minotaur's labyrinth" (68). In order to follow a narrative of detection, the protagonist must be able to investigate and follow a series of clues, to unravel the ball of yarn. In "Clues: Roots of an Evidential Paradigm," Carlo Ginzburg offers a qualitative study of the individual who seeks out "clues" and apparently insignificant data. Ginzburg argues that this epis-temological model of "conjectural knowledge" based on inference and guesswork has been emerging since the nineteenth century, and is predicated upon deduction: "though reality seems to be opaque, there are privileged zones—signs, clues—which allow us to pene-trate it" (123).

Dexter is obsessed with clues. Season 1 follows the Ginzburg model as Dexter analyses a variety of apparently insignificant clues that will lead him to the Killer. By episode four, it is apparent to

193

Dexter that the Killer is playing a game predicated upon Dexter's history. Looking through his photo album in "Let's Give the Boy A Hand" (1.4), Dexter finds a smiley face drawn on the back of a photograph of himself and Harry at the Angel of Mercy hospital. Pursuing his hunch, Dexter decides to go alone to the now-disused hospital and finds the partially amputated ice-rink nightwatchman, Tony Tucci.

Clues also form the third level of detective narration in Season 1. In addition to working with Miami PD to apprehend the Killer (level one), and making his own counter-investigation of the Killer (level two), Dexter also actively seeks out new "projects." "Shrink Wrap" (1.8) features a one-episode storyline in which Dexter investigates the apparent suicide of a number of highly successful Miami career women. Dexter reads the women's police files and studies photographs of the crime scenes, searching for a clue that will unite the apparently disparate "suicides" and reveal the "truth," that (as Dexter believes) they were all murdered. Dexter discovers that they all share the same therapist, Dr Emmett Meridian, and that Meridian gets his clients addicted to prescription drugs and then encourages them to commit suicide. In the course of his investigation, Dexter has several meetings with the man and finds them surprisingly useful, commenting, "I can't kill Meridian yet, I need another therapy session." He then secures the final clue, the video evidence needed to ascertain Meridian's guilt, and kills him.

While film noir partially descends from the hard-boiled detective novel, thereby having a certain influence on *Dexter*, it can be argued that the series also draws from the "Golden Age" classic detective and/or mystery model, originating in Edgar Allan Poe's amateur detective C. Auguste Dupin, and then made famous by Agatha Christie's Hercule Poirot, Dorothy L. Sayers' Lord Peter Wimsey, and Arthur Conan Doyle's Sherlock Holmes. Frank Krutnik makes a clear distinction between hard-boiled and golden age fiction, arguing that in hard-boiled fiction "ratiocination— the power of deductive reasoning—is replaced by action, and the mystery element is displaced in favour of suspense" (39). However, it can be argued that Dexter's mode of investigation mirrors traditional detective narratives, where the smallest of apparently innocuous clues can lead to the resolution of the case. Indeed,

Dexter can be viewed as a detective in the mold of Poe's Dupin. Popularized as a character in "Murders in the Rue Morgue" (1841) and "The Purloined Letter" (1844), Dupin moves on an intellectual plane beyond that of the beleaguered Parisian police force. In "Murders in the Rue Morgue," the narrator transcribes his conversation with Dupin: "'we must not judge of the means,' said Dupin, 'by this shell of an examination. The Parisian police, so much extolled for acumen, are cunning, but no more. There is no method in their proceedings, beyond the method of the moment'" (Poe 132). Dexter's projects are characterized by a failing on the part of the Miami PD. Either the murders have been misclassified as suicides, or, due to technicalities or lack of evidence, the killers have escaped justice. Mirroring Dupin, Dexter moves beyond the confines of the law (both literally and intellectually) to create his own forms of justice.

Detecting Voice-overs

The voices are back. Excellent.

(Dexter's voice-over in "Dex, Lies and Videotape," 2.6)

In her case study of *Double Indemnity*, Root notes that voice-over narration is a key characteristic in noir films (311), while Maureen Turim argues that the noir voice-over is the "transcription of a literary device—as the voice derived from the hard-boiled detective fiction . . . and the French Série noir" (171). The noirish trope of the protagonist's voice-over is regularly manifested in *Dexter*. Atypically for a contemporary American television series, Dexter is an extremely introverted lead character who possesses little ability to empathize with people, and lives day to day with the secret that he is a serial killer. The only people who discover his real identity—the antagonists Rudy Cooper (Season 1), Sergeant James Doakes and Lila West (aka Lila Tournay) (Season 2), and District Attorney Miguel Prado (Season 3)—are murdered by Dexter himself. Nevertheless, Dexter is able to project the appearance of normality while inwardly having deviant and murderous thoughts and desires. As such, to counter Dexter's secretive nature, the series makes extensive use of voice-over. The voice-over offers Dexter's real opinion on the events taking place around him, an opinion that is always at odds with his outward comments and demeanor. Examples of this include a scene with his adopted sister Debra Morgan in "The Dark Defender," when Debra states, "If Dad taught us one thing, it's the value of human life." While outwardly appearing to agree, Dexter's voice-over comes back with, "Yeah, but I think we had different homework assignments."

The dichotomy between Dexter's outward projection and inner subjectivity is further highlighted in "Love, American Style" (1.5), when Dexter has a conversation with a policeman. Dexter's girlfriend Rita Bennett is concerned as her Cuban friend, a maid at the hotel where they both work, is upset as her husband is missing. Dexter asks the policeman if many Cuban illegal immigrants have disappeared. The man explains that if the immigrants can't pay the release fee to the trafficker, they disappear, and states that "freedom is just another word for one more way to get fucked." Dexter inclines his head, and in voice-over says, "Sounds like someone's doing something very bad." He follows the man to the back of the police van and asks if they have any suspects. The man says there are several Cuban suspects, but they lack the evidence required for a conviction. Dexter looks down, and in voice-over muses, "If warrants were applied for, their names will be in the database." The man pats him on the back, misinterpreting Dexter's silence for emotional distress. He tells Dexter there is nothing he can do, and then walks out of shot. Dexter remains in the left-hand side of the frame in medium shot, as the police van drives off to the right. He smiles, and in voice-over reveals, "You'd be surprised."

This is a typical exchange between Dexter and another character, where Dexter's voice-over contradicts his outward appearance. In this sequence, Dexter's thoughts are communicated almost entirely in voice-over, creating an alternative version of events based on his decision to seek out and kill the illegal traffickers. The subjectivity implicit in the contradictory voice-over allows the audience to feel close to Dexter, to be on "the inside," and to know what the rest of the characters do not, that Dexter's urges to kill will shortly be satisfied again.

Dialogue is not always considered closely in Television Studies.

Christine Geraghty suggests that to provide a thorough aesthetic analysis of the medium, the formal dimensions need to be systematically examined. Analysts need to look beyond narrative patterns and reflect on the audio and visual dimensions of the television text, considering writing and dialogue, performance and characterization, and innovations in the medium (33–5). Enthusiastically taking up Geraghty's point that "it is surprising in a medium that is strongly associated in a variety of ways with talk, with 'overheard conversations' . . . that the tone and delivery of dialogue is often overlooked in favour of narrative progression" (34), I would argue that the utilization of voice-over in *Dexter* is particularly significant. The distinction between Dexter's vocal responses and contradictory voice-over create a multiple-level point of view. Dexter is at best monosyllabic, and at worst, mute. His inability to properly communicate with his peers is juxtaposed with his interior existence, which is revealed via the dialogic mechanism of the voice-over (in conjunction with flashbacks, dreams, and hallucinations) as a bloody house of horrors.

The Femme Fatale in *Dexter*

> Dexter (to Lila): You are more dangerous than my addiction will ever be
> ("Resistance is Futile," 2.9)

The mining of noir tropes changes in Season 2. The screen time allocated to flashbacks is reduced, and there is less focus on Dexter's interior world. Concurrently, the character arcs of Doakes, LaGuerta, Debra, and Angel are extended. Instead, Season 2 focuses on Dexter's interactions with recovering addict Lila, a classic femme fatale and the major antagonist of the Season. The literal meaning of the French term "femme fatale" is the "fatal woman", and "dictionary definitions of 'fatal' include: (1) causing or capable of causing death, (2) ruinous, disastrous, (3) decisively important, (4) destined, inevitable. The femme fatale carries all these levels of meaning, hence the easy slippage from deadliness to sexuality as a weapon" (Martin 206). Lila's role is signaled from the outset by her knowing, gently-mocking glances at Dexter in the Narcotics

Anonymous meetings, her skimpy clothing revealing her slim frame, and her ever-present red or black bra strap drooped loosely over her shoulder.

While the Miami PD and FBI's investigation of the Bay Harbor Butcher forms the first level of narration in Season 2, the dominant plotline is Dexter's interactions with Lila. Their meeting, developing relationship, the realization of her dangerous nature, and eventual death dominates both Dexter's thoughts and the development of the narrative. Again, this mirrors the classic mode of film noir, where Christine Gledhill argues that the "processes of detection—following clues and deductive intellection—are submerged by the hero's relations with the women he meets, and it is the vagaries of this relationship that determine the twists and turns of the plot" (28).

One of the central conceits of film noir is that the male protagonist becomes entangled with the femme fatale. In *Dexter*, this entanglement follows a straightforward linear trajectory: Dexter meets Lila at the Narcotics Anonymous meeting, she mentors him, and they grow increasingly close. Eventually Rita breaks up with Dexter, allowing him to have a sexual relationship with Lila, but Dexter rejects Lila and attempts to return to Rita and her family. The femme fatale storyline then reaches its conclusion as Lila discovers Doakes imprisoned at Santos Jimenez's cabin in the Everglades. Doakes tells Lila that Dexter is the Bay Harbor Butcher, and as a femme fatale, she delights in the news that her erstwhile lover is a serial killer. She promptly murders Doakes by setting off a gas explosion in the cabin, and decides to run away with Dexter, envisaging a *Bonnie and Clyde* (1967) outlaw existence. However, after complications put in place by Debra's persecution of Lila, Dexter tracks Lila to Paris and, in "The British Invasion" (2.12), murders her.

The characterization of Lila speaks directly to the fatal women of 1940s film noir. Lila is a complex character: beautiful, devious, intensely sexual but needy, paralleling Phyllis Dietrichson in *Double Indemnity*, Cora Smith in *The Postman Always Rings Twice*, and Kathie Moffat in *Out of the Past* (1947). Considered one of the finest of all film noirs, *Double Indemnity* was created from a Raymond Chandler script, in turn adapted from a James M. Cain story, and directed by Billy Wilder. Insurance agent Walter Neff falls in lust with housewife Phyllis (Barbara Stanwyck), who convinces Neff to kill her husband by making it appear that he died falling from a moving train, thus allowing them to claim double the life insurance money. As Phyllis, Stanwyck creates "one of the most powerful and disturbing noir portraits of a femme fatale—the destructive, duplicitous woman who transgresses rules of female behavior by luring men with the promise of possessing her sexually and then using them for her own, murderous, ends" (Root 311). Lila moves in the same murky, sexually charged waters as Phyllis. She lures Dexter into her world with her promise of understanding his "addictive" personality and then proceeds to manipulate him. She plants long, slow kisses on Dexter's lips after only their second meeting, the illicit action promising imminent transgressive sex.

Lila exhibits a number of character switches and, with each re-incarnation, grows more dangerous. She moves from caring mentor in "An Inconvenient Lie" (2.3), to sexualized mother figure in "The Dark Defender" (2.5), holding Dexter in her arms as he sobs after confronting Jimenez, his mother's killer. Her actions escalate: she progresses to bunny-boiler in "Morning Comes" (2.8), turning up unannounced at Dexter's work after he has ended their affair and then breaking into Rita's house, and fakes the role of the rape victim in "There's Something About Harry" (2.10). Over the course of the season, Lila is also revealed as a multiple arsonist. In "The Dark Defender," she admits to Dexter that she burned down her boyfriend/drug dealer's house when he was still inside; she torches her own apartment in "That Night, a Forest Grew" (2.7); in "The British Invasion" (2.12), she blows up the cabin with Doakes inside, then sets her apartment on fire (again) with Dexter, Cody, and Astor trapped inside.

Lila's death at the conclusion of "The British Invasion" is inevitable. She is a dangerous, volatile, and sensual woman, and patriarchal society will not allow her to escape her misdemeanors. This creates a somewhat conflicted ideological viewpoint when Dexter murders Lila. We are encouraged to root for the serial killer who stabs Lila in the heart, the same heart she gave over so completely to him, and yet his own crimes far outweigh her own. Lila is ruthlessly dispatched in a way that confirms her femme fatale status. Like Phyllis, Cora, Kathie, and the rest, the femme fatale only has three options by the film's conclusion: death, marriage, or a prison sentence, and whatever the outcome, her threat is contained.

Fearing Flashbacks: The Code of Harry

> Harry is the only one who saw me—really saw me. So he taught me to hide. And that's what kept me safe. But sometimes I'm not sure where Harry's vision of me ends and the real me starts.
>
> (Dexter's voice-over in "Let's Give the Boy a Hand," 1.4)

There are distinct structural similarities between *Dexter* and film noir in terms of modes of narration, particularly in the use of flashbacks. The main purposes of the flashback are to provide a subjective memory and to create narrative information. In *Flashbacks in Film: Memory and History*, Turim identifies investigative and confessional models as the two basic types of flashback. The investigative model "examines the past to solve a crime. It then leads us through a maze of clues and false leads constructed within the flashbacks" (172). The confessional structure is "characterised by the protagonist's retrospective examination of the ways he was introduced to his current criminality" (172). *Dexter* employs both types of flashback to create a seamless narrative. The flashbacks are propelled by Dexter's need to decipher clues that reveal his past, but, at the same time, they also provide subjective memories of his murderous apprenticeship under the tutelage of his adopted father, policeman Harry Morgan.

The flashbacks in the first half of Season 1 often feature Dexter as a teenager. This is a canny narrative tool, serving three purposes. First, the flashback reveals the world that Dexter inhabited while growing up. It also allows the audience to explore Harry's code. However, by presenting Deter as a fractious adolescent, his character is shown to reject or willfully misinterpret Harry's rules. As such, Dexter's behavior necessitates Harry patiently repeating his explanations to the traumatized teen, reinforcing Harry's code for the audience. As the season progresses and Dexter grows nearer the truth of his childhood traumas, the flashbacks increasingly move back through time, eventually portraying Dexter as a distressed young child covered in blood.

By uncovering Dexter's various repressed memories in Season 1, Dexter's story has, to a degree, been told. The only established plot-line left for the outset of Season 2 is that of Dexter's victims, explored through the Bay Harbor Butcher investigation. Bearing this in mind, it is unsurprising that Season 2 has a different approach to flashbacks. Used less frequently than in Season 1, they gradually reveal the extent of Harry's duplicitous nature: his constant lies, his affair with Laura Moser, Dexter's biological mother, and Harry's implication in her murder. Triggered by Dexter's search through police files, the flashbacks prove to Dexter that Harry is not infallible, while also suggesting the awful truth that Harry created Dexter as a killing machine, designed to murder suspects that evaded the law. This discovery makes Dexter's voice-over from Season 1, quoted at the header of this section, remarkably prescient.

From City Flat to Cozy Suburb: Dexter as Family Man

Nobody hurts my children.

> (Dexter's voice-over as he strangles pedophile
> Nathan Marten in "*The Lion Sleeps Tonight*," 3.3)

To conclude this essay a brief discussion of Season 3 is necessary. It can be argued that Season 3 continues to move away from the noirish origins of Season 1. This takes place in several crucial ways. First, at the level of detection, Dexter finds it increasingly difficult to stay ahead of Miami PD's investigations, commenting in "The Lion Sleeps Tonight" (3.3) that "this department is becoming annoyingly effective." This comes to a head in "Do You Take Dexter Morgan" (3.12), when Dexter kills the Skinner George King and literally throws him under the wheels of the approaching police car, then jumps out of a window to escape. As such, the gap between Dexter's knowledge as detective and Miami PD is narrowed, reducing his status as a noir protagonist who constantly outwits and stays ahead of the law.

201

Voice-overs continue but with a change in intent and tone: rather than pithy one-liners that offer an alternative presentation of Dexter's reality, they are increasingly polemic and poetic. This is an important distinction. To a degree, the voice-overs employed in earlier seasons could be construed as the thoughts inside Dexter's head, the fleeting ideas we all experience. The increasingly complex and verbose nature of voice-overs in Season 3 suggests knowing-ness on the part of the televisual text and a direct engagement with the audience.

As flashbacks can no longer be narratively justified (what is left of Dexter's and Harry's dark past that can be uncovered?), this narrative mechanism disappears in Season 3. Instead, a series of hallucinogenic embodiments of Dexter's thoughts takes place, depicting Dexter's real-time inner-world debates with Harry. Harry acts as Dexter's warped moral conscience, constantly warning him against opening up to Prado and counseling him against revealing the Code. These fantasy sequences take place in Dexter's living environment, but are constructed with hyper-real color and harsh white light that signals their alterity. Usually shot from Dexter's point of view with Harry talking into the camera, accompanied by occasional two-person shots, they offer an alternative presentation of Dexter's inner subjectivity, beyond the voice-overs.

Season 1 concluded with Dexter killing his brother Rudy/Brian. In Season 3 the family theme continues as an alternative, dark family develops in the brotherly relationship between Dexter and Prado. Replacing Rudy/Brian, Prado is aware of and accepting of Dexter's essential nature, telling Dexter "you and I are the same" (3.5). Prado's own darkness is reinforced by his nemesis, defense attorney Ellen Wolf, who tells LaGuerta that Prado doesn't follow the rules. In "The Damage A Man Can Do" (3.8) Dexter arranges for Prado to carry out the murder of a former American footballer, Billy Fleeter. Prado turns to Dexter and says, "Thank you for this, for letting me in. For showing me the way" (3.8). Through Fleeter's murder, Miguel and Dexter become blood brothers.

However, in "About Last Night" (3.9) Dexter discovers Wolf's corpse, and realizes that Prado is killing to satiate his own desires. This betrayal is further compounded when Dexter discovers that Prado's bloodied shirt is dosed with cow's blood, rather than

Freebo's, and that he has been manipulated: "I didn't create a monster; I was used by one" (3.9). Kidnapping Prado and binding him in the kill room, Dexter leans over him and whispers, "I killed my brother. I killed yours too" (3.11). As this demonstrates, the family is a recurrent trope across the series as a whole, and is particularly central to Season 3.

In addition, the serial arc of *Dexter* is revealed as circular, centered on a form of masochistic repetition-compulsion. Each season, one or more characters discover Dexter's secret, embrace him, and are murdered by him. By killing Prado, Dexter follows the pattern of Seasons 1 and 2, where Dexter kills the man (or woman) who accepts him for what he is. The killing of Prado also signals the restitution of Harry's code, as Dexter believes he was wrong to try to share his world with another. This is made explicit in voice-over dialogue bookending Season 3. In "Our Father" (3.1) Dexter announces that "My God is dead now", but in "Do You Take Dexter Morgan", Dexter is reconciled with Harry as he lies bound to the Skinner's table, saying, "Dad, I forgive you" (3.12).

By Season 3, there is a demonstrable move away from Season 1's noir origins and the transformation of Dexter is complete. Dexter is no longer represented as a quick-minded detective protagonist, easily outwitting the law; rather he struggles to stay ahead of Debra, Batista, and Masuka. As the title of this section also suggests, the rejection of noir in the third season can also be considered in terms of space and place. Dexter moves from living alone in his city flat, to spending most of his time staying with Rita, Cody, and Astor in the suburbs. Gender also plays its part in the paradigmatic shift: femme fatales no longer lurk around Dexter, and he chooses the wholesome pleasures of life with blonde-haired homemaker Rita.

Dexter moves from the "outside," the traditional space of the noir protagonist, to the "inside," presenting himself to the world as a family man. He embraces fatherhood, becomes a husband, and hopes for a happy life. The crisis points in the seasonal arc are much more mundane, focusing on issues around the family, wedding planning, and who to choose as best man. Indeed, one of the most exciting moments—Dexter's kidnapping—is revealed to be the beginning of his bachelor party organized by Masuka. Even specific kill plots feed into the wider narrative arc. Dexter's murder of pedophile Marten is a simplistic narrative mechanism that enables Dexter to fully realize his paternal affections for Cody and Astor, and accept his impending fatherhood with Rita's unborn child.

This essay has attempted to analyse the aesthetic qualities of the series in order to demonstrate how the first two seasons of *Dexter* explicitly draw on the film noir archetypes of the male anti-hero, the detective structure, voice-overs, the femme fatale, and flashbacks. However, it has been suggested that Season 3 represents a significant generic shift, moving away from the noir thriller and mutating into a frothy soap opera with a black heart. American soap operas (and related programmes such as *Desperate Housewives*) have always depicted the everyday darkness of suburban life, exploring the dichotomy between the exterior presentation of perfection and normality while, below the surface, indecency, depravity, and horror boil over. The descent from noir outsider to secretive suburbanite suggests that Season 4 will continue to mine the soap opera aesthetic, and *Dexter*'s film noir elision will be complete.

15.
The Art of Sp(l)atter: Body Horror in *Dexter*

Simon Brown and Stacey Abbott

> **Dexter:** I'm a very neat monster.
>
> ("Dexter," 1.1)

It has become commonplace over the years to suggest that television and the horror genre are incompatible bedfellows. The rationale is that the industrial restrictions imposed on network television, as well as TV's position as a domestic medium, interfere with its ability to fully engage with the conventions of the horror genre. Stephen King takes issue in *Danse Macabre* with how censorship and legislation restrict horror on television, as opposed to on film and in literature, from getting "the horror up front" and surviving instead on "innuendo and vapors" (215), while, according to Gregory Waller, the intrusion of commercial breaks not only disrupts any build-up of tension but reminds the audience of the real world beyond the horror text. As he argues, "[t]he commercial breaks in made-for-television movies serve to dissipate—to deny—horror by predicting the future and by insisting that problems are solvable, and happiness, safety, health, security, and pleasures are attainable" (159). Another obstacle to TV horror is television's inherent generic hybridity where shows such as *The X-Files, Buffy the Vampire Slayer*, and *Angel* merge horror with other genres like science-fiction, teen drama, and the detective genre respectively. This hybridity, like the commercial breaks, is seen as dissipating the horror. Furthermore, the networks' adherence to the "Least Objectionable Programming" (LOP) strategy, that ensures the broadest possible audience, makes the horror genre, described by Robin Wood "as the most popular and, at the same time, the most disreputable of Hollywood Genres" loved by aficionados and rejected by others, impossible on TV (77). This impossibility, therefore, stems from its inability to conform to the conventions of contemporary cinematic horror. In fact, within all this criticism, TV horror is distinguished from an ambiguously described form of "authentic" horror. For instance, Michael P. Levine and Steven Jay Schneider argue that *Buffy the Vampire Slayer* contains "no horror . . . at all" because it does not include what they describe as "true chills, uncanniness, or horror-proper," and yet they offer no explanation of what "horror-proper" is (201).

The implication of much of this criticism is that "horror-proper" is cinematic, explicit in terms of sex and violence, and narratively or thematically transgressive. As Rayna Denison and Mark Jancovitch have argued, the distinction between cinematic and television horror is usually described as follows:

> [i]f cinematic horror is claimed to be transgressive, dangerous and challenging, television horror is supposed to be frustrated by the limitations imposed by broadcasters, who are nervous of offending their audiences and prefer to simply confirm and reassure them instead. ("Introduction" to "Mysterious Bodies")

By this argument, perhaps, the most unlikely form of horror to appear on TV would be body horror, a sub-genre that emerged in the 1980s and which, according to Pete Boss, focused on "human tissue in torment, the body in profuse disarray" (15). Philip Brophy argues that this disarray is "conveyed through torture and agony of havoc wrought upon a body devoid of control" (10). It is "*showing* as opposed to *telling* that is strongly connected to the destruction of the body" (8). If TV horror really does have to negotiate the idea of reassuring an audience and providing them with the least objectionable programming possible, then such graphic display would necessarily be taboo.

There is, however, a developing movement within contemporary television scholarship toward reconsidering the relationship between TV and horror. Helen Wheatley's analysis of Gothic television reminds us of the medium's long-standing traditions of horror, albeit in a more culturally acceptable form through the

Gothic's emphasis on suggestion and its links to literature. As Matt Hills points out, the term Gothic often serves as a displacement term for "horror," allowing TV producers and critics to distance the program from horror while also suggesting that "'Gothic TV' is superior to devalued (or culturally inappropriate) TV horror" (119). Hills has also argued that, while there still exists a view that TV horror is a lesser form of the genre, it developed in the 1990s "towards showing more" through "generic and discursive hybridity, with 'horror' and 'TV' being brought together via the pursuit of niche, fan audiences" (127). This tendency "towards showing more" has tapped into a long-term televisual preoccupation with the body and horror which Denison and Jancovitch among others have identified, despite the fact that how this theme is conveyed has been affected by historical and institutional contexts of TV at the time (see "Mysterious Bodies"). This, combined with Hills' notions of generic and discursive hybridity, confirm that body horror on television is, and has been, alive and well.

Furthermore, the industrial contexts of contemporary television have changed since Waller and King made their initial claims, undermining these earlier arguments about horror and TV. For instance, American television is no longer defined by network programming, as the post-network, multi-platform landscape of contemporary TV has led to a much broader range of programming strategies beyond the "Least Objectionable" approach of the network era. In order to compete for audiences, TV channels led by HBO, a pay channel not bound by FCC regulations over content, are increasingly willing to push boundaries in terms of sex and violence. Furthermore, networks, netlets, and cable and pay-TV channels are specifically targeting smaller, loyal markets, making the horror aficionado an increasingly lucrative, while still niche, market (see Brown 2010). What all of this demonstrates is that TV and horror are not inherently incompatible. Donato Totaro, for example, has illustrated how the directors featured in *Masters of Horror*—a series deliberately aimed at horror-film fans with a particular emphasis on directors popular during the heyday of body horror—provide "some of the most outrageously intense, violent, sexual, controversial, and *political* horror to screen on television" while engaging "in a form of cinematic one-upmanship with their peers" (2010). This was made possible by the show's broadcast on Showtime, a premium cable channel not defined by the same censorship restrictions as network TV.

While the industrial context of *Masters of Horror* allows the series to boldly flaunt its credentials as horror to a niche audience, within network television the depiction of graphic body horror, most often associated with cinema, has been co-opted by more mainstream genres that possess a well-established history on TV. Medical dramas like *ER* and *Nip/Tuck*, and the police drama *24* reflect the conventions of body horror by showing the living body in extreme disarray and focusing on the pain of that process. Both *ER* and *Nip/Tuck* regularly represent the body in graphic physical distress, while *24* repeatedly contains scenes of physical torture and violence. Their ability to do this on primetime derives from the fact that these conventions are used in the service of more lofty thematic elements, respectively the ability of skilled physicians to salvage a body in torment, a critique of our modern obsession with beauty, and the defense of homeland security. These shows, arguably, do not revel in the disruption of the body for its own sake.

There is also a strand of forensic programs which equally focuses on the body in extreme disarray, but here the body is already dead, and notions of pain and suffering, though implicit, are absent. Series like *CSI* and *Bones* are interesting locations for graphic body horror through their depictions of the corpse, which Julia Kristeva describes as "the utmost of abjection . . . death infecting life" (4). Both of these shows regularly feature explicit displays of the damaged, deformed, and decaying body/corpse, photographed both internally and externally in extreme close-up and clinical detail. The boundaries of the body are repeatedly ruptured either through the initial injuries, decomposition, or procedural stripping of the body layer by layer in search of evidence in *Bones*, and, of course, through the *CSI* shot, in which the camera virtually penetrates the body to locate the point of injury or clinical inquiry. Deborah Jermyn has argued that *CSI* evokes a "fascination with exploring and exposing a 'gross' corporeality, revealing the liquids, the mucus, the organs that constitute our bodies" (88), while Elke Weissmann has demonstrated that *CSI*'s scenes of corpses "crawling with maggots, melting away in decomposition, discolored and mutilated . . . are clearly meant to disgust" but "also provide particular pleasures to the viewer . . . closer to those associated with the horror genre" ("The Victim's Suffering Translated: *CSI: Crime Scene Investigation* and the Crime Genre"). Significantly, Weissmann argues that this emphasis on the pleasures of the horror of the body shifts the focus in *CSI* (also applicable to *Bones*) from the crime to the victim, making the show less of a traditional whodunit and more of a "who-was-it-and-why-and-how-was-it-done-to-them?" It is this shift in focus that allows for *CSI* and *Bones* to co-opt the conventions of horror and justify them in the name of science, for as Deborah Jermyn among others has argued, the body in these series has become not simply a visual display of horror but rather a source of information and thus "speaks" to the scientists who examine them (83). These programs, therefore, justify their use of excessive graphic detail by presenting it as evidence necessary to solve the crime and ensure that justice is served. Having said this, these programs continue to revel in the spectacle of the grotesque body. The mainstream TV genres of the crime, police, and hospital drama, therefore, co-opt horror for their own purposes and force programs that want to be horror to raid, rework, and redefine the semantic and syntactic elements of the cinematic genre in order to create new forms of televisual horror. TV horror exists. You just need to know where and how to look for it.

In this chapter, we will therefore examine the hybrid forensic-police show/serial-killer drama *Dexter* as an example of TV horror. We will do this by exploring how the series negotiates its transgressive premise—in which blood-spatter expert Dexter Morgan lives by night as a vigilante serial killer—by both highlighting and downplaying its allegiance to the horror genre in order to create its own language of TV horror. Our approach to this subject will be threefold. We will first examine how *Dexter* acknowledges conventional horror aesthetics while also undermining these traditions and offering an alternative way of depicting the genre. We will then explore how the graphic representation of Dexter's crimes is consciously restricted throughout much of the series in order to invite audience identification with him despite his monstrous nature. While this may seem to be a denial of the show's roots in horror by seeming to soften the impact of Dexter's crimes and therefore confirming many of the criticisms leveled at TV horror, this strategy actually serves to enhance the horror by lending greater impact to those moments of visual excess when they do occur. Following on from this, we will address how seeing the world through Dexter's eyes creates a new understanding of horror in which murder is represented as art. In this manner, we will show how *Dexter* reconfigures for the television audience the Gothic aesthetic, the depiction of violence, and the mutilation of the body as represented by the art of sp(l)atter.

Dexter and the Aesthetics of Horror

On the surface, there is little about *Dexter* which seems to fit the series into standard definitions of the horror genre. For instance, in a direct reversal of Hills' claim that the Gothic often substitutes for horror on TV, *Dexter* deliberately subverts any sense of a Gothic mise en scène and instead locates its horror narrative within its incongruous bright and sunny Miami location. The show outlines its approach to horror in the very first episode when Dexter notes in his laconic voice-over that "there's something strange and disarming about looking at a homicide scene in the daylight of Miami. It makes the most grotesque killings look staged like you're in a new and daring section of Disneyworld; Dahmerland" (1.1). This is much more than a mere observation by our eponymous hero; it is a statement of the show's reconception of horror through the constructedness of its mise en scène. *Dexter* consciously manipulates mise en scène in order to subvert previous conceptions of horror and rearticulate its own approach to the genre.

To achieve this, the opening sequence of the series (1.1), in which Dexter stalks his next victim, grounds the show in familiar imagery of urban Gothic, beginning with the title card that changes from pristine white lettering against a black background to a more Gothic red, followed by a blood-red neon-soaked screen in which the reflection of a full moon appears. The red in this sequence evokes a sense of danger, alluding to violence and blood, while the other colors, blue and black, suggest darkness, night-time and secrecy. Dexter's voice-over speaks of compulsion, need, and hunger, not for food, but something "different now." He is filmed in a series of fragmented close-ups silently observing the people and streets around him, emphasizing not his identity but his point of view, alluding to such classic horror films as *Peeping Tom* as well as the slasher film tradition in which the point of view of the killer is aesthetically privileged. Coupled with the dark undercurrents of the series' haunting music, the atmosphere created in this sequence invokes the horror genre. Dexter is the unknown stalker, the dark human predator, every inch the serial killer. Shot from inside his car, he is a shadow isolated from the bright lights, loud music, and social atmosphere of the Miami which drifts past on the other side of his windscreen. The series is, in fact, littered with aesthetic moments that remind us that *Dexter* is horror, from the manner in which Dexter repeatedly emerges out of the shadows when he attacks his victims to the sound of his powertools and his victim's screaming as he cuts into them to the occasional glimpses of blood and body parts when he cleans up his crime scene.

These moments, however, are not emblematic of the entire series, which deliberately undercuts these conventions by introducing a new horror aesthetic. Dexter's everyday environment, in fact, conforms to few of these traditional tropes. His home is a neat and tidy space in which innocents can come and go with no inkling of the presence of his Dark Passenger, the only evidence being his tools hidden in a chest in the closet and the slides of his victims' blood (his only trophy) secreted behind the air-conditioning unit. Even Dexter's kill room is far from a terrifying dungeon of torture, what Carol Clover would describe as the "terrible place" in the style of *The Pit and Pendulum* or *The Texas Chainsaw Massacre* (78). Rather it is a sterile antiseptic space, never in the same location and constructed from clear plastic sheeting and decorated with the images of his victims' victims. This is a far cry from the traditional representation of the sociopathic killer in horror films, whose home, when revealed, is a clutter of lunatic bric a brac and Gothic décor. We might think here for example of Buffalo Bill's dungeon in *The Silence of the Lambs*, complete with skin suit and dark pit in which to hold his victims, or John Doe's apartment in *Se7en*, with its collection of graphic photos and obsessive journals.

The series, in fact, openly acknowledges Dexter's difference from conventional horror villains by surrounding him with characters

211

who are aesthetically aligned with these more traditional horror conventions. In Season 1, Neil Perry is mistakenly apprehended as the Ice Truck Killer, partly because the police enter his trailer to find it cluttered with files of morbid crime-related clippings, a wide selection of stuffed animal corpses, and the skeleton of his mother buried in his backyard, all clearly read as signifiers of his guilt and with deliberate echoes of *Psycho* (1.7). Likewise, the Ice Truck Killer's equally neat and seemingly normal apartment (he is after all Dexter's brother) is revealed to contain a refrigerated annex which is presented as a Gothic torture chamber with its rig for hanging victims upside down in order to bleed them dry. Even the unstable Lila's apartment in Season 2, with its grotesque sculptures, red walls, billowing curtains and, eventually, a painting of a monstrous Dexter, is classified as a Gothic space. Here the series acknowledges its origins in horror while also declaring its distinct approach to the genre. Dexter is a monster because he hides so unnoticeably within the daylight of Miami, and he achieves this by adopting the façade of normality. Similarly, in order for the series to be horror, it must equally conceal its horrific nature beneath the bright aesthetics of Miami through which the true horror of Dexter's nature periodically bursts.

Dexter, Violence, and Audience Identification

The notion that *Dexter* undermines the aesthetic conventions of horror in order to *be* horror stems from the fundamentally transgressive premise of the narrative, that its leading character and principal voice is a cold-blooded murderer with whom the audience must identify in order for the show to work. In order to facilitate this identification, just as the show downplays the Gothic aesthetic, it also downplays the explicit representation of body horror, choosing to reserve graphic display for particular moments of narrative or character significance.

The show protects the audience from seeing the full horror of what Dexter actually does by framing the murders so that they are concealed from view. The sounds of his power tools and his victims' screaming, along with the occasional glimpse of blood, make it clear what he is doing but do not risk breaking the identification by having the audience see too much. The show even goes so far as to acknowledge how our sympathies would be disrupted should too much be revealed. In a key moment in Season 2, Dexter remembers his father's response when he finally sees the truth of what he has created. Confronted by the sight of Dexter covered in blood and in the process of dismembering a body, Harry's response is visceral; he freezes, vomits, and begs Dexter to "stay away." This is not dissimilar to standard horror-movie reactions to the sight of the corpse, and the composition of this sequence is particularly abject as Harry, in close-up, vomits directly into the camera with Dexter, covered in blood, standing behind him. This repressed memory surfaces as a direct result of Doakes' reaction to witnessing Dexter in his ritual murderous act. Having been held captive by Dexter for several days, they have developed a rapport which is shattered when Dexter murders and dismembers a drug dealer in front of Doakes, albeit behind plastic sheeting. Like Harry, Doakes' response is visceral as he screams for Dexter to stop, and then recoils as the blood begins to seep onto the floor. Also like Harry, he tells Dexter to "stay away" (2.10).

Significantly for the audience, in these moments of revelation, the murderous act is split. With Harry, the audience witnesses a glimpse of the body in "profuse disarray," while, with Doakes, they see nothing, but hear the sounds of murder and dismemberment. While the explicit display of violence ruptures Harry and Doakes' ability to identify with Dexter, its withholding from the audience allows their sympathies to be maintained. The way in which the series negotiates its depiction of murder and the dismemberment of the body is crucial to maintaining the audience's sympathy for Dexter and to the world which they view through his eyes. In the first season, for example, the exploits of Dexter's Dark Passenger are kept largely hidden from the audience, and indeed given that Dexter is a blood-spatter analyst, unlike *Bones* and *CSI*, there is a conspicuous absence of blood or gore when the series begins. Seeing only from Dexter's perspective adds to this sense of disengagement, since Dexter himself is incapable of feeling any sense of horror at the acts of violence he sees and indeed perpetrates. It is only when events start to break through Dexter's emotionless veneer that the blood begins to flow.

The episode "Shrink Wrap" (1.8) is the first key moment when Dexter's path to understanding his past is conveyed through the increase in graphic display of body horror, marking a return to a more overt engagement with the types of horror conventions used in the first episode. It opens with the sound of thunder and the image of a large blood-spray pattern on the wall, picked out in a darkened room by flashlight. This is followed by a close-up of a woman's body, framed by the blood-streaked rim of the bath, and laying in crimson bathwater with her open mouth covered in blood. This crime scene is the first of the series where we see large amounts of blood, and once again the series draws attention to this fact by presenting it through a Gothic aesthetic (and in addition focusing on the nude figure of the dead woman, a rare glimpse of nudity which again adds to the unusually explicit nature of the scene), which is then subverted when Angel asks someone to turn the lights on and complains about power outages.

In this episode, Dexter stalks and kills a psychiatrist who has been using therapy to encourage women to commit suicide and then withholding their anti-depressant medication. The reasons for this conscious shift toward more explicit blood imagery only come to light as the episode, and subsequent episodes, unfold. In attempting to uncover the psychiatrist's guilt, Dexter undergoes a number of sessions in which he begins to drop his façade and reveal hitherto unexplored parts of himself (including a flash image of a child in a blood-soaked room), culminating in his finally admitting to someone else just what he is—a serial killer. Dexter then kills the therapist and, for the first time, his act of murder is accompanied by blood-letting, a pool which gradually forms under the twitching arm of the doctor's body while the actual killing takes place just off-camera. From this moment, Dexter is on a painful path to self-realization, and the blood-letting develops correspondingly.

In the later episode "Seeing Red" (1.10), Dexter collapses at a crime scene where the Ice Truck Killer has decorated a hotel room with the blood drained from his five victims. In a deeply abject sequence, Dexter, wearing full white forensic gear for the first time on the show (dryly noting to Masuka that they haven't gone prophylactic for some time), falls to the floor at the first sight of the room, emerging with his white suit covered in crimson blood. This moment is repeated several times, and intercut with the afore-mentioned image of a child crying in a similar pool of blood. It emerges that this is a repressed memory of the last time that Dexter could feel, when he, as a small child, watched his mother cut up with a chainsaw and was then locked for two days in a storage container two inches deep with blood. The sheer abject horror of this image is new for the audience, just as Dexter's reaction toward blood is new for him. Season 1 ends with a final blood-letting where Dexter slits the throat of the Ice Truck Killer, now revealed to be his long-lost brother, and hangs him up to let the blood drain out. This is the only time in the first series that we see Dexter actually cut someone on screen, and here, instead of being calm, he crouches, mortified in a corner, hyperventilating. This is a murder which Dexter actually feels, and thanks to the blood, the audience feels it, too.

In Season 1, therefore, the presence of blood indicates not violence so much as feelings. The more Dexter feels, the bloodier the scenes become, but again the image of blood and the act of murder or dismemberment remain largely separate. Indeed, as the series progresses and the depiction of Dexter committing murder becomes more commonplace, the use of blood continues to be restricted. Whereas in Season 1 his weapon of choice was an electric saw, by the end of the second season and into the third, we more commonly see Dexter either stab or garrotte his victims, and we also see him becoming more emotionally involved with the act. The murder of former lover turned killer Lila in "The British Invasion" (2.12) is both climactic and cathartic, but also strangely beautiful and moving with Dexter's "gift" of a spinal epidural to allow her no pain as he thrusts a knife through her chest. His stabbing of the drug dealer Freebo in Season 3's "Finding Freebo" (3.2) is depicted graphically, with first a shot from over Freebo's shoulder of Dexter stabbing him, and then a sustained shot over Dexter's shoulder of the knife buried in his neck. What is significant here is the anger on Dexter's face as he makes the thrust. In previous murders, the moment of death is seen, rather traditionally perhaps, as a moment of relief as the nagging voice of the Dark Passenger is finally quieted. But here Dexter is angry, his motion more passionate than calculated. The reason for this difference is that this murder is personal since Freebo is complicit in Dexter's killing an innocent. Equally personal is Dexter's killing of the pedophile who stalks Astor despite acknowledging that "He isn't a killer. He doesn't fit the code" (3.3), as well as the killing of Assistant District Attorney Miguel Prado (3.11) because he is becoming increasingly erratic and a danger to Dexter's freedom. Like Lila, Miguel both discovers Dexter's secret and accepts him regardless, but unlike with Lila, Dexter feels no connection with Miguel at the moment of death.

In this manner, the series makes use of three key components of horror—violence, blood, and emotion—but rarely at the same time in order to maintain the show's aesthetic distance from the horror. In maintaining this distance, however, *Dexter* does not deny its horror pedigree, but rather, like Dexter, creates a façade of respectability and narrative justification appropriate to its televisual context that enables the show to revel in its monstrous origins.

Dexter and the Art of Sp(l)atter

While *Dexter* is a show about murder and death in which horror is concealed by a mask of civility, this is but one strategy by which the show manipulates the conventions of horror. Interestingly for a series which features a forensic expert and scientist as its central character, unlike *Bones* and *CSI* which use the language of science to legitimize the fundamentally horrific nature of their subject matter, *Dexter* channels its explicit horror imagery through the language and representation of art.

This can be demonstrated by the hierarchy of killers that exists within the show. There are those who are worthy of the series', and therefore Dexter's, focus, and those who are not, as represented by the killers dispatched by Dexter on a semi-weekly basis. What distinguishes those deserving of our attention is how their meticulous control of their acts of murder borders on the artistic as seen through Dexter's eyes. The series uses Dexter's role as murderer, blood-spatter analyst, and crime-scene critic to express this concept of horror *as* art.[1]

To begin with, Dexter in his work environment is surrounded by images of violence transformed into art. The walls of his lab are adorned by prints of crisp red blood spatter on a white background which have been framed and mounted. Their presence on his wall creates a thematic link between art and the photographs of spatter which Dexter takes when he first visits a crime scene. Indeed, not just the act of photography but all of Dexter's on-site forensic work reconfigures the violence of death into the beauty of art. Having taken his photographs, the next stage of Dexter's investigation is to reverse-engineer the trajectory of the blood in the room to establish a three-dimensional plan of how the violence at the scene played out. Although from Dexter's perspective the purpose of this is to re-create the narrative of the crime, in visual terms his scientific analysis transforms the scene from an abject image of a familiar location drenched in blood and gore into an artistic delicate spider-web of soft red pieces of string. The first sequence where we see Dexter at his forensic work is the "hotel coke-head murder scene" in episode one (1.1). When Doakes shows Dexter pictures of the scene, Dexter responds by calling the work unprofessional and describing it as "child's play. Messy work. All that blood on the walls? Looks like a finger painting" (1.1). However, the crime scene is only revealed to the audience after it has been "Dexter-ized." Here the crisp white walls and sparse décor of the large room give the impression of a gallery space, in which the red patterns of Dexter's strings stand out as art. Dexter's commentary on the space is a critique of the murderer's work through the patterns of blood he leaves behind and is therefore couched in the language of art criticism, referring to "nice clear sprays of blood . . . no splashes, no drips" (1.1). This response is echoed in Season 3, where on seeing Dexter's work at his dead brother's crime scene, Miguel Prado remarks that it seems "like a piece of art" (3.1).

The colors white and red also feature heavily in Dexter's spatter room. This is a pure white room constructed by huge sheets of hanging paper in which Dexter, once more in his prophylactic white forensic gear, is able to test spatter patterns. Unlike the space for forensic examination and experimentation in *Bones* and *CSI*, which are represented as laboratory spaces for clinical scientific investigation, this space seems more like an artist's studio, the work Dexter does presented as interpretive rather than factual. When we first see this room in "Seeing Red," Dexter is trying to identify which power tool can create a specific spatter pattern by pouring blood substitute onto various tools and seeing how they project this substance onto the walls. This sequence is carefully composed using an artistic aesthetic. Shots of blood-drenched silver drills on a silver table look like art in themselves, while a shot of a white wall onto which red is suddenly sprayed in a vertical pattern from an unseen source is clearly designed to echo the creation of abstract art. When this room is later visited by Lila (2.5), who is herself an artist, producing mostly macabre and Gothic sculptures, she recognizes this space as an artist's space and asks for one of Dexter's spatter-pattern papers to take with her. Like Miguel, Lila contains a darkness within her which allows them both to recognize the artistry in Dexter's work. When Rudy (aka the Ice Truck Killer) visits the spatter room and sees Dexter in the process of testing blood-spatter patterns, creating his abstract art, he comments to Dexter, "So this is what you do for a living?" (1.10). Rudy, of course, knows who Dexter is and what he does. Implicit in this comment, as he casts an appreciative eye over the walls, is Rudy projecting his vision of Dexter's own kill room onto this space. He sees it as an artistic space because he also constructs his murder scenes as art.

While in his crime scene-related work, Dexter makes blood into art by effectively overwhelming its violent connotations, Rudy turns his crime scenes into art by removing the blood altogether, therefore negating any notions of gore or associations with body horror. The bodies are dismembered, packaged, and carefully composed as macabre sculptures. In at least three cases, he deliberately "frames" his victims. The first is found laying in an empty swimming pool (1.1), while later he places a body within a goal on a hockey rink (1.3). The severed fingertips found in the refrigerated truck are frozen in a block of ice which again acts as a frame (1.2). In "Let's Give the Boy a Hand" (1.4), he not only poses the severed body parts of Security Guard Tony Tucci, but also takes and leaves photographs of the poses at the scene. So, for example, Tucci's severed hand is presented as a carefully composed piece of macabre art, positioned as it is on a bloody beach towel and juxtaposed with the innocence of a child's bucket and spade. The accompanying photograph not only reworks this scene as photographic art, but also serves as his artistic reinterpretation of Dexter's family photos. Rudy is, is fact, an artist of sorts, having studied the human form at the

Sorbonne in Paris before moving into the field of prosthetics where, like Dexter, he creates art from horror, crafting new body parts to make whole again bodies in disarray. Deborah, seeing the work he has done on Tony Tucci's hand and foot (unaware of course that he removed the originals), says to him, "It's like living art, what you do" (1.7). Dexter for his part sees the flip side of Rudy's artistry. While the other detectives look at the Ice Truck Killer and see a monster, Dexter sees the craft and the beauty in the murderous work he does.

Dexter, of course, is the consummate artist of the show, and neither the Ice Truck Killer, nor Lila, nor Miguel Prado can match him. Unlike the Ice Truck Killer who displays his murder scene as art, Dexter leaves no murder scene for the police to find, carefully disposing of the evidence. When he does leave a body, as in the case of Miguel Prado, it is laid out by Dexter in a beautiful park which is shot with a series of soporific overhead dissolves (3.12). By contrast, the body of Ellen Wolf as left by Miguel is a mud-encrusted blue horror from beyond (or rather beneath) the grave (3.9). Lila may be a murderess, but her chosen method, death by fire, is messy and uncontrolled, not the work of a neat monster like Dexter.

Finally for Dexter, it is the murder that is art, and his audience is limited to his victim and to the televisual audience. Dexter stages his murders as performance art. He dresses the kill room as a narrative space, adorned with photographs and artifacts which tell the victims why they are there. The victims awake to find themselves naked and taped to a table, wrapped in plastic as Dexter confronts them with the evidence of their crimes. In this room, the audience is both witness and participant at once looking down on the space from above, seeing the artistry of the body laid in its wrappings, while at the same time being forced to look at Dexter from the victim's point of view. The murder represents the culmination of the performance. Once the victim is dead, there is nobody watching so the final act of the performance, the dismembering of the dead body, takes place off-screen. The horror lies in the art of the performance, not in the horror of the body in disarray.

John McCarty christened films that wallow in images of gore and the body in disarray as "splatter movies," a term that has come

219

to be associated with some of the "lowest" forms of cinematic horror. By being forced to negotiate the representation of the violence inherent in its premise, *Dexter*, searching for its status as TV horror, successfully reworks "low cinematic splatter" into the "art of sp(l)atter."

16.
From Silver Bullets to Duct Tape: Dexter versus the Traditional Vigilante Hero

Stan Beeler

The American psyche has a deeply rooted understanding of justice which insists that the rule of law must be, from time to time, adjusted by individuals who compare existing legislation to a template of "natural justice."[1] The very foundations of the United States depend on a tale of revolt against unjust taxation. It is not, therefore, surprising that the mythology of the nation as expressed in its popular culture abounds with tales of men who, when faced with evildoers wrapped in the protection afforded by a weak or corrupt legal system, take justice into their own hands. Although this theme is not completely absent from what one might refer to as higher literature, it is most often present in media in the realm of popular culture: comic books, popular novels, radio programs, and television.[2] The Showtime series *Dexter* has taken the narrative paradigms that are used in the construction of the popular-culture vigilante hero and given them an ironic twist which reveals some of the underlying ethical complexities of the tradition.

The vigilante hero of American popular culture comes in a number of distinct packages that have separate characteristics suitable to their roles. Some use a mask[3] and perform their tasks in secret. Characters of this sort can have super-powers or simply be unusually adept at their law-enforcement tasks. Others follow the pattern of the private detective, a cynical and hardened man who attempts to bring his personal sense of justice to a corrupt world. These private-eyes do not hide their true identities, but work in the shadowy world between law-enforcement professionals and the life of a criminal. Although they collaborate with law enforcement to bring criminals to justice, they are just as often threatened with imprisonment for their cavalier disregard for legal formalities. Dexter, in a frightening, madcap fashion, partakes of some elements of both traditions.

Masked figures from popular culture like The Lone Ranger and Batman exist outside the normal process of law. They hide their true identity so that they may continue their "good work" unhindered by the legal system that they generously choose to augment. It is commonly accepted that the masked vigilante will ensure that there is a clear demarcation between his personal life and his public function. While masked, they exist in a subliminal state with no real legal existence and, while unmasked, they are law-abiding members of society. The masked heroes often justify this secrecy as a means to protect their friends and families from the vengeance of criminal adversaries, but it is also clear that a more open course of action would result in prosecution and imprisonment.

The hidden hero usually selects his secret identity so that it does not arouse suspicion. As John Cawelti indicates in his "Myths of Violence in American Popular Culture," the secret identity of this sort of figure is usually quite prosaic:

> In fact, in his other identity, he is generally some respectable member of [. . .] society. As superhero, he gains no personal advantage or satisfaction from his heroic deeds beyond his basic and automatic concern to make justice prevail. Thus, he is purely reactive, a symbolic embodiment of the general principle that the criminal is certain to meet his nemesis. (531)

Although Dexter is clearly "a respectable member of society" during the day, there are a number of excursions from the traditional paradigm that make his character—both in Jeff Lindsay's novels and the television series—a truly twenty-first-century post-modern hero. While Dexter is a respected professional with apparently normal family relationships, he never really considers himself to be a solid citizen. Rather like Superman, who is an alien pretending to be the human Clark Kent, Dexter's life as a working man is more of a mask than his secret identity. It is the normal world that puzzles Dexter, and, through his reflections on the matter, his audience.

While Dexter's night work as a somewhat heroic bringer of justice follows in the tradition of the masked hero and therefore requires a secret identity, Dexter's employment as a forensic technician for the Miami police force is closer to the tradition of the hard-boiled private-eye. Like a private-eye, he is unofficially related to the law-enforcement community, but has no true authority to act. As such, the plot structures and characterization in *Dexter* owe a lot to the detective story. Yet, unlike the detective heroes penned by Raymond Chandler and Dashiell Hammett,[4] Dexter's public identity is not one that we would immediately consider a man of action. He is shy, retiring, and more likely to be considered by his friends and his targets as a victim than an aggressor. In other words, he is closer to the alter-ego of a superhero than the world-weary, hard-boiled detective. However, as a blood-spatter expert, Dexter is part of a contemporary trend which idolizes the technical and scientific aspects of law enforcement. The *CSI* franchise, *Bones*, as well as the series *Numb3rs*, typify this shift in the heroes of American popular culture.[5] The highly skilled technicians and scientists that dominate this sub-genre are more likely to carry an identity card than a badge, and if they carry a gun, it is not a part of their official job description. Nevertheless, like the private detectives of an earlier tradition, they always seem to turn up when the criminal is finally brought to justice. Thus, Dexter manages to have the unobtrusive secret identity required by the masked hero while eliciting his contemporary audience's fascination with unofficial law enforcement by a dispassionate and scientifically distanced view of the intensely violent aspects of contemporary life.

In popular culture precedents, the vigilante hero does not require a great deal of moral soul-searching before moving forward in his search for justice. In contrast, the ethical universe represented by Dexter's narrative is subtly textured and humorous in its representation of this man who "takes the law into his own hands." One might think that a series like *Dexter* would alienate any potential audience through its graphic representation of violence. This is not the case, because the writers have employed a strategy that prevents the audience from being overwhelmed by the sheer horror of the subject material. Like the other forensic experts that abound in contemporary popular culture, Dexter manages to present the unthinkable aspects of violence in a forthright manner through the power of abstraction:

> What we see when we view the isolated human foot on the forensics table of the show *Dexter* is of course not a whole body at all but its lacunae or negative dimension, that is to say, the very lack of the rest of the body. Hall, who plays the role of Dexter, is similarly defined by the advertising for the show as a character whose psychology is assembled from many parts. (Holzapfel 2–3)

By abstracting the body parts from a once-living being,[6] the series manages to avoid the feelings of disgust that are so important to the graphic depiction of violence more common in slasher films. Dexter's status as a composite being—created by a similar process of abstraction—is even more interesting. His internal monologue, which is presented in voice-over format, reveals his technique for blending in with his non-psychopathic colleagues and relatives; he simply imitates what he considers to be a normal person's emotional response for any given situation. He assembles his behavior from observed paradigms. As Dexter's character is assembled from various components—loyal son, reliable brother, competent scientist, and violent psychopath—he is able to attract an audience on numerous levels while providing a logical justification for a truly post-modern sense of alienation.

Because he is so good at his own peculiar art of protective mimicry, Dexter's daytime behavior is indistinguishable from anyone else working at a similar job. In fact, Dexter appears substantially more normal to his co-workers than his fellow forensic scientist, Vince Masuka. The fact that he is apparently a "normal guy" is overshadowed by the fascination his work holds for the contemporary American audience. Unlike other masked heroes of American popular culture, Dexter's prosaic public existence is as interesting to the audience as his life as an heroic avenger. Dexter brings criminals to justice both day and night. This divergence from tradition serves two functions; it provides an element more appropriate to contemporary tastes than the hackneyed trope of the private detective, and it allows the writers to develop parallel plotlines that are a distorted mirror image of a common story. For example, the first season's plot arc—the search for the Ice Truck Killer—has a rich narrative based on the ineffectual police efforts to capture Rudy/Brian juxtaposed with the intertwined plot-line delineating Dexter's search for a kindred spirit. Dexter spends his days in the lab and on the crime scenes using his technical skills to find some clue to his brother's identity in the bloodless corpses and horrifying scenes of torture and murder. After work hours, he follows the subtle hints that are, in effect, direct messages from one killer to another. In "Crocodile" (1.2), Brian leaves a dismembered doll in Dexter's freezer to provide insight into his *modus operandi*. In "Let's Give the Boy a Hand" (1.4), he begins to leave body parts posed in scenes snatched from Dexter's family photos to empha-size their familial relationship. The level of moral complexity that this aspect of the series brings to the audience transcends the usual black-and-white representation of hero versus villain found in Dexter's popular culture antecedents. In fact, as J.M. Tyree so astutely observes, "[The] tone never seems mad, however, because in *Dexter* normal life is portrayed as so fundamentally screwed up. . . . In *Dexter*, normal life is portrayed as so demented that a serial killer's personality is not very much different than anyone else's" (83). Although this might lead one to suspect that Dexter's view of the world is close to the cynicism of his hard-boiled detective antecedents, there is actually an essential difference. Dexter is not contemptuous of the mundane existence of his friends and colleagues. In fact, he wants desperately to belong to it. Unfortu-nately, every time he approaches another person, things go wrong.

Dexter's complex and rather humorous character development is predicated on a serial killer who is relentless in his acquisition of family ties despite the fact that he often muses on his self-defined role as a sociopath: someone who is unable to develop real feelings for others. Although Dexter at first exhibits many of the character-istics of a sociopath, his behavior over the course of the series would indicate that he develops true feelings for his adopted sister Debra Morgan, his acquired family—Rita Bennett and her children, Astor and Cody—and his workmates Angel Batista, Vince Masuka, and even his boss, Lieutenant LaGuerta. The depth of these supposedly artificial feelings is revealed during the climactic final episode of Season 1 in which his biological brother, Brian, tempts Dexter with the opportunity to ritualistically murder Debra. Dexter resists this temptation and murders Brian so that Debra can be safe. Although Dexter mourns the fact that he has killed the only person who can really understand him, it is clear from his actions that he has assimilated the moral template that his adoptive father Harry has given him. The Code of Harry has become so internalized that it has become an effective super-ego. There is, however, a substantial deviation between the characterization of Dexter in Jeff Lindsay's novels and his representation in the series. In the novels, the sense of black humor is much stronger, as Dexter goes through the process of courting and marrying a woman for whom he has no true feelings. Lindsay's Dexter compares his own emotional situation with his adoptive father when contemplating the education of Cody: "I was not Harry, could never be anything like Harry. Harry had run on love, and I had a completely different operating system" (299). In the television series, we see Dexter is clearly developing a genuine relationship with Rita. Although he first becomes involved with her because her previous experience with a violent husband has made Rita unwilling to enter into a sexual relationship, when Rita initiates sex, Dexter is at first bemused and then becomes a willing participant. This aspect of Dexter's television persona is much closer to the superhero represented by popular culture than Lindsay's genial psychopath. His mundane existence is relatively close to that of any other member of the society that he seeks to protect. There are, of course, sly variations on the mild-mannered lifestyle of the off-duty superhero Dexter. For example, he has a sexual affair with his Narcotics Anonymous sponsor, Lila, and feels more guilt about betraying Rita than he does for his dozens of murders.

Although, in the television series, Dexter seems to be developing a human face through involvement with others, the cheerful psychopath does not have an easy path toward becoming a "real boy." Each season of Dexter finds our hero recognizing aspects of himself in the violent adversary provided by the current plot arc. In Season 1, it is his brother Brian who tempts him with the joy of killing untrammeled by the ethical considerations of finding an appropriately evil victim. In Season 2, it is Lila Tournay, the addict with anger-management problems, and, in Season 3, it is Miguel Prado, a vigilante lawyer who has difficulty distinguishing between his own desires for personal vengeance and the public good. These three adversaries are important to Dexter's strange development as an ethical being. Unlike the villains that can be found in the Batman or Lone Ranger series, Dexter's opponents test his ethical rather than his physical prowess.

> Dexter: I never really got the whole superhero thing, but lately it seems we have a lot in common; tragic beginnings, secret identities, part-human, part-mutant . . . arch-enemies. (2.5)

This line is delivered in a voice-over as Dexter takes a swab sample from two action figures at a crime scene in a comic-book store. As he says "arch-enemies," there is an eye-line match from Dexter to a brief close-up of Sergeant Doakes. The implication is that Dexter considers Doakes to be his greatest adversary.[7] This is actually a misconception on Dexter's part. Although Doakes openly dislikes Dexter and wishes to prove him guilty of some crime, he does not really threaten Dexter's moral existence—except that he tempts Dexter to break Harry's moral code and kill an innocent. Fortunately for Dexter's moral development, Lila conveniently steps up and performs the execution that Dexter cannot. Unlike Doakes, Brian, Lila, and Miguel are unequivocally represented as tempters, villains far more worthy of the ironic complexity of Dexter's world. The name of this episode, "The Dark Defender," is derived from a lurid poster on the wall of the shop representing a hooded figure holding a dripping blade while crouching over a pile of corpses. The murder victim, Danny, had intended to create a graphic novel with a hero based on Dexter's exploits as the Bay Harbor Butcher. As the victim's colleague says: "Danny had this great idea to put a spin on this vigilante serial killer we got running around . . . His blade of vengeance turns wrong into right." Dexter's response is typical of the macabre humor of the series. He is at first intrigued with the notion, then deflates it with a wry internal comment: "Naw, Miami's too hot for all that leather." Nevertheless, the next scene is a dream—shot in black and white to emphasize the surreal comic-book nature of the sequence—in which Dexter, dressed as the Dark Defender, walks in on his mother's murder and heroically dispatches the three men who took part in her bloody execution. Throughout this episode, the image of Dexter in the hood of the Dark Defender is replicated in a number of inventive variations. When Lila comes to visit him at work, Dexter is in a white room attempting to reproduce the blood-splatter effect of the comic-book shop murder with a dummy full of red syrup. He is posed as the negative image of the poster from the comic-book shop, the dark background and dark hooded costume replaced with a translucent white raincoat hood against the white walls of the blood-splatter room. And just in case we did not notice that *Dexter* presents violence as art, Lila asks for one of the sheets of "blood"-splattered paper for her "found art" projects.

Even before the arrival of Lila—who is an artist by profession—in Season 2, visual art plays an important role in the aesthetic impact of *Dexter*. The series is characterized by its high-quality cinematography; the use of color—especially blood red—is hyper-real. The city of Miami explodes with vibrant, yet somehow over-ripe, visual stimuli.[8] The brightly, highly saturated primary color, comic-book visual aspects of the series provide a counterpoint to the ethical distortion of *Dexter*'s plot-line. There are no half-tones in Dexter's life; misdeeds result in bloody retribution. Violence and murder are an integral component of both the public and the secret aspects of our hero's life, and he moves from frame to frame like a masked avenger. The climax of "The Dark Defender" episode presents Dexter beating the old man responsible for his mother's death while musing aloud: "Isn't this what heroes do? Avenge lost loved ones?" The grizzled old murderer is laid out on a bright green pool table, his blood sharply defined by contrast with the primary colors of the setting. Yet Dexter cannot bring himself to kill the old man because the ethical framework of his constructed identity does not allow for personal vengeance. He breaks off the encounter and goes back to his hotel room, where he is comforted by a nearly naked Lila. The fact that this emotional infidelity bothers Dexter more than murder is part and parcel of the distorted ethical structure of the series.

Perhaps the most significant aspect of Dexter's divergence from the typical masked hero is that Dexter, unlike The Lone Ranger and Batman or even the cynical private detective, takes an unholy glee in the gory mechanics of his efforts to redress the imbalance of the justice system. This is the primary reason why each season's neme-sis is so threatening. Every one of them tempts Dexter with the promise of release from his self-imposed restrictions. Brian, Lila, and Miguel bring into question the rigorous moral template provided by Dexter's step-father Harry. After all, Dexter is a masked hero with very special problems. Unlike the popular-culture heroes that provide the narrative template for this series, he does not want to stop with the minimum amount of violence required to accom-plish his ends:

> Superheroes rarely kill the criminals they overcome; instead they knock them out and turn them over to the police, or, like the Lone Ranger, they shoot the gun out of the villain's hand with silver bullets or some other mystical weapon and then call the sheriff. For all his dazzling capacities, marvelous weapons, and fantastic disguises, the superhero is a transcen-dent agent of society. (Cawelti 531)

This is definitely at odds with Dexter's rather disconcerting pleas-ure in the violence of his acts of justice. Although Dexter's powers are similar to Batman and the Lone Ranger in that they are in no way supernatural,[9] unlike these popular-culture antecedents, Dexter needs to act in order to satisfy his own desire for murder. It is the highly personalized nature of Dexter's desire to kill that makes him such an unusual commentary upon the pop-culture avenger.

Dexter's calamitous character flaw—an almost complete lack of empathy for others—means that he must find some way to main-tain a buffer between his desires and society's expectations. Time and time again, we are reminded that despite his perverse soul, Dexter practices a strict moral procedure that only allows him to punish the guilty—the oft-mentioned "Code of Harry." The hero's code has a long tradition in the American popular culture: "Though the Code is an unwritten law, engraved only on the hearts of its adherents, it is, nevertheless, a stringent set of moral rules concern-ing, above all, the proper uses of individual violence" (Cawelti 536).

This sort of moral code is present primarily in American-style detective fiction. Dexter's foster-father, Detective Harry Morgan, has developed this code of behavior for Dexter as a defense mechanism—it is Harry's means of assuring himself that Dexter will not follow the path of so many other serial killers. Harry's code is based on a principle of altruism with a strong admixture of self-preservation. Dexter is never allowed to kill for personal reasons; his victims are chosen because they present a threat to society as a whole. In the regional context of the series, they tend to be people who prey on the innocent and defenseless citizens of Miami. In his desire to physically strike down the enemies of society, Dexter is "[u]nlike the superhero. The vigilante does kill . . . [H]is violence is dramatically climactic. It either represents an escalation of the villain's acts of violence or it is performed with some striking skill or style" (Cawelti 532). Dexter is trained by his step-father to prepare for each killing with hours of research, and he is sure never to leave a trace of his activity behind because he is a forensic scientist by profession. In "An Inconvenient Lie" (2.3), Sergeant Doakes reveals another of Dexter's special skills: "I know you studied martial arts in college, but I don't know what a lab geek needs with advanced jujitsu." Like Batman, Dexter is completely prepared to do battle with the forces of evil.

However, the real problem is that the evil that Dexter must battle is internal as well as external. In the beginning of the series, Dexter is revealed to have all of the psychological earmarks of a garden-variety psychopathic mass-murderer. He does not appear to have real emotions; he simply imitates the actions of others in emotional situations. The one true emotion that he seems to have is a pleasure in the suffering and death of others. These characteristics manifest early in Dexter's life and may be attributed to the horrific trauma of witnessing his mother's bloody murder while he was still a toddler. Dexter openly admits that, without his adoptive father's insistence on guilty victims, he would have become a common serial killer like his brother Brian. Despite this significant digression from the established pattern of the comic-book hero, Dexter does prevail. He slowly learns to care for others; he defeats the adversaries who would corrupt him, and his life gradually begins to merge with the normal existence from which he was excluded.

Appendix A: Episode Guide

Episode Number	Episode Title	Writer	Director	Original US Airdate
Season 1				
1.1	"Dexter"	James Manos, Jr	Michael Cuesta	Oct. 1, 2006
1.2	"Crocodile"	Clyde Phillips	Michael Cuesta	Oct. 8, 2006
1.3	"Popping Cherry"	Daniel Cerone	Michael Cuesta	Oct. 15, 2006
1.4	"Let's Give the Boy a Hand"	Drew Z. Greenberg	Robert Lieberman	Oct. 22, 2006
1.5	"Love American Style"	Melissa Rosenberg	Robert Lieberman	Oct. 29, 2006
1.6	"Return to Sender"	Timothy Schlattman	Tony Goldwyn	Nov. 5, 2006
1.7	"Circle of Friends"	Daniel Cerone	Steve Shill	Nov. 12, 2006
1.8	"Shrink Wrap"	Lauren Gussis	Tony Goldwyn	Nov. 19, 2006
1.9	"Father Knows Best"	Melissa Rosenberg	Adam Davidson	Nov. 26, 2006
1.10	"Seeing Red"	Kevin Maynard	Michael Cuesta	Dec. 3, 2006
1.11	"Truth Be Told"	Timothy Schlattman and Drew Z. Greenberg	Keith Gordon	Dec. 10, 2006
1.12	"Born Free"	Daniel Cerone and Melissa Rosenberg	Michael Cuesta	Dec. 17, 2006
Season 2				
2.1	"It's Alive"	Daniel Cerone	Tony Goldwyn	Sept. 30, 2007
2.2	"Waiting to Exhale"	Clyde Phillips	Marcos Siega	Oct. 7, 2007
2.3	"An Inconvenient Lie"	Melissa Rosenberg	Tony Goldwyn	Oct. 14, 2007
2.4	"See-Through"	Scott Buck	Nick Gomez	Oct. 21, 2007

Episode Number	Episode Title	Writer	Director	Original US Airdate
2.5	"The Dark Defender"	Timothy Schlattman	Keith Gordon	Oct. 28, 2007
2.6	"Dex, Lies, and Videotape"	Lauren Gussis	Nick Gomez	Nov. 4, 2007
2.7	"That Night A Forest Grew"	Daniel Cerone	Jeremy Podeswa	Nov. 11, 2007
2.8	"Morning Comes"	Scott Buck	Keith Gordon	Nov. 18, 2007
2.9	"Resistance is Futile"	Melissa Rosenberg	Marcos Siega	Nov. 25, 2007
2.10	"There's Something About Harry"	Scott Reynolds	Steve Shill	Dec. 2, 2007
2.11	"Left Turn Ahead"	Timothy Schlattman and Scott Buck	Marcos Siega	Dec. 9, 2007
2.12	"The British Invasion"	Daniel Cerone (teleplay) Daniel Cerone and Melissa Rosenberg (story)	Steve Shill	Dec. 16, 2007
Season 3				
3.1	"Our Father"	Clyde Phillips	Keith Gordon	Sept. 28, 2008
3.2	"Finding Freebo"	Melissa Rosenberg	Marcos Siega	Oct. 5, 2008
3.3	"The Lion Sleeps Tonight"	Scott Buck	John Dahl	Oct. 12, 2008
3.4	"All in the Family"	Adam Fierro	Keith Gordon	Oct. 19, 2008
3.5	"Turning Biminese"	Timothy Schlattman	Marcos Siega	Oct. 26, 2008
3.6	"Si Se Puede"	Charles H. Eglee	Ernest Dickerson	Nov. 2, 2008
3.7	"Easy as Pie"	Lauren Gussis	Steve Shill	Nov. 9, 2008
3.8	"The Damage a Man Can Do"	Scott Buck	Marcos Siega	Nov. 16, 2008
3.9	"About Last Night"	Melissa Rosenberg (teleplay); Scott Reynolds (story)	Tim Hunter	Nov. 23, 2008
3.10	"Go Your Own Way"	Timothy Schlattman	John Dahl	Nov. 30, 2008
3.11	"I Had a Dream"	Lauren Gussis and Charles H. Eglee	Marcos Siega	Dec. 7, 2008
3.12	"Do You Take Dexter Morgan"	Scott Buck	Keith Gordon	Dec. 14, 2008

Appendix B: Novel Guide

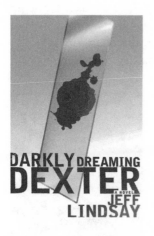

The first novel in the series, *Darkly Dreaming Dexter* (2004) introduces us, through its first-person narrative, to Dexter Morgan, a blood-spatter expert for the Miami Metro Police Department who is himself a serial killer. Following the code that he learned from his foster-father Harry, Dexter, however, only kills other killers. With the help of Deb, his ambitious, determined, frequently foul-mouthed sister, Dexter tries to break the case of a serial murderer who leaves body parts with no blood and who seems to know him a little too well.

In Lindsay's 2005 follow-up, Dexter returns to face a sadistic killer who leaves his victims disturbingly maimed and dismembered. This time, the killer has unusual ties to Sergeant Doakes and to Deb's new love interest, federal agent Kyle Chutsky. Dexter, meanwhile, has personal problems of his own, as somehow his girlfriend Rita seems to think that they are engaged and he is beginning to have some strange suspicions about her children, Cody and Astor.

As Dexter prepares for his wedding to Rita, he suddenly finds himself investigating a new wave of killings, killings so bizarre that they have even scared off his Dark Passenger. Dexter also has difficulty dealing with Rita's kids, Cody and Astor, who have a similar inclination toward homicide and are looking for Dexter to school them in the ways of serial murder. With *Dexter in the Dark* (2007), Lindsay takes the series in a more supernatural direction, as both Dexter and the reader learn about the true nature of his Dark Passenger.

The latest novel in the series (2009) brings a newly married Dexter into the art world, as he squares off against a serial killer with a different and decidedly darker kind of aesthetic. While Cody and Astor want to continue their training and Deb wants to confront Dexter about his crimes, this case poses the greatest threat yet—to his code, to his family, and to the very anonymity that makes his murders possible.

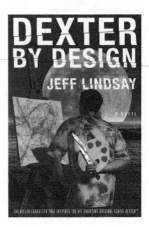

Bibliography

Abbott, Stacey, ed. *The Cult TV Book*. London and New York: I.B.Tauris, forthcoming, 2010.

Allison, Deborah. "Catch Me If You Can, Auto Focus, Far From Heaven and the Art of Retro Title Sequences." *Senses of Cinema* 26 (May–June 2003). 6 February 2009
http://archive.sensesofcinema.com/contents/03/26/retro_titles.html

Alston, Joshua. "Too much of a bad thing; No one on TV can be merely good or evil anymore. That's why we're suffering from antihero overload." *Newsweek* 153.2 (2009).
http://proquest.umi.com.ezproxy.mtsu.edu/pqdlink?Ver=1&Exp=01 –16–2014&FMT=7&DID=1621785541&RQT=309

Aunt Sally. "'Help Yourself' in Style." *Sunday Times Magazine* 13 May 2007: 39.

Baldick, Chris. *In Frankenstein's Shadow: Myth, Monstrosity, and Nineteenth-Century Writing*. New York: Oxford UP, 1987.

Bass, Saul. *Bass on Titles*. Pyramid Films, 1977.

——."Movement, Film, Communication." *Sign, Image and Symbol*. Ed. Gyorgy Kepes. London: Studio Vista, 1966. 200–5.

Bataille, Georges. *Eroticism*. San Francisco: City Lights Books, 1986.

Bobbitt, Rebecca. "RE: dexter's lab." E-mail to James Francis. 21 January 2009.

Bonnycastle, Kevin. "Not the Usual Suspects: The Obfuscation of Political Economy and Race in *CSI*." Byers and Johnson, 149–76.

Boss, Pete. "Vile Bodies and Bad Medicine." *Screen* 27.1 (1986): 14–25.

Bould, Mark. *Film Noir: From Berlin to Sin City*. London: Wallflower Press, 2005.

Braphy, Philip. "Horrorality—the Contextuality of Contemporary Horror Films." *Screen* 27.1 (1986): 2–13.

Braxton, Greg. "Cop-Show Streets Get Meaner." *Los Angeles Times* 12
March 2002. 23 March 2009
http://articles.latimes.com/2002/mar/12/entertainment/et-braxton12

Brown, Simon. "Cult Channels: Showtime, FX and Cult TV." Abbott,
2010.

Brown, Wendy. "Neo-liberalism and the End of Liberal Democracy."
Theory & Event 7.1 (2003).

——. "Neoliberalism, Neoconservatism, and De-Democratization."
Political Theory 34 (2006a): 690–712.

——. *Regulating Aversion: Tolerance in the Age of Identity and Empire.*
New Brunswick: Princeton UP, 2006.

Burke, Edmund. *A Philosophical Enquiry into the Origin of our Ideas of
the Sublime and Beautiful.* [1757] Oxford: Oxford UP, 1990.

Butler, Judith. *Giving an Account of Oneself.* New York: Fordham UP,
2005.

Byers, Michele. "Post *CSI*-TV: The Ecstasies of Dexter." *FlowTV*
1 December 2006. 1 December 2008 http://flowtv.org/?p=91

—— and Val Johnson. *"The* CSI *Effect:" Television, Crime, and
Governance.* Lexington, 2009.

Cain, James M. *Double Indemnity.* 1943. London: Orion, 2002.

——. *Mildred Pierce.* 1941. London: Orion, 2008.

——. *The Postman Always Rings Twice.* 1934. London: Orion, 2005.

Carroll, Noël. Foreword. *The Frankenstein Film Sourcebook.* By Caroline
Joan ("Kay") S. Picart, Frank Smoot, and Jayne Blodgett. Westport:
Greenwood, 2001. vii–x.

Cassuto, Leonard. "Rooting for Serial Killers: The Strange Case of
Dexter." *Columbia University Press Blog* 16 October 2008. 15
November 2008. http://www.cupblog.org/?p=412

Cawelti, John G. "Myths of Violence in American Popular Culture."
Critical Inquiry 1.3 (1975): 521–41.

Cerone, Daniel, Clyde Phillips, and Sarah Colleton. "DVD Audio
Commentary: Born Free" *Dexter: The First Season.* DVD. Showtime,
2007.

Chamberlain, Daniel, and Scott Ruston. "*24* and Twenty-First Century
Quality Television." *Reading 24: TV against the Clock.* Ed. Steven
Peacock. London: I.B.Tauris, 2007. 13–24.

Chandler, Raymond. *The Big Sleep.* 1939. London: Penguin, 2005.

——. *Farewell My Lovely.* 1940. London: Penguin, 2005.

Chin, Vivian. "Buffy? She's Like Me, She's Not Like Me—She's *Rad*."
Athena's Daughters. Eds Frances Early and Kathleen Kennedy.
Syracuse: Syracuse UP, 2003. 92–102.

Cleto, Fabio. *Camp: Queer Aesthetics and the Performing Subject*. Ann Arbor: Michigan UP, 1999.

Clover, Carol J. "Her Body, Himself: Gender in the Slasher Film." *The Dread of Difference: Gender and the Horror Film*. Ed. Barry Keith Grant. Austin: Texas UP, 1996. 66–113.

Collings, David. "The Mother and the Maternal Thing: Mary Shelley's Critique of Ideology." *Frankenstein*. 2nd ed. Ed. Johanna M. Smith. Boston: Bedford, 2000. 280–95.

Dean, Flannery. "Dex appeal: The curious charm of TV's most popular serial killer." *CBC News* 24 September 2008. 23 January 2009 http://www.cbc.ca/arts/tv/story/2008/09/24/f-dexter-third-season.html

Denison, Reyna, and Mark Jancovitch. "Introduction" to "Mysterious Bodies." *Intensities: The Journal of Cult Media Special Issue* 4 (2007). 21 January 2009 http://intensities.org/Essays/Jancovich_Intro.pdf

DeWolf-Smith, Nancy. "The Good, the Ugly and the Bad." *Wall Street Journal* 29 September 2006: W5. 3 March 2009 http://online.wsj.com/article/SB115949032468577451.html?mod=2_1168_1

Dolan, Marc. "The Peaks and Valleys of Serial Creativity: What Happened to/on *Twin Peaks*." *Full of Secrets: Critical Approaches to Twin Peaks*. Ed. David Lavery. Detroit: Wayne State UP, 1994. 30–50.

Eggerton, John. "PTC Pushes CBS Affiliates to Drop Dexter." *Broadcasting and Cable* 1 May 2008. 7 March 2009 http://www.broadcastingcable.com/article/113541–PTC_Pushes_CBS_Affiliates_to_Drop_Dexter.php

Eick, Dennis. *Programmplanung*. Konstanz: UVK, 2007.

Erdem, Tuna. "CFP: 'It Has Happened Before, It Will Happen Again': The 'Third' Golden Age of Television Fiction." *Independent Scholars*. 2007. 10 January 2009 http://www.independentscholars.org/s/show.aspx?id=34

Evans, Dylan. *An Introductory Dictionary of Lacanian Psychoanalysis*. Hove and New York: Brunner-Routledge, 2003.

Faith, Karlene, and Yasmin Jiwani. "The Social Construction of 'Dangerous' Girls and Women." *Marginalization and Condemnation*. Eds Bernard Schissel and Carolyn Brooks. Halifax: Fernwood, 2002. 83–107.

Fiedler, Leslie. *Love & Death in the American Novel*. New York: Anchor, 1960.

Foucault, Michel. "Governmentality." *The Foucault Effect: Studies in*

Governmentality. Eds Graham Burchell, Colin Gordon, and Peter Miller. Chicago: Chicago UP, 1991. 87–104.

——. *The Will to Knowledge: The History of Sexuality*. Volume 1. Trans. Robert Hurley. London: Penguin, 1998.

Frank, Nino. "Un nouveau genre 'policier': l'aventure criminelle." *L'Ecran Français* 61 (1946): 8–9, 14.

Freccero, Carla. "Historical Violence, Censorship, and the Serial Killer: The Case of *American Psycho*." *Diacritics* 27.2 (1997): 44–58.

Fukuyama, Francis. *America at the Crossroads: Democracy, Power and the Neoconservative Legacy*. New Haven: Yale UP, 2006.

Garland, David. "The Limits of the Sovereign State: Strategies of Crime Control in Contemporary Society." *The British Journal of Criminology* 36.4 (1996): 445–71.

Garvin, Glenn. "You gotta love this charming serial killer." *Miami Herald* 1 October 2006: NA. *General OneFile*. Gale. Suffolk Community College – SUNY. 1 March 2009 http://lib1.lib.sunysuffolk.edu:2053/itx/start.do?prodId=ITOF

Geffner, David. "First Things First." *Filmmaker* Fall 1997. 6 February 2009 http://www.filmmakermagazine.com/fall1997/firstthingsfirst.php

Geraghty, Christine. "Aesthetics and Quality in Popular Television Drama." *International Journal of Cultural Studies* 6.1 (2003): 25–45.

Gilbert, Sandra M., and Susan Gubar. "Mary Shelley's Monstrous Eve." Shelley 225–40.

Gillette, Amelia, et al. "Inventory: 22 TV Opening-Credit Sequences That Fit Their Shows Perfectly." *The Onion's A.V. Club*. 18 March 2007. 8 March 2009 http://www.avclub.com/articles/inventory-22–tv-openingcredit-sequences-that-fit-t,1809/

Ginzburg, Carlo. *Clues, Myths and the Historical Method*. Baltimore, MD: Johns Hopkins Press, 1989.

Gledhill, Christine. "*Klute*1: A Contemporary Film Noir and Feminist Criticism." Kaplan 20–34.

Gregory, André and Wallace Shawn. *My Dinner with André*. New York: Grove Press, 1981.

Guider, Elizabeth. "Int'l TV banks on yanks." *Variety* 12 November 2006. 5 December 2008 http://www.variety.com/article/VR1117953753.html?categoryid=14&cs=1

Haggins, Bambi. "Darkly Dreaming of Dexter: If Loving Him Is Wrong I Don't Want To Be Right." *FlowTV* 16 November 2007. 5 March 2009 http://flowtv.org/?p=942

Halberstam, Judith. *Skin Shows: Gothic Horror and The Technology of Monsters*. Durham: Duke UP, 1995.

Hall, Peter. "Opening Ceremonies: Typography and the Movies, 1955–1969." *Architecture and Film*. Ed. Mark Lamster. New York: Princeton Architectural Press, 2000. 129–39.

Hammett, Dashiell. *The Maltese Falcon*. London: Orion, 2002 [1930].

Havrilesky, Heather. "Finale Wrap-Up: *Dexter*." *Salon.com* 15 December 2008. http://www.salon.com/ent/tv/review/2008/12/15/dexter/index.htm

Hayward, Susan. *Key Concepts in Cinema Studies*. 2nd ed. London: Routledge, 2000.

Henriques, Diana B. "Madoff Will Plead Guilty; Faces Life for Vast Swindle." *New York Times* 10 March 2009: A1. 28 March 2009 http://www.nytimes.com/2009/03/11/business/11madoff.html

Henriques, Ron. "*Hannibal Rising*." *LatinoReview.com* 8 February 2007. 27 March 2009 http://www.latinoreview.com/theatrical-reviews/235

Hibberd, James. "Parents Television Council Denounces CBS's 'Dexter' Plan." *Advertising Age* 5 December 2007. 1 February 2009 http://adage.com/hibberd/post?article_id=122424

Hills, Matt. *The Pleasures of Horror*. London and New York: Continuum, 2005.

Hoeveler, Diane Long. "*Frankenstein*, feminism, and literary theory." *The Cambridge Companion to Mary Shelley*. Ed. Esther Schor. Cambridge: Cambridge UP, 2003. 45–62.

Holzapfel, Amy Strahler. "The Body In Pieces: Contemporary Anatomy Theatres." *PAJ: A Journal of Performance and Art* 30.2 (2008): 1–16.

Jermyn, Deborah. "Body Matters: Realism, Spectacle and the Corpse in *CSI*. "*Reading* CSI: *Crime TV Under the Microscope*. Ed. Michael Allen. London: I.B.Tauris, 2007. 79–89.

Jiwani, Yasmin. *Discourses of Denial: Mediations of Race, Gender, and Violence*. Vancouver: UBC Press, 2006.

Kaplan, E. Anne, ed. *Women in Film Noir*. 2nd ed. London: British Film Institute, 1998.

Kilgour, Maggie. "Dr Frankenstein Meets Dr Freud." *American Gothic: New Interventions in a National Narrative*. Eds Robert K. Martin and Eric Savoy. Iowa City: Iowa UP, 1998. 40–53.

King, Neal. "Brownskirts: Fascism, Christianity, and the Eternal Demon." South 197–211.

King, Stephen. *Stephen King's Danse Macabre*. New York: Everest House, 1981.

Kolker, Robert. *A Cinema of Loneliness: Penn, Stone, Kubrick, Scorsese,*

Spielberg, Altman. 3rd ed. Oxford: Oxford UP, 2000.

Kooistra, Paul. *Criminals as Heroes: Structure, Power, and Identity*. Bowling Green, OH: Bowling Green S U Popular P, 1989.

Kristeva, Julia. *Powers of Horror: An Essay on Abjection*. Trans. Leon S. Roudiez. New York: Columbia UP, 1982.

Krutnik, Frank. *In a Lonely Street: Film Noir, Genre, Masculinity*. London: Routledge, 1991.

Lacan, Jacques. *The Seminar. Book II: The Ego in Freud's Theory and in the Technique of Psychoanalysis, 1954–1955*. Trans. Sylvana Tomaselli. New York and Cambridge: Cambridge UP, 1998.

——. *The Seminar. Book VII: The Ethics of Psychoanalysis, 1959–60*. Trans. Dennis Porter. London: Routledge, 1992.

Lavery, David. "Apocalyptic Apocalypses: The Narrative Eschatology of *Buffy the Vampire Slayer*." *Slayage*: *The Online International Journal of Buffy Studies* Number 9 (2003). http://www.slayageonline.com/essays/slayage9/Lavery.htm

——. "*Lost* and Long Term Television Narrative." *Third Person: Authoring and Exploring Vast Narratives*. Ed. Pat Harrigan and Noah Wardrip-Fruin. Cambridge, MA: MIT Press, 2009.

——, and Robert J. Thompson. "David Chase, *The Sopranos*, and Television Creativity." *This Thing of Ours: Investigating The Sopranos*. New York: Columbia UP, 2002. 18–25.

Leitch, Thomas. "Nobody Here But Us Killers: The Disavowal of Violence in Recent American Films." *Film and Philosophy* 1 (2001). 22 August 2002 www.hanover.edu/philos/film/vol_01/leitch.htm (site now discontinued).

Levine, Michael P. and Schneider, Stephen Jay. "Feeling for Buffy: The Girl Next Door." South 294–308.

Lindsay, Jeff. *Darkly Dreaming Dexter*. 2004. New York: Vintage, 2006.

——. *Dearly Devoted Dexter*. 2005. New York: Vintage, 2006.

——. *Dexter in the Dark*. New York: Doubleday, 2007.

——. "Jeff Lindsay speaks to Al Karim for *Shots Ezine*" *Shots: The Crime and Mystery Ezine* 2004. 7 March 2009 http://www.shotsmag.co.uk/interviews2005/jeff_lindsay/jlindsay.html>

Longworth, James L., Jr. "Martha Williamson: Visionary." *TV Creators: Conversations with America's Top Producers of Television Drama*. Syracuse: Syracuse UP, 2002: 55–82.

Martin, Angela. "'Gilda Didn't Do Any of Those Things You've Been Losing Sleep Over!': The Central Women of 40s Film Noirs." Kaplan 202–28.

McCarty, John. *Splatter Movies: Breaking the Last Taboo*. New York: FantaCo Enterprises, 1981.

Meeks, Kenneth. "Racism and Reality in *NYPD Blue*." *What Would Sipowicz Do?* Ed. Glenn Yeffeth. Dallas: BenBella Books, 2004.

Mill, John Stuart. *Utilitarianism*. 2nd ed. Ed. George Schor. Indianapolis: Hackett, 2001.

Miller, Frank, writer, and David Mazzucchelli, artist. *Batman: Year One*. New York: DC Comics, 2005.

Moi, Toril. *Sexual/Textual Politics: Feminist Literary Theory*. London: Taylor & Francis, 1985.

"Mysterious Bodies." *Intensities: The Journal of Cult Media* Special Issue 4 (2007). 21 January 2009 http://intensities.org/Issues/Intensities_Four.htm

Naremore, James. *More Than Night: Film Noir in Its Contexts*. London: California UP, 1998.

Nelson, Robin. "Analysing TV Fiction: How to Study Television Drama." *Tele-Visions: An Introduction to Studying Television*. Ed. Glen Creeber. London: British Film Institute, 2006. 74–86.

Newcomb, Horace. "*Magnum*: The Champagne of TV." *Channels of Communication* (May/June 1985): 23–6.

Ono, Kent A. "To Be a Vampire on Buffy, The Vampire Slayer: Race and ("Other") Socially Marginalizing Positions on Horror TV." *Fantasy Girls: Gender in the New Universe of Science Fiction and Fantasy Television*. Ed. Elyce Rae Helford. Lanham, MD: Rowman and Littlefield. 163–86.

Phillips, Clyde. *Dexter 25: SHORunner*. Showtime On Demand. 2008.

Poe, Edgar Allan. *Selected Tales*. London: Penguin, 1994.

Poovey, Mary. "The Lady and The Monster." Shelley 251–61.

"PTC: High Time for CBS to Pull *Dexter* "*parentstv.org*. 25 April 2008. 7 March 2009 http://www.parentstv.org/PTC/news/release/2008/0425.asp

"PTC to CBS: Do Not Air *Dexter* on Broadcast TV." *parentstv.org*. 30 Jan. 2008. 7 March 2009 http://www.parentstv.org/PTC/news/release/2008/0130.asp

Rajiva, Mythili. "Troping Mr Johnson: Reading Phallic Mastery and Anxiety on Season One of *CSI: Crime Scene Investigation*." Byers and Johnson, 177–99.

Reeves, Jimmie L., Mark C. Rodgers, and Michael Epstein. "Re-Writing Popularity: The Cult *Files*." *Deny All Knowledge: Investigating The X-Files*. Eds David Lavery, Angela Hague, and Marla Cartwright. Syracuse: Syracuse UP, 1996.

Rizzo, Carita. "Till Death Do They Part?" *TV Guide* 3 November 2008: 38–9.

Root, Jane. "Film Noir." *The Cinema Book*. 3rd ed. Ed. Pam Cook. London: British Film Institute, 2007. 305–15.

Rucker, Allen. *The Sopranos: A Family History*. New York: New American Library, 2000.

Scanlon, T.M. *What We Owe to Each Other*. Cambridge: Harvard UP, 1998.

Schmid, David. "The Kindest Cut of All: Adapting Thomas Harris's *Hannibal*." *Literature/Film Quarterly* 35.1 (2007): 389–95.

———. *Natural Born Celebrities: Serial Killers in American Culture*. Chicago: Chicago UP, 2005.

Schrader, Paul. "Notes on Film Noir." *Film Genre Reader III*. Ed. Barry Keith Grant. Austin: Texas UP, 2003. 229–42.

Schütte, Jörg and Eric Karstens. *Praxishandbuch Fernsehen*. Wiesbaden: Vs Verlag, 2005.

Sepinwall, Alan. "After hours, he makes a killing." *Star-Ledger (Newark-NJ)* 29 September 2006: 059. *Custom Newspapers*. Gale. Suffolk Community College – SUNY. 1 March 2009 http://lib1.lib.sunysuffolk.edu:2053/itx/start.do?prodId=SPN.SP03

Shelley, Mary. *Frankenstein; or, The Modern Prometheus*. Ed. Paul J. Hunter. New York: Norton, 1996.

"Showtime's Critically-Acclaimed Drama *Dexter* Premieres Sunday, Feb. 17, 10:00–11:00 p.m. on the CBS Television Network." *Showtime Official Site*. 7 January 2008. 7 March 2009 http://www.sho.com/site/announcements/20080107Dexter.do

"Showtime's Serial Killer, Dexter, Inspires Some Bloody Interesting Items You Can Own." *if it's hip, it's here*. 17 November 2008. 1 December 2008 http://ifitshipitshere.blogspot.com/2008/11/showtimes-serial-killer-dexter-inspires.html

Simpson, Philip L. *Psycho Paths: Tracking the Serial Killer Through Contemporary American Film and Fiction*. Carbondale: Southern Illinois UP, 2000.

Snell, Bruno (1953) cited in Jay, Martin. *Downcast Eyes: The Denigration of Vision in Twentieth Century French Thought*. London: California UP, 1994.

Sontag, Susan. "Notes on 'Camp.'" *Camp: Queer Aesthetics and the Performing Subject: A Reader*. Ed. Fabio Cleto. Ann Arbor: Michigan UP, 1999. 54–65.

South, James B., ed. *Buffy the Vampire Slayer and Philosophy: Fear and*

Trembling in Sunnydale. Chicago and LaSalle, Illinois: Open Court Press, 2003.

Spicer, Andrew. *Film Noir*. Harlow: Longman, 2002.

Stanley, Alessandra. "He Kills People and Cuts Them Up. But They Deserve It. Besides, He's Neat." *New York Times* 29 September 2006: E24.5 March 2009 http://www.nytimes.com/2006/09/29/arts/television/29dext.html?_r=2&ref=television&oref=slogin

Statistisches Bundesamt. "Gebiet und Bevölkerung—Ausländische Bevölkerung." *Statistisches Bundesamt* (official website). 1 October 2008. 5 December 2008 http://www.statistik-portal.de/Statistik-Portal/de_jb01_jahrtab2.asp

Storm, Jonathan. "A creepy premise, appealing character." *Philadelphia Inquirer* 1 October 2006: H01. 5 March 2009 http://www.avsforum.com/avs-vb/showpost.php?p=8553539&postcount=16192

sugarboots. "Dexter Haiku." *Dexter Wiki*. 22 March 2009 http://dexterwiki.sho.com/page/Dexter+Haiku?t=anon

Summerscale, Kate. *The Suspicions of Mr Whicher, or, The Murder at Road Hill House*. London: Bloomsbury, 2008.

Sutherland, John. "1000 Novels Everyone Must Read: Crime." *The Observer* 18 January 2009: 5.

Thompson, Philip. *The Grotesque: The Critical Idiom*. London: Methuen, 1972.

Thomson Media Control. 15 January 2009. http://www.media-control.de/

Thoret, Jean Baptiste. "The Aquarium Syndrome: On the Films of Michael Mann." Trans. Anna Dzenis. *Senses of Cinema* 19 (2002). 3 March 2009 http://pandora.nla.gov.au/pan/10772/20050309–0000/www.sensesofcinema.com/ contents/01/19/mann.html

——. "Gravity of the Flux: Michael Mann's *Miami Vice*." *Senses of Cinema* 42 (2007). Trans. Sally Shafto. http://archive.sensesofcinema.com/contents/07/42/miami-vice.html

Totaro, Donato. "Masters of Horror." Abbott, 2010.

Tulloch, John and Manuel Alvarado. *Doctor Who: The Unfolding Text*. London: Macmillan, 1983.

Turim, Maureen. *Flashbacks in Film: Memory and History*. London: Routledge, 1989.

Tyree, J.M. "Spatter Pattern." *Film Quarterly* 67.1 (2008): 82–5.

Vowell, Sarah. "Please Sir May I Have a Mother?" *Salon.com* 2 February 2000 http://www.salon.com/ent/col/vowe/2000/02/02/vowell_wb/index.html

Waller, Gregory A. "Made-For-Television Horror Films." *American Horrors: Essays on the Modern American Horror Film.* Ed. Gregory A. Waller. Urbana and Chicago: Illinois UP, 1987. 145–61.

Weed, Peter. "Using Movie Title Sequences Effectively." *Moviemaker* Summer 2007. 6 February 2009 http://www.moviemaker.com/editing/article/using_movie_title_sequences_effectively_20071227/

Weissmann, Elke. "The Victim's Suffering Translated: *CSI: Crime Scene Investigation* and the Crime Genre." *Intensities: The Journal of Cult Media* Special Issue 4 (2007). 21 January 2009 http://intensities.org/Essays/Weissmann.pdf

Wheatley, Helen. *Gothic Television.* Manchester: Manchester UP, 2006.

Williams, Linda. "When the Woman Looks" cited in Jancovich, Mark (Ed.). *Horror: The Film Reader.* London: Routledge, 2004.

Winthrop, Delba. "Aristotle and Theories of Justice." *American Political Science Review* 72.4 (1978): 1201–16.

Wood, Robin. *Hollywood from Vietnam to Reagan.* New York: Columbia UP, 1986.

Zizek, Slavoj. *Welcome to the Desert of the Real.* London: Verso, 2002.

Teleography

Bones. Creator Hart Hanson. Perf. Emily Deschanel, David Boreanaz, Michaela Conlin, T.J. Thyne, and Tamara Taylor. Fox. 2005–present.

Buffy The Vampire Slayer. Creator Joss Whedon. Perf. Sarah Michelle Gellar, Nicholas Brendon, Alyson Hannigan, Anthony Head, James Marsters, and Michelle Tractenberg. WB, UPN. 1997–2003.

CSI: Crime Scene Investigation. Creators Ann Donahue and Anthony E. Zuiker. Perf. William Petersen, Marg Helgenberger, George Eads, Paul Guilfoyle, Eric Szmanda, and Jorja Fox. CBS. 2000–present.

Dallas. Creator David Jacobs. Perf. Larry Hagman, Linda Gray, Patrick Duffy, Ken Kercheval, Victoria Principal, and Steve Kanaly. CBS. 1978–1991.

Desperate Housewives. Creator Marc Cherry. Perf. Nicollette Sheridan, Teri Hatcher, Felicity Huffman, Marcia Cross, and Eva Longoria Parker. ABC. 2004–present.

Dexter's Laboratory. Creator Genndy Tartakovsky. Perf. Kathie Soucie, Frank Welker, Allison Moore, Christine Cavanaugh, and Jeff Bennett. Cartoon Network. 1996–2003.

Grey's Anatomy. Creator Shonda Rhimes. Perf. Ellen Pompeo, Sandra Oh, Katherine Heigl, Justin Chambers, and Patrick Dempsey. ABC. 2005–present.

I Love Lucy. Perf. Lucille Ball, Desi Arnaz, Vivian Vance, and William Frawley. CBS. 1951–7.

Miami Vice. Creator Anthony Yerkovich. (Exec. Producer Michael Mann.) Perf. Don Johnson, Philip Michael Thomas, Edward James Olmos, Olivia Brown, and Saundra Santiago. NBC. 1984–9.

Numb3rs. Creators Nicolas Falacci and Cheryl Heuton. Perf. David Krumholtz, Rob Morrow, Judd Hirsch, Alimi Ballard, and Peter MacNicol. CBS. 2005–present.

NYPD Blue. Creators Steven Bochco and David Milch. Perf. Dennis Franz, David Caruso, Jimmy Smits, Rick Schroder, Kim Delaney, and Mark Paul-Gosselaar. ABC. 1993–2005.

Prison Break. Creator Paul Scheuring. Perf. Wentworth Miller, Dominic Purcell, Amaury Nolasco, Robert Knepper, Sarah Wayne Callies, and William Fichtner. Fox. 2005–9.

The Shield. Creator Shawn Ryan. Perf. Michael Chiklis, Benito Martinez, Walton Goggins, Kenny Johnson, C.C.H. Pounder, Jay Karnes, and David Rees Snell. FX. 2002–8.

The Sopranos. Creator David Chase. Perf. James Gandolfini, Edie Falco, Michael Imperioli, Lorraine Bracco, Tony Sirico, Steve Van Zandt, Dominic Chianese, and Aida Turturro. HBO. 1999–2007.

24. Creators Robert Cochran and Joel Surnow. Perf. Keifer Sutherland, Carlos Bernard, Mary Lynn Rajskub, Dennis Haysbert, Elisha Cuthbert, and James Morrison. Fox. 2001–present.

The Wire. Creator David Simon. Perf. Dominic West, John Doman, Wendell Pierce, Lance Reddick, and Deirdre Lovejoy. HBO. 2002–2008.

Filmography

American Psycho. Dir. Mary Harron. Perf. Christian Bale, Justin
  Theroux, Josh Lucas, Chloë Sevigny, and Reese Witherspoon. Lions
  Gate, 2000.
Analyze This. Dir. Harold Ramis. Perf. Robert De Niro, Billy Crystal,
  Lisa Kudrow, and Chazz Palminteri. Village Roadshow Pictures,
  1999.
The Big Sleep. Dir. Howard Hawks. Perf. Humphrey Bogart, Lauren
  Bacall, and John Ridgely. Warner Bros, 1946.
Bonnie and Clyde. Dir. Arthur Penn. Perf. Warren Beatty, Faye Dunaway,
  Michael J. Pollard, and Gene Hackman. Warner Bros, 1967.
Citizen Kane. Dir. Orson Welles. Perf. Joseph Cotten, Dorothy
  Comingore, and Orson Welles. RKO, 1941.
Copycat. Dir. John Amiel. Perf. Sigourney Weaver, Holly Hunter,
  Dermot Mulroney, William McNamara, and Harry Connick, Jr.
  Regency, 1995.
Double Indemnity. Dir. Billy Wilder. Perf. Fred MacMurray, Barbara
  Stanwyck, and Edward G. Robinson. Paramount, 1944.
Freaks. Dir. Todd Browning. Perf. Wallace Ford, Leila Hyams, Olga
  Baclanova, and Roscoe Ates. MGM, 1932.
In a Lonely Place. Dir. Nicholas Ray. Perf. Humphrey Bogart, Gloria
  Grahame, and Frank Lovejoy. Columbia, 1950.
Key Largo. Dir. John Huston. Perf. Humphrey Bogart, Lauren Bacall,
  Edward G. Robinson, Lionel Barrymore, and Claire Trevor. Warner
  Bros, 1948.
The Maltese Falcon. Dir. John Huston. Perf. Humphrey Bogart, Mary
  Astor, and Peter Lorre. Warner Bros, 1941.
Miami Vice. Dir. Michael Mann. Perf. Colin Farrell, Jamie Foxx, Li
  Gong, and Naomie Harris. Universal, 2006.

My Dinner with André. Dir. Louis Malle. Perf. Wallace Shawn and André Gregory. Saga, 1981.

Natural Born Killers. Dir. Oliver Stone. Perf. Woody Harrelson, Juliette Lewis, Tom Sizemore, and Robert Downey, Jr. Warner Bros, 1994.

Out of the Past. Dir. Jacques Tourneur. Perf. Robert Mitchum, Jane Greer, Kirk Douglas, and Rhonda Fleming. RKO, 1947.

The Postman Always Rings Twice. Dir. Tay Garnett. Perf. Lana Turner, John Garfield, Cecil Kellaway, and Hume Cronyn. MGM, 1946.

Psycho. Dir. Alfred Hitchcock. Perf. Anthony Perkins, Janet Leigh, Vera Miles, John Gavin, and Martin Balsam. Shamley, 1960.

The Public Enemy. Dir. William A. Wellman. Perf. James Cagney and Jean Harlow. Warner Bros, 1931.

The Roaring Twenties. Dir. Raoul Walsh. Perf. James Cagney, Priscilla Lane, Humphrey Bogart, and Gladys George. Warner Bros, 1939.

Serial Mom. Dir. John Waters. Perf. Kathleen Turner, Sam Waterston, Ricki Lake, and Matthew Lillard. Polar Entertainment, 1994.

Se7en. Dir. David Fincher. Perf. Brad Pitt, Morgan Freeman, Kevin Spacey, and Gwyneth Paltrow. New Line, 1995.

The Silence of the Lambs. Dir. Jonathan Demme. Perf. Anthony Hopkins, Jodie Foster Scott Glenn, and Ted Levine. Orion Pictures, 1991.

Taxi Driver. Dir. Martin Scorsese. Perf. Robert De Niro, Jodie Foster, Harvey Keitel, Cybill Shepherd, and Peter Boyle. Bill/Phillips, 1976.

The Untouchables. Dir. Brian DePalma. Perf. Kevin Costner, Sean Connery, Charles Martin Smith, Andy Garcia, Robert De Niro. Paramount, 1987.

Endnotes

Introduction

1 This ethical dilemma recalls creator Shawn Ryan's analysis of the problematic nature of Vic Mackey on *The Shield*: "What would people want if their safety could be more guaranteed? It's something that comes up in the pilot: What people really care about is walking to their car without being mugged, and coming home to find their stereo still there. If that means some cop has to rough up a few people, then it's don't ask, don't tell" (Braxton).

Chapter 1

1 As Lindsay told interviewer Al Karim, "Believe it or not, I think P.G. Wodehouse was an influence" ("Jeff Lindsay Speaks").

2 Lindsay also told Al Karim that he "wrote a column that was in 3 or 4 newspapers for about 5 years. It was called 'Fatherhood'" ("Jeff Lindsay Speaks").

3 In his review, Henriques specifically said, "Novelist Thomas Harris clearly fell in love with Hopkins's portrayal of the character he created and with the release of *Hannibal* turned his supporting villain into a sympathetic hero" ("*Hannibal Rising*").

4 Madoff recently pled guilty to running a Ponzi scheme that cost investors billions of dollars and that was, as the *New York Times* noted, "perhaps the largest fraud in Wall Street's history" (Henriques, "Madoff Will Plead").

Chapter 2

1 Growing up, Chase was "a fan of television's *The Untouchables* (1959–1963), which he watched with his father" (Lavery and Thompson 20), but he "fell out of love with TV probably after *The Fugitive* went off the air" (Rucker, also cited in Lavery and Thompson 19).

2 See the Introduction, note 1.

Chapter 3

1 I am indebted to Douglas Howard for this insight.

Chapter 4

1 "Superstar" (4.17) or "Normal Again" (6.17) or "Storyteller" (7.16).
2 I have in mind "Expose" (3.14), of course, which winks at the viewer throughout about its stand-alone extermination of Paolo and Nikki, additions to the cast summarily rejected by its fan base and buried alive at the episode's end.
3 In an interview with James Longworth (67), *Touched By an Angel* showrunner Martha Williamson insists the single greatest detriment to the production of quality television is the sheer number of episodes required—ordinarily 22—by a network television series. She speaks with envy of the premium channel agenda—ordinarily 12 or 13—of her friend David Chase (*The Sopranos*).
4 For a more historical account of the classification of types of television series, see my own "*Lost* and Long-Term Television Narrative."
5 Tulloch and Alvarado identify a closely related narrative form which they deem the episodic serial, series which exhibit continuity between episodes but only for a limited and specified number (ix). The subject of their study, *Doctor Who*, serves as an example, as does another famous British series, *The Prisoner*. And Newcomb uses a different designation for essentially the same narrative manifestation: cumulative narrative. Like the traditional series and unlike the traditional open-ended serial, each installment of a cumulative narrative has a distinct beginning, middle, and end. However, unlike the traditional series and like the traditional serial, one episode's events can greatly affect later episodes. As Newcomb puts it, "Each week's program is distinct, yet each is grafted onto the body of the series, its characters' pasts" (quoted in Reeves, Rodgers, and Epstein 30).
6 Jeff Lindsay's novels are, of course, first-person narratives and an obvious inspiration for the television series' use of voice-over.

Chapter 5

1 As Daniel Chamberlain and Scott Ruston note, "Generally speaking, exemplars of the mature quality television genre have announced their distinction with a clearly identifiable cinematic visual style that can be read as an intentional contrast to the videographic or blank style of standard television programming. . . . As the quality genre has taken shape, it has become axiomatic that quality television aims for an association with cinema as a superior art form to television" (16–17).

In terms of programs seeking to acquire quality status through an appropriation of high-end style for "meretricious gain," I am thinking primarily of British productions like *Hustle* (BBC 2004–ongoing) and *New Tricks* (BBC 2003–ongoing), but also USTV works such as *Bionic Woman* (NBC 2007) and *Terminator: The Sarah Connor Chronicles* (Fox 2008–ongoing).

2   Thank you to Douglas Howard for his insightful observation of one of this episode's and series' related concerns:

'In "Our Father," when Dexter goes through the crime scene with Miguel, Miguel sees his blood-spatter work with the red string as a "kind of art." Dexter, on the other hand, sees it more as a "narrative," and this may well explain his interest in crime scenes as well as his interest in other killers. The surface betrays the deeper story within. As someone who has been trained in reading these surfaces, Dexter is always curious to follow that "narrative thread" and to learn the story that will be explained and who's responsible. His nemeses from Seasons 1–3—Brian, Lila, Miguel—all are people, like Dexter himself, with truths or stories beneath the surface, and each season's arc largely works around Dexter's attempt to reveal their true characters, to reveal what lies beneath.

Chapter 6

1   Noël Carroll notes that, as a myth, *Frankenstein* "has been played and replayed in countless variations . . . [by new generations] ready to relocate and adjust for their own times the significance of the tale of the creature brought back from the dead" (vii). Chris Baldick adds, however, that this "series of adaptations, allusions, accretions, analogues, parodies, and plain misreadings which follows upon Mary Shelley's novel is not just a supplementary component of the myth; it *is* the myth" (4).

2   David Collings points out that Victor studies "in defiance of his father's prohibition, as if replaying the [O]edipus complex in his intellectual pursuits" (281).

3   In discussing psychoanalytic readings of the novel, Diane Long Hoeveler also makes this point, that, "[i]n creating the monster, Victor attempts to undo the death of his mother" (52).

4   Sandra Gilbert and Susan Gubar describe his dream as "the primal kiss that incestuously kills both 'sister' and 'mother'" (234).

5   A similar scene takes place in *Dexter in the Dark*, when Dexter is

bothered by a student in his PE class. A janitor later finds the student in the biology lab "securely taped to the table with a swatch of grey duct tape over his mouth, and Dexter standing above him with a scalpel, trying to remember what he had learned in biology class the day they dissected the frog" (113).

6 As Dexter notes in *Dexter in the Dark*, "the Harry Code had been set up to operate in the cracks of the system, in the shadow areas of perfect justice rather than perfect law" (16).

7 Frank Miller's analysis of Batman, whom Lundy actually compares to the Bay Harbor Butcher in "Dex, Lies, and Videotape," also works as a justification for Dexter: "He wants the world to be a better place, where a young Bruce Wayne would not be a victim . . . In a way, he's out to make himself unnecessary. Batman is a hero who wishes he didn't have to exist" (*Batman: Year One* 101). Whether Harry planned on having Dexter avenge her or not, Dexter's killings could also, ultimately, be read as an attempt to prevent that first killing, his mother's death, and his creation. In "The Dark Defender," Dexter even dreams of heroically saving his mother in the storage container by disposing of her attackers.

8 The closest that we get to seeing this instability in Season 1 is when Harry admits, after the death of Davey Sanchez, that his "world feels out of control" (1.2).

9 In this context, Dexter's assertion that he "killed his father" in "There's Something About Harry" recalls the creature's reaction to Victor's death at the end of *Frankenstein:* "That is also my victim!" (153).

10 Rather than dealing with this emptiness, Jeremy decides to kill himself in jail. As a teen, Dexter also risks killing himself just "to feel alive" (2.1), a feeling that he briefly gets when his garbage bags are discovered on the ocean floor at the start of Season 2.

11 Dexter immediately relates to Miguel's story about his alcoholic father, who, for all of his son's success, still thought of him as "a failure" (3.3), and his friendship with Miguel develops, in part, because they both are dealing with this kind of disappointment.

12 As Ramon Prado explains to Dexter in the final episode, he was actually the one who "did that to [their] father," but Miguel "made it his story" and incorporated it into his own "legend" (3.12), another lie that reveals the truth about Miguel's character.

13 After Miguel's first kill, the dream version of Harry, again an imaginative construct of Dexter's psyche, expresses the conflict and the competition between father and son as he hopes that Dexter is "a stronger man" and better able to bear the "heavy burden" of teaching

Miguel the code (3.8). Miguel, however, is not the first killer that Dexter "creates." When Lila kills Doakes, Dexter also compares himself to his father; as he tells her, "I'm more like my father than I've ever imagined. I created a monster of my own" (2.12). In both cases, Dexter must subdue these killers, since they cannot be controlled and since their crimes fall outside the code.

14 As Beth Johnson insightfully notes in her chapter, "Dexter's mother is startlingly similar in appearance to Rita" (83). This connection also recalls the Oedipal issues in *Frankenstein*, a text that turns on the attempt to possess the mother. Gilbert and Gubar agree that "female-ness ... is at the heart of [the novel]," although they suggest that, through "his single most self-defining act," Victor "transforms him[self] into [the original mother,] Eve" (232).

15 The creature's request "to be pardoned" after Victor's death again comes to mind here.

Chapter 7

1 In Jeff Lindsay's novel (2005) *Darkly Dreaming Dexter*, Dexter's Oedipal issues are arguably addressed via Dexter's relationship with his (foster)-sister, Deb. In Chapter 27, as Brian encourages Dexter to murder Deb, Dexter refers to Deb as "mommy": "A drop of sweat rolled across Deborah's forehead and into her eye. [...] I closed my eyes. The room dove around me, got darker, and I could not move. There was Mommy watching me, unblinking. I opened my eyes. My brother stood so close behind me I could feel his breath on my neck. My sister looked up at me, her eyes as wide and unblink-ing as Mommy's. And the look she gave me held me, as Mommy's had held me. I closed my eyes; Mommy. I opened my eyes; Deborah" (267).

Chapter 8

1 Lila claims to "see" Dexter for who he really is, and for a brief time he believes her. But after she manipulates and seduces him, he soon discovers she is more of a monster than he is and ultimately doesn't confide in her about his secret. (She finds out from Doakes.)

2 DNA proved Dexter's biological father was Joe Driscoll, but it is never established whether or not he was also Brian's father. Given the lack of keepsakes in Joe's house to remind him of Brian and that Joe didn't bequeath his house to both of them, it is possible Dexter and Brian are only half-brothers.

Chapter 10

1 The relationship between Lindsay's novels and the television series is a complex one and deserves an essay in its own right. Although I will draw a number of comparisons between these two sources in this essay, my purpose in doing so is not to argue or imply that *Dexter* the series should be regarded as a failed or inaccurate adaptation of its source material. Rather, I make these comparisons in order to draw attention to the fact that the changes made to Lindsay's books (both in terms of what the series leaves out and what it adds) are symptomatic of what it takes to make *Dexter* the series such a phenomenal success. For a more general discussion of the issues raised by adapting written murder narratives to film, see my 2007 article, "The Kindest Cut of All: Adapting Thomas Harris's *Hannibal*," *Literature/Film Quarterly* 35.1 (2007): 389–95.

2 See Byers for an interesting comparison between *CSI* and *Dexter*. Byers praises the latter show for problematizing "the binary structures of good and evil and truth and lies that we are pushed to accept by *CSI*."

3 To return for a moment to the theme of guilt and innocence, it's worth noting another significant difference between Lindsay and *Dexter* the series at this point. In Lindsay's work Deb, Dexter's sister, comes to learn of his need to kill. By contrast, the series continues to "protect" Deb from such knowledge, thus maintaining her innocence. This puts the audience member in an even more privileged position in relation to Dexter. In *Dexter*, everyone who knows or discovers Dexter's secret is either dead (Harry) or is killed (Doakes, Lila, Miguel, and Rudy/Brian). We are the only ones who share this knowledge with Dexter and live. What better way to reinforce audience identification with this character?

4 The fact that Miguel Prado is an Assistant District Attorney, and thus a representative of the system, indicates affinities between *Dexter* and other television crime dramas with criminal/legal themes. Like many of the main characters in series such as *The X-Files, CSI, Law & Order*, and *The Wire*, Dexter is himself part of the system (as a blood-splatter analyst for Miami Metro Homicide) and external to that system (because of his killings). This ambiguous placement gives audiences the option of both identifying with Dexter as a maverick, as the epitome of a peculiarly American brand of individualism, while also toying with the idea that Dexter's violence is systemic, or rather, is what the system needs to function effectively. Although *Dexter* is not interested in pursuing the destabilizing implications of the systemic nature of Dexter's homicides, the implications remain, nonetheless.

Chapter 11

1 While quite peripheral within the domain of *Buffy* studies, this critique has been made by scholars like Ono (2000), Neal King (2003), Levine and Schneider (2003), and Chin (2003), who variously argue that *Buffy* stages particular forms of cultural critique which overlay deeper and more pernicious narratives that reify existing hierarchical structures, particularly those that pertain to "race."

2 In "Easy as Pie" (3.7), Dexter is put on the case of Albert Chung, an Asian-American murderer resented by Vince Masuka, the one Asian-American character who regularly appears on the series. The episode plays on ideas about racial stereotypes by making Chung look like Masuka, and by having Masuka acknowledge that, in taking off his shoes before entering the home of his murder victims, Chung is engaging in clichéd behavior. The fact that he has now left sock rather than shoe prints leaves Masuka to remark: "and Asians are supposed to be smart."

3 I would add here identities in the broadest sense.

Chapter 12

1 The United States is "founded" on violence: the Indians, the myth of pioneers conquering the Wild West, the Civil War. No one denies that America is proud of its history. Its Puritan heritage, on the other hand, makes open sexuality a problem. Germany, too, has a more than violent past, but to take pride in this or to enjoy any kind of violence is utterly forbidden since World War II and the Holocaust. The social (and sexual) revolution during the sixties provided an allowed source of revolutionary "wildness" for German society.

2 The Bauer Verlagsgruppe holds another 31.5 per cent of RTL2; the other 31.5 per cent is held by the Tele München Group and the Walt Disney Company.

3 I can only allude to the numerous reasons why German shows do not function—to go into the details would swell this article to explosion: not enough competition between the stations and between public, commercial, and Pay-TV broadcasters, no showrunner system (script writers and directors are working almost independently of one another), no courage to try out new things, and a much smaller market than in the US, which restricts the possibilities of refinancing. American broadcasters also earn about ten times more out of advertising than German ones, business people without knowledge of programming are put in charge of TV stations, and German programs are generally too boring, too tame, and lacking a strong sense of cinematic history.

4 The new interest in US shows is constantly growing stronger. Besides the A-shows by US networks, cable products like USA's *Monk*, TNT's *Nightmares and Dreamscapes*, and Sci Fi's *Eureka* are also very popular. Not only are Western European countries "infected," but the whole East as well: Russia and Poland spend more money on US programs than Latin America. HBO and AXN can be received in almost every Eastern European country; even Japan's appetite has been whetted, now that the first two seasons of *Lost* on DVD have made an immense profit: Japan is currently planning on buying several licensed products. The international enthusiasm for these shows is a rather new phenomenon; up until now, there have only been two or three American shows at a time that were successful in the rest of the world.

5 FSF stands for "Freiwillige Selbstkontrolle Fernsehen." This is something like the German FCC (the telecommunications regulatory agency), but a "light" version.

Chapter 15

1 Indeed in Season 2, Dexter sees himself and his vigilante crimes immortalized in comic art as The Dark Defender (2.5).

Chapter 16

1 Aristotle used the term natural justice to distinguish a concept of right that was distinct from what was "just by law." Natural justice is thought to be somehow inherent in the world and to transcend legislative law: "He [Aristotle] insists that the politically just, while conventional, is only partly conventional and is also partly natural" (Winthrop 1207).

2 The reasons for this are numerous and complex, but one might attribute a major impetus for popular culture's delight in the topos to the underlying suspicion that the upper classes have hijacked the legal system to their own advantage.

3 Dexter does not normally use a mask in the television series. However, in the novels he does: "From my gym bag I pulled a white silk mask and dropped it over my face, settling the eyeholes snugly" (*Dexter in the Dark*, 25).

4 Chandler's detective hero Philip Marlowe and Hammett's Sam Spade were instrumental in the development of the hard-boiled fiction genre. Their protagonists were world-weary men whose reaction to a generally corrupt society was characterized by a desire to maintain personal honor.

5 *CSI: Crime Scene Investigation* (2000–) is a crime drama based in Las

Vegas, Nevada which follows the adventures of a team of forensic investigators. *Bones* (2005–) is a series based on the novels of forensic anthropologist Kathy Reichs. *Numb3rs* (2005–) is a detective series developed by Ridley and Tony Scott that focuses on the solution of crimes by the unlikely team of an FBI agent and his mathematician brother. All of these series attempt to integrate a modern perspective on the use of science in crime detection with more traditional television police drama. While they owe a great deal to the dispassionate approach to detection of Conan Doyle's Sherlock Holmes novels, they emphasize the macabre violence of the crimes presented in a very contemporary fashion.

6   In Season 1, Dexter comes across body parts that have been abstracted from a still-living victim. In "Let's Give the Boy a Hand" (1.4), Rudy/Brian leaves a severed hand that belongs to a man who has been a suspect in the Ice Truck killings.

7   This scene paraphrases Jeff Lindsay's novel: "Every superhero must have an archenemy, and he [Sergeant Doakes] was mine" (*Dearly Devoted Dexter*, 17). Lindsay and the creators of the Showtime series play with the genre expectations of their audience, providing a moral complexity not found in tales of other secretive heroes.

8   Like *Miami Vice* (1984–9), *Dexter* presents the city of Miami in all its color-rich tropical glory. *Miami Vice* was one of the first television shows to take advantage of the advances in television's technical capabilities, both visual and auditory. *Dexter* matches the exuberance of *Miami Vice*'s rock soundtrack with bright songs with a Cuban/Latin feel.

9   This is not exactly accurate if we consider Dexter as he appears in Jeff Lindsay's novels. In the third novel of the series, *Dexter in the Dark*, Dexter becomes aware of a supernatural entity, Moloch, that he identifies as his Dark Passenger. In the previous novels and in the television series, this Dark Passenger can be seen as a convenient way for Dexter to identify his compulsion to murder, but, in this novel, Moloch is acknowledged as a separate by others.

Index

AGF 159
Alvarado, Manuel 45, 250
Alston, Joshua 185
American Psycho xv, xxiv, 22, 31, 39, 40, 179, 180–2
Analyze This 186
Angel 162, 164, 205
anti-hero xiv, 16, 43, 54, 58, 178, 189, 190, 192, 204
Aristotle 256
art xx, xxiv, 3, 10, 13, 27, 49, 51, 53, 54, 55, 56, 80, 81, 129, 136, 147, 179, 181, 192, 197, 204, 205–220, 224, 228, 250, 251, 256
Aunt Sally 80

Baldick, Chris 251
Bass, Saul xxi, 27–9, 30, 39
Bataille, George 81
Bateman, Patrick xvii, 40, 179, 180–2, 185
Batista, Angel 21, 105, 197, 203, 214, 225
Batman xxiv, 222, 227, 228, 229, 230, 252
the Bay Harbor Butcher 42, 44, 89, 90, 149, 152, 192, 198, 201, 227, 252
Bennett, Astor 71, 91, 94, 95, 96, 108, 138, 139, 141, 183, 184, 199, 203, 204, 216, 225
Bennett, Cody 7, 71, 91, 94, 95, 96, 108, 138, 139, 141, 199, 203, 204, 225, 226
Bennett, Paul 80, 84, 126, 138, 139, 152, 154, 181
Bennett, Rita xvi, 7, 45, 47, 48, 57, 58, 69, 71, 72, 73, 74, 75, 79, 80–2, 83–4, 85, 88, 90, 91, 92, 93, 94, 95, 96, 101, 107, 108, 109, 112, 126, 128, 129, 138, 139, 141, 148, 152, 153, 154, 179, 181, 182, 183, 184, 186, 187, 188,

196, 198, 199, 203, 204, 225, 226, 253
Benz, Julie 45, 47–8
The Big Sleep 192
blood xiii, xiv, xviii, xx, xxiv, 6, 7, 12, 30–5, 36, 37, 39, 41, 44, 49, 52, 53, 56, 61, 67, 68, 71, 75, 77, 82, 83, 86, 97, 99, 100, 104, 106, 107, 108, 112, 118, 132, 140, 148, 149, 168, 175, 176, 177–8, 179, 180, 181, 185, 187, 197, 201, 202, 210, 211, 212, 213, 214, 215, 216, 217, 218, 227, 228, 230
blood spatter xxiv, 6, 44, 61, 78, 82, 83, 85, 117, 132, 147, 168, 177, 179, 183, 209, 213, 216, 217, 218, 223, 228, 251, 254
brotherhood 96–113, 148–9
Bobbitt, Rebecca 177–8
Bogart, Humphrey 4, 189, 192
Bones xvi, xix, xxiv, 76, 208, 209, 213, 216, 217, 223, 257
Bonnie and Clyde 135
Bonnie and Clyde (film) 198
Bonnycastle, Kevin 143, 144
Bould, Marc 190, 191
Brown, Wendy 145, 152, 155–6
Buffy the Vampire Slayer 43, 46, 162, 166, 205, 206, 255
Bundy, Ted 135
Burke, Edmund 78
Burroughs, Edgar Rice 11
Byers, Michele 144, 254

Cagney, James 15, 190
Cain, James M. 190, 198
Californication 167, 168
camera work 34, 36, 40, 41, 50, 51, 52, 53, 55,

56, 178, 202, 208, 213, 214

Camilla 19, 73, 111, 112

cannibalism xv, 13

capital punishment 11, 22

Carroll, Noël 251

Cassuto, Leonard 138

Cawelti, John 222, 229, 230

CBS xviii–xix, 22–3, 46, 142, 144

Cerone, Daniel 109

Chamberlain, David, and Scott Ruston 250

Chandler, Raymond 190, 192, 198, 223, 256

Chase, David 15, 17, 19, 249, 250

Clerval, Henry 70

Clover, Carol 211

clue 180, 193–5

the Code of Harry xv, xviii, xxii, xxiv, 65, 66, 67, 70, 72, 73, 75, 77, 81, 85, 91, 92, 93, 94, 95, 96, 97, 100, 102, 103, 106, 107, 110, 111, 117–128, 130, 131, 136, 138, 141, 146, 147, 149, 150, 151, 152, 153, 155, 179, 181, 184, 200–1, 202, 203, 216, 226, 227, 229–30, 252, 253

"College" (*Sopranos* episode) 14, 17, 20

Colleton, Sara 109

Collings, David 69, 74, 251

color 27, 31–2, 33, 34, 35, 40–1, 49, 50, 51, 52, 56, 83, 202, 208, 210, 217–18, 228, 257

comedy xxiv, 9, 16, 175–88

comic books 12, 192, 221, 227, 228, 230, 256

consequentialism xxiii, 128–31

Cooper, Kyle 39

Cooper, Rudy (see also Brian Moser, the Ice Truck Killer) xxii, 38, 40, 69, 96, 100, 123, 140, 148, 149, 150, 195, 202, 218, 219, 225, 254, 257

Copycat 40

CSI xvi, xvii, xxiv, 6, 144, 161, 162, 164, 165, 166, 170, 208, 209, 213, 216, 217, 223, 254, 256

cumulative narrative 250

Dahmer, Jeffrey 135, 170, 210

Dallas 46, 163

the Dark Defender 47, 61, 192, 227–8, 252, 256

the Dark Passenger xviii, xx, 8, 48, 77, 78, 90, 112, 188, 211, 213, 215, 257

Darkly Dreaming Dexter xix, 3, 4, 44, 46, 63, 65, 69, 109, 138, 140, 253

Deadwood xvi, xx, 76

Dearly Devoted Dexter xx, 65, 257

Death Wish 137

Derrick 166

Desperate Housewives 47, 162, 204

DeWolf-Smith, Nancy xiv, xix

Dexter by Design xx, xxi, 13

Dexter Episodes—

"About Last Night," 73, 95, 106, 107, 112, 202–3, 219

"All in the Family," 69, 104, 105–6

"Born Free," xiv, 86, 88, 98–9, 100–1, 102, 103, 107, 108, 111, 187, 188, 140, 187

"The British Invasion," 42, 45, 57, 63, 69, 70, 90–1, 141, 151, 198, 199, 215, 253

"Circle of Friends," 69, 86, 100, 212, 219

"Crocodile," 78, 82, 161, 225

"The Damage a Man Can Do," 72, 94, 95, 102, 106, 107, 202, 252–3

"The Dark Defender," 65, 73, 101, 109, 191–3, 196, 199, 218, 227–8, 252, 256

"Dex, Lies, and Videotape," 65, 195, 252

"Dexter," xv, xvi, 14, 17–18, 22, 23, 24, 49, 50, 51, 53, 54, 56, 57, 63, 64, 68, 69, 78, 79, 80, 88, 98, 100, 108, 119, 138, 191, 205, 210, 217, 218

"Do You Take Dexter Morgan," 201, 203

"Easy as Pie," 255

"Father Knows Best," 76, 83, 84, 100

"Finding Freebo," 71, 73, 93, 181, 215

"Go Your Own Way," 73, 94, 95, 108, 112

"I Had a Dream," 43, 73–4

"An Inconvenient Lie," 69, 88, 199, 230

"It's Alive," 63, 108, 252

"Left Turn Ahead," 63, 68, 75, 101, 104

"Let's Give the Boy a Hand," 85, 97–8, 111, 193, 194, 200, 218, 225, 257

"The Lion Sleeps Tonight," 71, 93, 94, 101, 102, 105, 107, 183, 184, 201, 216, 252

"Love American Style," 64, 68, 137, 196

"Morning Comes," 89, 199

"Our Father," 50, 56, 57, 65, 66, 72, 91, 92, 102, 154, 203, 217, 251

"Popping Cherry," 65, 86, 96, 104, 218

"Resistance is Futile," xiii, 90, 197

"Return to Sender," 98, 182, 185–6

"See-Through," 69, 89

"Seeing Red," 83, 86, 103, 181, 214, 217, 218

"Shrink Wrap," xvii, 64, 79, 82, 84, 137, 186–7, 194, 214

"Si Se Puede," 72, 92, 98, 105, 106, 107, 112
"That Night a Forest Grew," 199
"There's Something About Harry," xvi, 66–7, 199, 213, 252
"Truth Be Told," 84, 85
"Turning Biminese," 71–2, 93, 94, 103, 106, 202
"Waiting to Exhale" 69, 108–9, 111, 150–1
Dexter in the Dark xx, 7, 12, 61, 251, 252, 256, 257
Dexter's Laboratory xxiv, 175, 178, 184
Digital Kitchen 30
Disavowal xv, xvi, xxiii, 135–6, 139
Doakes, Sgt James xvi, xvii, xx, 19, 21, 37, 42, 45, 46, 67, 90, 109, 110, 147, 149–50, 152, 153, 154, 170, 178, 183, 195, 197, 198, 199, 213, 217, 227, 230, 253, 254, 257
Doe, John 179, 182, 183, 185, 211
Dolan, Marc 44, 45, 46
Donovan, Mike 51–4, 57, 122, 138
Double Indemnity 190, 195, 198
Doyle, Arthur Conan 194, 257
Driscoll, Joe 84, 253
Dubbing xxiii, 158, 169, 170
Dupin, Auguste 194, 195

Ellis, Bret Easton 40
England (United Kingdom, Great Britain, British, English) xxiii, 43, 80, 88, 89, 129, 141–2, 158, 162, 165, 193, 250, 251
Erdem, Tuna 76
Estrada 65
Evans, Dylan 80, 82, 87, 92, 93, 94
Everyman 182

Faith, Karlene, and Yasmin Jiwani 148
Farewell My Lovely 192
fatherhood 8, 71, 75, 93, 94, 112, 183, 203, 204, 249
femme fatale 189, 191, 197–200, 203, 204
Fiedler, Leslie 48
film noir xxiv, 189–204
flashback 18, 47, 66, 78, 82, 93, 109, 118–19, 176, 186, 187, 189, 191, 197, 200–1, 202, 204
Fleeter, Billy 72, 95, 106, 202
flexi-narrative xxi, 46
Foucault, Michel 79, 152, 155
Frank, Nino 190

Frankenstein (film-1931) 63
Frankenstein (novel) xxii, 61–77, 251, 252, 253
Frankenstein, Elizabeth (nee Lavenza) 62, 70
Frankenstein, Victor xxii, 61–77, 251, 252, 253
Frankenstein, William 70
Frankenstein's creature 62, 63, 66, 68, 69–70, 73, 74, 76 251, 252, 253
Freaks 188
Freebo 104, 106, 107, 110, 112, 181, 203, 215–16
Freud, Sigmund 80, 82, 83, 85, 87, 92
Fukuyama, Francis 145

Gabbard, Glenn 17
Galt, Clemson 106
Garland, David 143
Garvin, Glenn xvii
Geffner, David 28–9, 39
Geraghty, Christine 197
Germany (German) xviii, xxiii, 157–71, 255
Gilbert, Sandra, and Susan Gubar 251, 253
Ginzburg, Carlo 193
Gledhill, Christine 198
the Gothic 50, 63, 89, 190, 206–7, 210–11, 212, 214, 218
Greenblatt, Robert 16, 17
Grey, Johnny 132
Grey's Anatomy 47, 166, 177

Haggins, Bambi xviii
Halberstam, Judith 68
Hall, Michael C. 6, 9, 10, 30, 47, 170, 175
Hall, Peter 27, 29
Hammett, Dashiell 190, 192, 223, 256
Harris, Thomas 9, 140, 249, 254
Harron, Mary 31, 40, 182
Harry's nurse 65
Havrilesky, Heather 45
Hawks, Howard 192
Hayward, Susan 191
HBO xiv, xix, 17, 30, 144, 169, 207, 256
Henriques, Ron 9, 249
Hills, Matt 207, 210
Hitchcock, Alfred 27
Hoeveler, Diane Long 251
Holmes, Sherlock 194, 257
horror xxiv, 177–8, 205–20
Hughes, Dorothy B. 190

Humbert, Humbert xv, xvii

I Love Lucy xxiv, 181
the Ice Truck Killer xx, 10, 23, 37, 38, 40, 44, 46, 86, 96, 98, 100, 108, 109, 123, 124, 125, 126, 140, 175, 178, 193, 212, 214, 215, 218, 219, 225
identification 34, 36, 39, 40, 75, 135, 137, 139, 140, 142, 176, 185, 209, 212–16, 254
imaginary father 92, 93, 95
In a Lonely Place 189, 192

Jermyn, Deborah 208, 209
Jimenez, Santos 65, 198, 199
Jiwani, Yasmin 146
Jung, Carl Gustav 11, 75

Kabel1 159, 160, 163, 164
Kilgour, Maggie xv
King, George (see also the Skinner) 110, 152, 153, 201
King, Stephen 205
Kolker, Robert 51, 56
Kooistra, Paul 135
Kristeva, Julia 208
Krutnik, Frank 190, 194
Kühn, Axel 169

Lacan, Jacques 85, 87, 90, 92, 93, 94
LaGuerta, Lt Maria xx, 10, 21, 37, 44, 109, 124, 147, 153, 197, 202, 225
Lau, Amy 132
Lavery, David xxi–xxii, 249
Lecter, Hannibal xv, xvii, 9, 13, 135, 140, 179, 180, 185
Leitch, Thomas M. 135–6, 139
lighting 40, 41, 49, 189, 190, 191
liminality 29, 36
Lindsay, Jeff xix–xx, xxi, xxiv, 3–13, 23, 44, 45, 61, 63, 69, 109, 137, 138–40, 222, 226, 249, 250, 253, 254, 257
Little Chino 111
Lolita xv
the Lone Ranger xxiv, 222, 227, 228, 229
Lost 43, 166, 250, 256
Lundy, Special Agent Frank xiii, 252

Mackey, Vic 17, 19, 77, 249
Malle, Louis 47
The Maltese Falcon 190, 192

Mann, Michael xxii, 55–6
Manos, James, Jr xvi, xix, xxi, 5, 14–24, 45
Marlowe, Philip 192, 256
Marten, Nathan 73, 111, 183–4, 201, 204
masculinity xxiii, 146, 147, 148, 150, 151, 152, 153, 154
Masuka, Vince xvi, 10, 73, 75, 182, 185–6, 203, 214, 224, 225, 255
Matthews, Tom xiii, 67
McCarty, John 219
McCloud, Frank 192
Meridian, Dr Emmett xvii, 82, 84, 110, 137, 186–7, 194
Miami xiv, xvii, xviii, xx, xxii, 6, 43, 49, 50, 51, 55, 74, 80, 88, 101, 128, 129, 130, 141, 147, 149, 152, 153, 194, 210, 211, 212, 227, 228, 230, 257
Miami Metro Police Department xvi, 73, 117, 128, 129, 193, 194, 195, 198, 201, 223, 254
Miami Vice (film) xxii, 50, 55
Miami Vice (television series) xxii, 50, 55, 163, 257
Milch, David 15, 19
Mildred Pierce 190
Mill, J.S. 129
Millennium xvi
Miller, Frank 252
Moffat, Kathie 198
Moi, Toril 87
Moloch 257
Montgomery, Robert 192
Morgan, Deb (Debra or Deborah) 18, 21, 45, 66, 72, 74, 86, 89, 91–2, 95, 96, 97, 98–9, 100, 101, 102–4, 106, 109, 112, 123, 126, 128, 140, 141, 148, 153, 154, 170, 175, 178, 179, 180, 182, 187, 196, 197, 198, 203, 219, 225–6, 253, 254
Morgan, Dexter xiii–xxiv, 3, 5–6, 7, 8, 10, 11, 12, 13, 16–19, 21, 23, 24, 30–42, 43–8, 49–54, 56, 57–8, 61, 63–9, 70–6, 77, 78–95, 96–113, 117–30, 133, 136–42, 145, 147–56, 170–1, 175–88, 189, 191–204, 209–19, 222–30, 251, 252, 253, 254, 255, 256, 257
Morgan, Harry xiv, xx, xxii, 8, 18–19, 37, 47, 61, 63–9, 70–6, 77, 82, 83, 84, 85–6, 88, 91, 92, 93–4, 95, 96, 97, 98, 99, 100, 101, 103, 104, 106, 107–8, 110, 111, 112, 118–19, 123, 124, 128, 129, 136, 138, 139, 140, 141, 176, 179, 181, 184, 186, 187, 191, 194,

200–201, 202, 203, 213, 226, 227, 229–30, 252, 254

Moser, Brian("Biney") xiv, xvi, xix, xx, xxii, 10, 65, 86, 87, 88, 93, 96–113, 140, 148, 149, 150, 153, 154, 178, 202, 225–6, 227, 229, 230, 251, 253, 254, 257

Moser, Laura xiv, 18, 61, 65, 66, 68, 72, 73, 75, 82, 83–4, 85, 86, 88, 93, 95, 99, 100, 109, 111, 112, 118, 119, 123, 148, 149, 199, 201, 219, 227, 228, 230, 253

mother fixation xxii, 83

MOW (monster of the week) 46

"Murders in the Rue Morgue" 195

Nabokov, Vladimir xv

Narcotics Anonymous 84, 88, 198, 226

Naremore, James 190, 192

narrative xv, xix, xxi-xxii, xxiii, 4, 14, 27, 28, 29, 30, 32, 36, 37, 40, 41, 42, 43–8, 64, 66, 69, 76, 134, 136, 143, 144, 146, 148, 149, 170, 178, 186, 187, 189, 191, 193, 194, 197, 198, 200, 202, 203, 204, 206, 210, 212, 216, 217, 219, 221, 223, 225, 229, 250, 251, 254, 255

Neff, Walter 198–9

Nelson, Robin 45, 46

neoliberalism xxiii, 143–56

New Tricks 251

Newcomb, Horace 45

9/11 xxiii, 19, 133, 140, 144

Numb3rs 223, 257

NYPD Blue xvi, 15, 145

Oedipus complex xxii, 61, 62, 68, 69, 70, 71, 74, 77, 82, 83, 87, 92, 253

opening title sequence xv, xxi, 27–42, 44, 176–8

the Other xvi, xxiii, 12, 48, 90, 101, 136, 139, 140, 141, 143, 145–7, 151, 153–4, 155, 156, 183

Out of the Past 198

Parents Television Council (PTC) xix, 21, 142

Peeping Tom 211

Perry, Neil 212

Petrulio, Fabian 17

Phillips, Clyde 45, 47, 48, 75

The Pit and the Pendulum 211

Poe, Edgar Allan xvii, 4, 194, 195

Poovey, Mary 63

Post Mortem 161, 164

The Postman Always Rings Twice 190, 198

Prado, Miguel xvi, xix, xxii, 37, 43, 46, 47, 71, 72, 73, 74, 75, 92, 93, 94, 95, 96–97, 101–8, 110–13, 124–5, 128, 129, 137–8, 140, 152–3, 154, 178, 181, 195, 202, 216, 217, 218, 219, 226, 227, 229, 251, 252, 253, 254

Prado, Oscar 58, 66, 73, 102, 104, 105, 111, 141

Prado, Ramon 76, 98, 102, 103, 104, 105, 110, 125, 252

Premiere 157, 164, 168, 169, 171

Prison Break 44, 76

The Prisoner 250

private detective/private eye xxiv, 192, 221, 223, 224, 228

Pro7 159, 160, 163, 164

Profiler xvi

Psycho 15, 212

psychoanalysis xxii, 78–95, 251

The Public Enemy 190

Puritans 133–4, 255

quality television xx, 76, 162, 250

race 146, 255

real father xxii, 92, 94, 95

Reichs, Kathy xix, 257

ritual xiv, xv, xxii, xxiv, 23, 32, 35, 39, 52, 53, 58, 73, 91, 92, 136, 151, 177, 213, 226

The Roaring Twenties 190

Robinson, Edward G. 190

Root, Jane 190, 195, 199

RTL 159, 160, 161, 163, 164, 165, 166

RTL2 157, 159, 160, 161, 163, 166–9, 170, 255

Ryan, Shawn 17, 23, 249

Ryness, Juan 66, 67

Sanchez, Davey 64, 67, 252

Sayers, Dorothy L. 194

Scanlon, T.M. 127

Schlesinger, Warner Bros President Jeff 162

Schrader, Paul 191

Scorsese, Martin 50–1, 52

Seger, Hans 169

Sepinwall, Alan xvii

serial killer xiii, xv, xvi, xvii, xviii, xxii, xxiii, 6, 7, 8, 16, 20, 21, 22, 23, 38–40, 43, 44, 47,

50, 53, 61, 65, 67, 69, 70, 71, 78, 79, 96, 99, 117, 123, 130, 131, 132–3, 135–6, 140, 142, 147, 148, 150, 152, 167, 168, 169, 170, 175–6, 179, 180–3, 185, 187, 188, 195, 198, 199, 209, 211, 214, 225, 227, 230
serial narrative 43, 44, 46
Serienjunkies 162
Se7en xv, 22, 39, 40, 179, 182–3, 211
Seventh Heaven 76
Shelley, Mary 62, 63, 66, 77, 251
The Shield xx, xxi, 14, 16, 17, 19, 21, 23, 76, 166, 249
Showtime xvii, xviii, xix, xx, xxiii, 3, 6, 14, 16, 17, 132, 142, 157, 175, 184, 208, 221, 257
The Silence of the Lambs xv, 22, 140, 179–80, 211
Simpson, Philip L. 179
Sipowicz, Andy 144, 145
Six Feet Under 30, 166, 175
the Skinner xix, 43, 48, 73, 74, 75, 98, 110, 152, 178, 201, 203
slasher films 211, 224
"the Slice of Life" 48, 54
Smith, Cora 198
Snell, Bruno 86
soap opera xxiv, 204
The Sopranos xiv, xx, xxi, 14, 15, 16, 17, 21, 47, 76, 186, 250
Soprano, Tony xiv, 17, 19, 76, 77
Spade, Sam 190, 192, 256
Spicer, Andrew 189, 190, 191
Stanley, Alessandra xvii
Stanwyck, Barbara 199
Steele, Dixon 189, 192
Storm, Jonathan xvii
sublimation xxii, 79–80
Summerscale, Kate 193
Superman 222
symbolic father 92–3

Tarzan 11
Taxi Driver 50, 51
television ratings 157, 158, 159, 160, 161, 164, 165, 166, 167
the Ten Commandments 65, 121
The Texas Chainsaw Massacre 211

Thoret, Jean Baptiste 55–6
Tirone, Romeo 189
Totaro, Donato 207
Touch of Evil 190
Tournay, Lila (a.k.a. Lila West) xvi, xix, 37, 44, 46, 69, 79, 88–90, 96, 110, 129, 141–2, 150, 152, 153, 195, 197, 198–9, 212, 215, 216, 218, 219, 226, 227, 228, 229, 251, 253, 254
Tucci, Tony 111, 194, 218, 219
Tulloch, John 45, 250
Turim, Maureen 195, 200
Turner, Ethan 71, 103
24 44, 76, 161, 163, 166, 167, 168, 208
Tyree, J.M. 189, 225

the United States (America, American) xx, xxiii, 18, 19, 48, 132–7, 141–2, 143–4, 150, 155, 157, 159, 160, 162–3, 165, 167, 170, 190, 195, 202, 204, 207, 221, 223, 224, 229, 254, 255, 256
The Untouchables (film) xv
The Untouchables (television series) 15
utilitarianism 129

vigilantism xix, xxiii, xxiv, 43, 112, 136, 137, 146, 147, 148, 156, 209, 221, 222, 223, 226, 227, 230, 256
voice-over xv, xvi, 16, 47, 54, 78, 91, 118, 119, 126, 148, 170, 189, 191, 193, 195–7, 200, 201, 202, 203, 204, 210, 224, 227, 250
Vowell, Sarah 43
VOX 160, 161, 164, 165

Walton, Robert 62, 63, 68, 74
Weissmann, Elke 208–9
Wilder, Billy 198
Williamson, Martha 250
Winter, (PTC President) Tim xix
The Wire 144, 254
Wodehouse, P.G. 4, 249
Wolf, Ellen 72, 73, 95, 106, 112, 124, 153, 202, 219
Woolrich, Cornell 190
Writers' Strike xviii, 168

Zizek, Slavoj 152, 156